Early Praise for
Mac Kung Fu, Second Edition

Keir Thomas has compiled one of the most useful and interesting assembly of Mac tips and tricks available today. Packed with how-to insights and easy-to-follow steps, *Mac Kung Fu, Second Edition* is a knowledgeable guide to have by your side every step of the way.

➤ **Mike Riley**
  Advanced technologist and author of *Programming Your Home*

Mac Kung Fu, Second Edition contains a plethora of excellent Mac advice. It is accessible to new users, and even experienced Mac enthusiasts will find ways to make their lives simpler and more efficient.

➤ **Loren Sands-Ramshaw**
  Orglist

All levels of Mac users will enjoy this book. I particularly like the types of tips that the book offers that boost productivity, customize the working environment, and just make using a Mac more fun!

➤ **Fred Daoud**
  Author of *Stripes...and Java Web Development Is Fun Again*

Mac Kung Fu

Over 400 Tips, Tricks, Hints, and Hacks for Apple OS X

Keir Thomas

The Pragmatic Bookshelf

Dallas, Texas • Raleigh, North Carolina

Many of the designations used by manufacturers and sellers to distinguish their products are claimed as trademarks. Where those designations appear in this book, and The Pragmatic Programmers, LLC was aware of a trademark claim, the designations have been printed in initial capital letters or in all capitals. The Pragmatic Starter Kit, The Pragmatic Programmer, Pragmatic Programming, Pragmatic Bookshelf, PragProg and the linking *g* device are trademarks of The Pragmatic Programmers, LLC.

Every precaution was taken in the preparation of this book. However, the publisher assumes no responsibility for errors or omissions, or for damages that may result from the use of information (including program listings) contained herein.

Our Pragmatic courses, workshops, and other products can help you and your team create better software and have more fun. For more information, as well as the latest Pragmatic titles, please visit us at *http://pragprog.com*.

The team that produced this book includes:

Jackie Carter (editor)
Potomac Indexing, LLC (indexer)
Kim Wimpsett (copyeditor)
David J Kelly (typesetter)
Janet Furlow (producer)
Juliet Benda (rights)
Ellie Callahan (support)

Printed in the United States of America.
ISBN-13: 978-1-937785-07-9
Printed on acid-free paper.
Book version: P1.0—November 2012

Contents

Acknowledgments

Many thanks to those who reviewed *Mac Kung Fu, Second Edition* prior to publication: Daniel Bretoi, Ed Burnette, Trevor Burnham, Fred Daoud, Ian Dees, Isaac Dudney, Mike Riley, and Loren Sands-Ramshaw. Their comments, corrections, and suggestions made this an infinitely stronger book.

Thanks to Jonathan Wood for the loan of his Apple remote control, and my apologies for not returning it sooner!

Thanks to Jacquelyn Carter for expertly guiding me through my third book with Pragmatic Bookshelf, and, of course, thanks to all those switched-on individuals at Pragmatic who run perhaps the most extraordinary and amazing publishing outfit I've had the privilege of working with.

Finally, thanks to the Whowf for love and encouragement when I needed it most.

then skip that particular tip and perhaps return to it later when you feel more confident.

The tips were written for Mountain Lion and newer releases of OS X. That isn't to say many won't work on previous releases of OS X. However, I've tested the tips only against Mountain Lion, and some terminology changed in this release. If you do intend to use the book with an older release, some common sense will go a long way.

For All Macs—No Add-Ons Required!

All this book requires is a Mac computer running OS X. Nothing else. You might own a MacBook, MacBook Pro, MacBook Air, iMac, Mac Mini, or Mac Pro. It doesn't matter, although a handful of tips talk about getting the most from portable Macs.

No tip requires you to buy more software. All the tips enhance, harness, or tweak built-in functionality. A small fraction of the tips discuss downloading some add-in software to add vital functionality that's missing from OS X, but the software mentioned is nearly always free of charge.

Sharing

If you'd like to share some of the tips from this book on your blog, then feel free. It's unlikely my publisher will be too happy if you take liberties, but sharing a couple of tips you've found useful can only be a good thing. If you do, it would be great if you could mention the book and provide a link to the book's official web page—see below.

Online Resources

You can find this book's official web page at http://pragprog.com/book/ktmack2/mac-kung-fu. There you can report any errata in the book as well as make suggestions for future editions. You can also get involved in a discussion with other readers in the book's official forum and ask me questions. We'd love to see you there!

Keir Thomas
November 2012

CHAPTER 1

Getting the Most from the Tips

This book contains more than 400 tips, and you can jump in anywhere. They're in no particular order, and you don't have to start at the beginning! If you're looking for tips on a particular topic or function of OS X, use the index at the back of the book.

Mixed in with the tips are sidebars that concisely explain features of OS X you might have overlooked. The goal is to introduce you to key productivity features of OS X.

There are also a handful of "supertips" scattered throughout the book, which are collections of many smaller tips under a single heading, covering a particular app or technology. The aim is to provide a one-stop destination for learning about secret or hidden features.

Whichever path you choose when reading, here are some notes to help you get the most from the tips.

1.1 Activating Secret Settings via Typed Commands

Some tips involve typing configuration commands within a Terminal window in order to activate secret or experimental settings. Unfortunately, there's no way to avoid this, but don't worry—it's not as difficult as it might sound, and it definitely isn't dangerous.

Using the command line is surprisingly straightforward. Just type what you see on the page, and then hit Return. Make sure you type the command exactly as it appears, and read through a second time to check. Of course, if you're reading *Mac Kung Fu* as an ebook on your Mac,[1] you can simply copy and paste the command straight in.

---

1. Amazon offers a Mac version of its Kindle software: http://www.amazon.com/gp/kindle/mac.

Most of these commands make changes only to your user account. Other users won't be affected. Tips that affect the entire system are clearly marked!

After hitting `Return` when you are typing commands, you won't see anything like "Command completed!" or "OK." If you see no feedback, that's a good sign—it means everything worked. If there's an error, it probably means you've mistyped. OS X is usually clever enough not to make any changes should that happen. Just try again.

Sometimes commands are too long to fit on one line of the book—an inherent limitation of both printed and electronic books. In such a case, the remainder of the line is indented beneath it, and you should type the entire line, hitting `Return` only at the end of the last line. You should usually type a space after the end of each line that overflows to the next, but it's always clear when you shouldn't. Using your common sense will once again provide dividends.

Usually you'll be shown the command that activates the secret feature discussed in the tip, followed by the command that turns it off again should you want to do so.

1.2 Using the Apple and Application Menus

Some tips refer to the *Apple menu*. Other tips refer to the *application menu*. The Apple menu is the menu at the top left of the screen, signified appropriately enough by the Apple logo.

The application menu is the menu to the right of this, usually named after the application in question and in bold text.

The *main menu* simply refers to the entire menu bar along the top of the screen.

1.3 Making a Time Machine Backup

It's generally good advice to make use of the Time Machine backup utility, if you aren't already doing so. Even better advice is to have Time Machine perform a backup before undertaking some tips in this book that tweak system files. To do so, click the Time Machine icon at the top right of the screen, and select Back Up Now from the menu that appears.

1.4 Using the Mouse or Trackpad

Some tips require you to right-click to access special, context-sensitive menus. If you're using a standard PC mouse with two (or more) buttons, you'll find the right mouse button works fine. If you're using an Apple-manufactured mouse or trackpad, there are a variety of ways to right-click, as follows:

- Hold down `Control` and left-click in the usual way.

- If you're using a trackpad, bunch two fingers together and click (or tap if you've enabled tap-to-click in System Preferences).

- If you're using an Apple Magic Mouse, open System Preferences (Apple menu→System Preferences), click the Mouse icon, and then check Secondary Click. From then on, you can press the top-right side of the mouse to right-click.

- If you're using an Apple mouse (formerly called the Apple Mighty Mouse), open System Preferences (Apple menu→System Preferences), click the Mouse icon, and change the drop-down menu pointing to the top right of the mouse to read Secondary Button. See Figure 1, *Activating right-clicking with an Apple mouse*, on page 4.

Several tips in this book make reference to trackpad gestures. In nearly all cases, these gestures require a multitouch trackpad, such as the stand-alone Magic Trackpad or the glass "buttonless" trackpads that have been featured in the MacBook series since late 2008.

1.5 Having an Admin Account

Most tips presented here assume you will be using an admin account. This is the standard type of account created when you first set up your Mac. If you share your Mac with somebody else, the other user might have created a standard account or even one managed with parental controls for you to use. You'll need to speak with this person about getting a full admin account before proceeding with the tips.

1.6 Logging Out and Back In

Sometimes you'll have to log out and then back in again to make the changes active. To do this, save all your files, click the Apple menu, and then choose the Log Out option. On the main login screen that subsequently appears, click the icon representing your user account, and enter your password when prompted.

1.7 Using Program Windows

In this book I make frequent reference to common program window elements. Most are obvious, but to avoid confusion and get more details, see the following list (and check out Figure 2, *Program window controls referenced in this book*, on page 5):

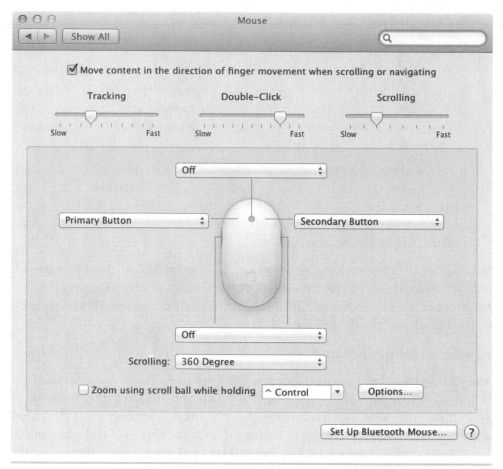

Figure 1—Activating right-clicking with an Apple mouse

1. Tabs: Clicking each tab button takes you to a different sheet with a different page of options. The currently selected tab button is darkened.

2. Checkboxes: Clicking puts a check in the box, activating that particular feature. Clicking again removes the check, deactivating that feature. Multiple checkboxes can be selected.

3. Radio buttons: Like checkboxes, clicking in the circle activates that feature. The difference is that with radio buttons, you can select only one choice within the options offered.

4. Drop-down lists: Clicking a drop-down list shows a menu from which you can select an option.

5. Padlock: When the padlock is locked in a System Preferences window, only trivial options can be edited. Clicking the padlock will prompt you for your login password and only then allow access to all other options.

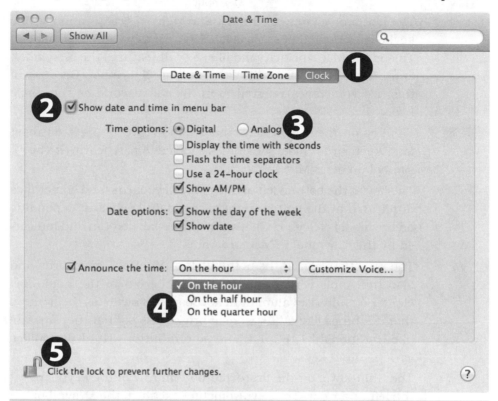

Figure 2—Program window controls referenced in this book

1.8 Using the Mac Keyboard and Shortcuts

Lastly, a word about the Mac keyboard. Over the years, the various Mac modifier keys have been renamed a few times, leading to some confusion. Further confusion is caused by the fact that different countries refer to the keys in different ways.

Throughout this book I simply refer to the keys by the names that appear on modern American English Mac keyboards—Command or Option, for example.

If you see something like Command+Space, that's an instruction to hold down the Command key and then hit Space. Another example is Option+Command+D, which is an instruction to hold down Option and Command before hitting the D key.

For reference purposes, you might find the following table useful. It explains the location and alternative names of the Mac's various function keys.

Key	Description
Command	The key immediately to the left and right of Space on most Mac keyboards. Sometimes this is labeled with the word *Cmd* instead. This is the Mac's primary modifier key. It features the ⌘ symbol, and on older keyboards it also uses the symbol. Because of this, it's sometimes referred to in the wider world as the *Apple key*.
Option	The key on the second left (and second right) of Space on most Mac keyboards, also sometimes labeled *Alt*. It features the ⌥ symbol on older Mac keyboards.
Control	The key at the bottom left of most Mac keyboards (and sometimes duplicated at the bottom right of the main keyboard, depending on the model of keyboard). It's sometimes labeled *Ctrl* and indicated by the ^ symbol in Mac programs.
Fn	The Function key, at the bottom left of MacBook keyboards and also the Apple wireless keyboard; at the left of the home key cluster on full-sized aluminum keyboards. It switches the hotkeys that do things like adjust screen brightness so that they operate like traditional F1, F2, F3, and so on, buttons. It also modifies various other keys.
Shift	The Shift keys, on the first-from-bottom row of the keyboard, at the left and right. The keys sometimes feature the ⇧ symbol.
Tab	The Tab key, located to the left of the main QWERTY row of keys. It sometimes has the symbol ⇥.
Return	The Return/Enter key, used to end a line of text and begin a new one, as well as to complete typed commands. It sometimes has the symbol ↵.
Delete	The Delete key, used to erase a character behind the cursor and located at the top right of the main keyboard beneath the Eject key. On PC keyboards this is often called Backspace, but in the world of Apple computers (and this book) it's referred to as Delete. (This key is also different from the *forward* delete key, indicated by Delete ⌦, and found on full-sized Mac keyboards within the home key cluster.)
Eject	The Eject key, located at the top right of the main keyboard on some MacBook computers and featuring the standard eject symbol

Key	Description
	(MacBook Air and MacBook Pro Retina computers, which lack an optical drive, have the power button in this location). It is used to eject CDs/DVDs from the CD/DVD-ROM drive.
Cursor keys	The cursor keys (indicated by arrow symbols like ←, →, ↑, and ↓) are located at the bottom right of MacBook keyboards and Apple wireless keyboards and in the right third of wired keyboards.

Several tips in this book refer to default OS X keyboard shortcuts for Mission Control. You might find the shortcuts you use are slightly different. To switch to the defaults, open System Preferences (Apple menu→System Preferences), click the Keyboard icon, and then ensure the Keyboard Shortcuts tab is selected. In the list on the left, select Mission Control, and then click the Restore Defaults button. You can then quit System Preferences.

Deactivating for iTunes

The previous method works for most OS X apps, although Safari and iTunes are two exceptions. It appears it's impossible to turn it off in Safari, but you can disable rubber-band scrolling iTunes by quitting the iTunes if it's open and then opening Terminal and typing the following:

```
defaults write com.apple.iTunes disable-elastic-scroll -bool YES
```

Should you decide you'd like to reactivate rubber-band scrolling in iTunes, you should quit the app and then use the following command within Terminal:

```
defaults delete com.apple.iTunes disable-elastic-scroll
```

Tip 3

Stop Scrollbars from Disappearing

In recent versions of OS X, the once reliable notion of scrollbars appearing at the right and (sometimes) bottom of the screen has seen some attention from Apple's software engineers.

In OS X Mountain Lion the scrollbars are invisible unless you scroll the document or simply place two fingers on the trackpad. This leaves those who like to click and grab the scroller in the lurch, because if you move the mouse cursor to where the scrollbar usually is, there's nothing there—both the vertical and horizontal scrollbars (if the window has one) remain invisible!

Within System Preferences (Apple menu→System Preferences), you can opt to always have the scrollbar always visible—click the General icon, and select Show Scroll Bars. This is certainly a solution but not an elegant one.

Viewing Scrollbars When the Cursor Hovers Over Them

Luckily there's a secret setting that allows the best of both worlds—it will cause the scrollbars to appear when your mouse cursor hovers over the edge of the window (or bottom, if the document you're viewing scrolls horizontally). Otherwise, the scrollbars be invisible unless you're scrolling through the document, as mentioned earlier.

To activate the secret setting, open Terminal, and type the following:

```
defaults write -g NSOverlayScrollerShowOnMouseOver -bool TRUE
```

Then log out and back in again for the changes to take effect. Note that if this doesn't seem to work and you're using a standard PC mouse, you might also have to switch the Show Scroll Bars setting in System Preferences, as mentioned earlier, to When Scrolling.

Deactivating Scrollbars-on-Hover

To deactivate the new feature, again open a Terminal window, and type the following:

```
defaults delete -g NSOverlayScrollerShowOnMouseOver
```

Then log out and back in again for the changes to take effect.

Tip 4

Make Your Mac Speak with Siri's Voice

At the time of this writing, the iPhone tool Siri hasn't yet been integrated with OS X (although OS X has a dictation tool that you can activate via the Dictation & Speech component of System Preferences). However, you can install Siri's voice files to OS X Mountain Lion and use its built-in speech tools to have the Siri voice talk to you upon request, such as reading aloud highlighted text.

Activating the Siri Voice Files

Here are the steps needed to switch to the Siri voice files:

1. Open System Preferences (Apple menu→System Preferences), and click the Dictation & Speech icon.

2. When the Dictation & Speech pane appears, click the Text to Speech tab.

3. Click the System Voice drop-down list, and select Customize.

4. In the drop-down dialog box, scroll down and select Samantha, which will be under the English (United States) heading. Then click OK. (If you're British, you might want to select the Daniel voice under the English [United Kingdom] heading to get the default British Siri voice; Australian users should select Karen under the English [Australia] heading.)

5. You'll be asked if you want to download and install a new voice. Agree to do so.

6. The voice will now be downloaded and installed, although be aware that it's almost half a gigabyte in size so might take some time to come down the line. Once it's finished, select it within the System Voice drop-down list within System Preferences.

Testing the New Voice

You can test the new voice within Safari or TextEdit by highlighting a paragraph of text and then clicking Edit→Speech→Start Speaking. Note that it takes a few seconds for Speech to start the first time you use it, and you might have to quit and restart the app in question for the new voice to start working. See also Tip 290, *Make Your Mac Speak*, on page 310.

Under the Dictation & Speech heading of System Preferences, you can activate other spoken helpers, such as speaking dialog boxes when they appear. These are primarily designed to help the partially sighted or blind, but they can be fun to play around with!

If you get tired of the Siri voice, you can switch to any of the other voices using the System Voice drop-down list, as described earlier. The default voice is Alex.

Tip 5

Supertip: Dictate Like a Pro

OS X Mountain Lion includes speech recognition, which you can activate by opening System Preferences (Apple menu→System Preferences), selecting Dictation & Speech, and clicking the On radio button on the Dictation tab.

Using it is very simple—just tap the `Fn` key twice (or one of the `Control` keys if you're using a full-sized external keyboard) and then speak. Double-tap the key again when you've finished.

Specifying Capital Letters, Spacing, and Line Breaks

Here's how to specify capitalization when dictating:

- Capitalizing a word: Say "cap" before the word you to capitalize. For example, to enter the phrase "We should all read the good Book," you would say, "We should all read the good *cap* Book."

- Using title case (capitalizing the start of each word): Say "caps on" before the words you want in title case and then say "caps off" after. For example, for the phrase "The Town of Bath is Lovely in Spring," you'd say "*caps on* the town of bath is lovely in spring *caps off.*"

- Block capitals: To capitalize an entire word (the equivalent of using Caps Lock when typing), say "all caps." For the phrase "I need the report RIGHT NOW," you'd dictate "I need the report *all caps on* right now *all caps off.*" An individual word can be put in capitals by just saying "all caps" before it: "I need the report *all caps* now and not later" produces "I need the report NOW and not later."

- All lowercase: To dictate words without any capitalization whatsoever, use "no caps" in the same way as described for "all caps." Dictating "I want to live in *no caps on* new york *no caps off*" produces "I want to live in new york."

- Prevent hyphenation: OS X's Dictation feature is clever enough to hyphenate words that need it, but you can stop it from doing so by saying "spacebar": "This is a low *spacebar* budget enterprise" will produce "This is a low budget enterprise."

- Force hyphenation: Should you say something you think should be hyphenated but OS X's Dictation doesn't realize, you can simply say "hyphen" —"He was a no *hyphen* good man" will type "He was a no-good man."

- Remove spaces altogether: To create a sentence or series of words without spaces between them (*compounding* words), use "no space." As with the dictation terms earlier, it can be used singularly to indicate two words should be joined, or it can be turned "on" and "off" before and after a series of words: "We are best *no space* friends" will type "We are bestfriends"; saying "We are *no space on* best friends forever *no space off*" will type "We are bestfriendsforever."

- Inserting line breaks: To insert a line break, just say "new line." To insert a paragraph break (that is, an empty line before the following sentence), just say "new para."

Specifying Punctuation, Symbols, and Numerals

In most cases, inserting punctuation is intuitive and obvious. Saying "full stop" or "period" will insert that symbol, for example. Saying "copyright sign" will insert a copyright symbol, and saying "at sign" will insert @. Saying "inverted question mark" will produce the ¿ symbol.

OS X will automatically insert "curly quotes" but if you specifically want a noncurly quotation mark, say "backquote."

Currency symbols, including the dollar, must be followed by "sign" if not used with numbers: to say "$31" you can simply say "thirty-one dollars" but to type "We need more $," you would have to say "We need more *dollar sign*."

You can also insert a long dash by saying "em dash." To insert ellipsis (…), say either "dot dot dot" or "ellipsis."

Should you want to use Roman numerals, just say them as you would normally preceded by numeral: "The year of my birth was *numeral* MCMLXXII." Similarly to inserting an actual number rather than the word for the number (that is, "5" rather than "five"), say "numeral" beforehand: "He reported there were *numeral* five of them" will type "There were 5 of them."

Inserting Emoticons

What if you want to indicate your vague emotional state via clever use of punctuation? Apple has thought of that. Simply saying "smiley face," "winky face," and "frowny face" will insert :-), ;-), and :-(, respectively.

Navigating Around Text

Although navigating the cursor through text is best done via the keyboard or mouse, the dictation tool offers two commands to move the cursor: "next line" will move the cursor to the next line of text, while "next paragraph" will move it to the next paragraph.

Tip 6

Get Rid of Files—Securely

Whenever you empty the trash, the files are deleted in the standard way; that is, the OS X filesystem makes the space they occupied available for another use. However, the actual content of the files sticks around on the disk until it's overwritten, and it can be recovered using one of the many third-party file recovery tools available.

To avoid this, you can securely empty the trash, which involves writing over the data with zeroes so that it can't be recovered (at least outside of a high-tech crime lab), but bear in mind that the files might still exist in your Time Machine backup (see Tip 307, *Make Time Machine Forget a File*, on page 322).

Note that if your Mac has a solid-state hard disk (SSD), such as those fitted to MacBook Air and Retina MacBook Pro computers, securely erasing files or the trash in the ways described next is ineffective and likely unnecessary because SSDs employ TRIM to clean up old data.[1] The best method of protecting an SSD (or any kind of storage disk) from data snoops is to encrypt its contents—see *Exploring OS X: FileVault*, on page 232.

Securely Emptying the Trash

To securely empty the trash, simply click and hold the trash icon in the Dock until the context menu appears (or right-click the Dock icon). Let go of the mouse button and then hold down the Command key. The menu will change to read Secure Empty Trash. Click to do so. You can also open a Finder window and click the Secure Empty Trash entry on the Application menu.

Be aware that deleting files securely takes significantly longer than deleting unsecurely. With a very full trash can, it might take hours. The work of securely emptying the trash will take place in the background, however.

Always Emptying the Trash Securely

To always securely empty the trash, open a Finder window and click the Application menu and then Preferences. Then click the Advanced tab, and check Empty Trash Securely.

Wiping Individual Files

While there's no built-in method of securely obliterating individual files on the desktop, short of moving them to the trash and then selecting to securely empty it, you can use the command-line tool srm to delete files and then overwrite the space with random data. srm is perhaps one of the most dangerous commands available on your Mac, however, so use it carefully!

Next I explain how to use it at the command line, before explaining how it can be used to create a simple Automator service for use in Finder windows and on the desktop.

---

1. See http://arstechnica.com/security/2011/03/ask-ars-how-can-i-safely-erase-the-data-from-my-ssd-drive/, although if you've fitted a third-party SSD to your Mac, see also http://www.groths.org/?page_id=322.

Using srm at the Command Line

Open Terminal (open Finder, select the Applications list, and then double-click Terminal in the Utilities folder), and at the command prompt type srm. Then drag and drop from a Finder window onto the Terminal window the file you'd like to eradicate. For example, if I wanted to delete file.txt from my desktop, after I'd dragged and dropped it onto the Terminal window, I'd see the following:

```
srm /Users/keir/Desktop/file.txt
```

Then hit Return to complete the command and eradicate the file. As with all Terminal commands, if you see no output, then everything has worked fine. Depending on the size of the file, deletion should take no more than a few seconds.

The srm command is intended to be a secure version of the basic rm Unix command. Therefore, securely deleting a directory and its files can be achieved with srm -rf followed by the directory name and path. However, when deleting many files in this way, it's useful to add the -v (verbose) switch so you get a progress display and can confirm when each file is deleted. In other words, the command for deleting a directory would be srm -rfv .

Creating a GUI Secure Delete Tool

Using Automator you can create a service that appears on the menu that appears whenever you right-click a file and offers a secure delete function powered by srm. Here's how to set it up:

1. Start Automator, which you'll find near the top of the Applications listing within Finder. When it starts, click the Service icon within the Choose a File Type For Your Document dialog box, and then click the Choose button. If this dialog box doesn't appear, click File→New.

2. In the Automator program window, click in the search field above the second column from the left, and type Run Shell Script. This will filter the list beneath to one item, which you should drag to the right side of the program window, dropping it over the area containing the text Drag Actions or Files Here to Build Your Workflow.

3. At the top right of the window, alongside the heading Service Receives Selected, you'll see two drop-down lists alongside each other: Text and Any Application. Change the first to Files or Folders and the second (on the right) to Finder.

4. Under the Run Shell Script heading, change the Pass Input drop-down to As Arguments.

5. In the large text area beneath the Run Shell Script heading, delete what's already there, and type the following; for an example from my test system, see Figure 4, *Creating a secure delete GUI tool*:

```
for i in "$@"
do
srm -rf "$i"
done
```

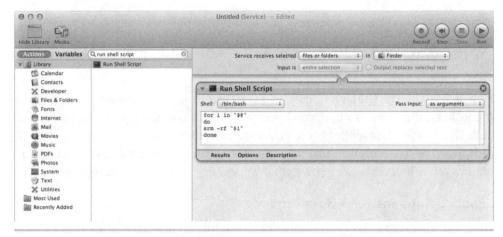

Figure 4—Creating a secure delete GUI tool

6. Click File→Save. Because this is a service, there's no need to specify a destination for the file. However, you will need to type a filename. This is what will appear in the menu when you right-click files, so something illustrative like Secure Delete will do. Click the Save button in the dialog when you're done.

7. Once the service has been saved, you can quit Automator.

You can now test your new service—right-click a file/folder (or a selection of them), and select Secure Delete from the menu. Alternatively, you may have to click Services→Secure Delete. After a few seconds, the file or folder will simply disappear and will be gone forever (it *won't* go to the trash!).

Bear in mind two things: first, there's no status update when deleting files this way, and second, large files or large collections of files might take some time to be deleted. Deleting will take place in the background, so, once started, you can get on with other things.

Also bear in mind as mentioned earlier that there's no way to undo file/folder deletion that's done this way—it's an extremely thorough way of eradicating data!

To remove your Secure Delete service, open a Finder window, and hit `Shift`+`Command`+`G`. In the dialog box that appears, type ~/Library/Services. Then drag the Secure Delete service file to the trash. Then log out and back in again.

Tip 7

Auto-answer FaceTime Calls

Here's a neat tip that enables the FaceTime app to automatically answer incoming calls from contacts you specify. You can use it if you're happy having calls from specified colleagues, friends, or family automatically answered, although be careful because there'll be nothing stopping these incoming callers from instantly seeing what's happening in front of your computer!

Enabling Auto-answer on FaceTime

Here are the steps required to enable automatic answering of calls on Face-Time:

1. Start by opening FaceTime if it isn't already open, and log in. Then look for the contact details of the individual(s) you'd like to enable auto-answering for. This will be listed in your Contacts or Favorites list and will probably be an email address. Write the details down, and then quit FaceTime.

2. Open a Terminal window (open Finder, select the Applications list, and then in the list of applications double-click Terminal within the Utilities folder), and type the following line:

    ```
    defaults write com.apple.FaceTime AutoAcceptInvites -bool TRUE
    ```

3. Then type the following line, and at the end type the FaceBook ID of the individual or device you want to auto-answer when they call. For example, if the contact FaceTime ID is keir@example.com, you'd type the following:

    ```
    defaults write com.apple.FaceTime AutoAcceptInvitesFrom -array-add
        keir@keirthomas.com
    ```

If the FaceTime ID is a cell phone number, you need to type it after the command without any spaces. For example, if the FaceTime ID was the cell phone number +1 555 123 1234, you'd type the following:

```
defaults write com.apple.FaceTime AutoAcceptInvitesFrom -array-add
    +15551231234
```

Restart FaceTime, and you should find calls from the FaceTime IDs you added are automatically answered!

You can repeat step 3 and add more FaceTime IDs to the list.

Removing Auto-answer Entries

To remove a FaceTime ID from the auto-answer list, you can use the following command, but unfortunately this removes *all* of the entries you might have added using the previous commands.

Quit FaceTime, open a Terminal window, and type the following two lines:

```
defaults delete com.apple.FaceTime AutoAcceptInvites
defaults delete com.apple.FaceTime AutoAcceptInvitesFrom
```

If you have Xcode installed and are competent using its Plist editor, you can manually remove individual auto-answer entries from the FaceTime preferences file, which is found in the ~/Library/Preferences/com.apple.FaceTime.plist file.

Tip 8

Instantly Add Movies and Music to iTunes

If you use third-party software to download music and movies to your computer, you'll be familiar with the rather lengthy process needed to add them to your iTunes library—you have to start iTunes, then ensure the correct music or movie list is visible, and finally drag and drop the files onto the program window....

However, there's a hidden folder you can use to import music and movies straight into iTunes. All you need to do is configure any app you use to download files straight into this folder, and they will be instantly imported—even if iTunes isn't running at the time.

To find the folder, open Finder, hit Shift+Command+G, and then type ~/Music/iTunes/iTunes Media/. One of the folders you should see will be Automatically

Add to iTunes. As its name suggests, any files copied into this folder will be added to iTunes automatically. Assuming you have kept the default preferences setting of iTunes organizing your media folders, any files placed there will be moved out of the folder and automatically filed within the Music folder whenever iTunes is running, so it should appear empty most of the time.

You can create a desktop alias of the folder by clicking and dragging it to the desktop, before pressing `Option`+`Command` and releasing the mouse button. You can then simply drag and drop files onto the alias instead.

Tip 9

Be a Messages App Keyboard Wizard

Because the Messages app is all about typing and because reaching for the mouse or trackpad can be a distraction, keyboard shortcuts are essential. Here are some of the more useful:

Shortcut	Description
`Control`+`Command`+A / I / O / W	Set your status as available (A), invisible (I), away (W), or offline (O).
`Command`+1	Show buddies list.
`Control`+`Tab`	Move between conversations listed on the left of the Messages window (if two or more conversations are listed).
`Option`+`Up` / `Down`	Cycle through things you've already typed and sent —useful if you need to repeat something said earlier in the conversation. Hit `Return` to resend the message.
`Option`+`Command`+B	Show the entry within Contacts of the person you're chatting to; if they have no entry within your address book, you'll instantly create a new one.
`Shift`+`Command`+I	Show profile details of the person you're chatting to, and set audio alerts/bounce the Messages icon in the Dock/run an AppleScript when they perform various actions, such as come online or send you a message.

Shortcut	Description
Option + Command + E	Compose a new email to the individual in Mail, provided an email address is associated with the individual's IM chat account.
Option + Command + L	Show a list of recent and ongoing file transfers (to transfer a file, drag and drop it onto the conversation within the Messages window, or hit Option + Command + F to open a dialog box where you can select a file).
Shift + Command + K	Add a timestamp to the conversation, similar to that which appears when you initially go online and start chatting with somebody—useful if you want to record when something was said.
Option + Command + K	Permanently delete conversation—cannot be undone.
Shift + Command + E	Open video effects window so you can apply special effects to any video conversation (click the camera icon at the top right of the chat window to start video conversation; note that Messages docsn't support video calls on all chat protocols).

Tip 10

Store Absolutely Any File in iCloud

The built-in Preview app lets you add images and PDFs to its iCloud store (click File→Open to add files), which are what the app usually displays on most Macs, but that's not all it'll accept for upload. It'll also store (and let you view!) Microsoft Office documents, such as Word, Excel, and PowerPoint files. Strangely, however, it won't accept more primitive office document formats such as rich-text files (those with an .rtf extension) or comma-separated value spreadsheets (those with a .csv extension).

It's worth bearing in mind that, just like with Finder windows, you can hold down Option to copy a file to iCloud, rather than moving it there, which is the default behavior.

Note that the range of image files Preview will accept for upload to iCloud is very broad—you can save Photoshop (.psd) documents there, for example, and view them within Preview.

TextEdit accepts any kind of file for upload to its iCloud storage area—from MP3 files and movies to images—even though it can't open them (attempting to open, say, a movie will produce a screen full of seemingly random characters, although you can still watch the movie in Quick Look by selecting it in the iCloud listing and hitting `Space`).

TextEdit's egalitarian approach to iCloud makes it an ideal way of transferring files from one Mac to another via iCloud, provided they're both logged in to the same iCloud ID—just drag and drop the file onto the TextEdit window of the first computer, and then drag and drop it from TextEdit's iCloud listing to a Finder window on the other Mac.

Tip 11

Use a Secret, Alternative Cut and Paste

Ever had something important held in the clipboard, like a picture, yet wanted to quickly cut and paste some text within a document? OS X actually contains two clipboards, although the second is much more primitive than the main one and will cut and paste only text. You won't find it on any menus, either, and it is available only via two keyboard shortcuts. You can use it in the usual way by highlighting some text, using `Control`+`K` to cut the text, and pressing `Control`+`Y` to paste the content in the new position. (Note that's `Control` and not `Command`; longtime Unix/Linux users will, of course, recognize this secondary clipboard as an implementation of the kill and yank tools found in the likes of Emacs.)

There's no "copy" option, unfortunately, although you can emulate this by cutting the text with `Control`+`K` and then immediately pasting it back in with `Control`+`Y`, before moving to the new position where you'd like the text to be inserted and again pasting with `Control`+`Y`.

Only plain text is copied—any formatting such as bold or italics is lost. Additionally, although it should work fine within most OS X applications, it probably will not work if you cut text from one app to paste into another app

—in my testing, each app seemed to have its own private secondary clipboard. However, the only way to find out for sure is to give it a try!

Tip 12

Correct Misspellings or Typos Without the Mouse

Although in many OS X apps you can right-click a misspelled or mistyped word to see suggested replacements (that is, words that are underlined in red or blue), you can also simply move the cursor to the end of the word using the cursor keys and then wait a second until a list of suggested replacements appears beneath. Hit the Down cursor key and then the Left/Right cursor keys to select a replacement, before hitting `Return` to select the one you're happy with (or hit `Esc` to quit the replacements menu). If no list appears, it's probably the case that OS X has no suggestions for that particular misspelling or typo.

Tip 13

Create iCloud Folders

Here's a tip that will be obvious to anybody who owns an iPad or iPhone but possibly a revelation to anybody else.

Apps that let you save files within iCloud, such as TextEdit and Preview, allow you to create folders within iCloud to help organize documents. But there's no New Folder button. Instead, you can create a new folder by dropping one file on top of another (provided either file isn't locked). You'll immediately be prompted to enter a name for the new folder. Simple!

You can add new items to the folder by dragging and dropping them on top, just like in Finder. Note that you can also elastic-band select many files at once.

To delete the folder, you'll need to empty it of all its contents by either dragging the files out or deleting them. Then the folder will vanish.

Note that there are a couple of caveats. First, iCloud folders aren't like those on your hard disk because you can't create another folder within them. All each folder can contain are files. Second, note that any file that's locked (see Tip 199, *Lock Files for Safety*, on page 222) can't be added to an iCloud folder until it's unlocked.

Tip 14

See What Folders You've Accessed Recently

Want to see a list of folders or places you've recently accessed in Finder? Just click and hold the back button at the top left of the Finder window. In the list that appears, you can click any of the folders to jump straight to that location.

You can also click and hold the forward button to select one of the folders or places later in your history—in other words, that you previously visited *after* visiting that folder! (Note: This also works in most web browsers, where clicking and holding back or forward will show a list of your most recently accessed websites.)

Tip 15

See Bluetooth Signal Strength

If you use any Bluetooth devices with your Mac, such as a keyboard or mouse, there are a variety of ways you can view the strength of the signal between your Mac and the device(s).

Using System Preferences to View Signal Strength

To get the most information, you can use System Preferences (Apple menu→ System Preferences). Once it's open, click the Bluetooth icon, and then select the Bluetooth device in the list while holding down Option—see Figure 5, *Viewing the signal strength of a Bluetooth peripheral*, on page 27. You'll see a number along with a familiar signal bar display that you might be used to with your cell phone or Wi-Fi signal.

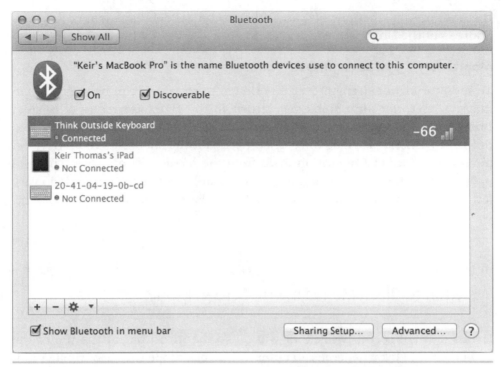

Figure 5—Viewing the signal strength of a Bluetooth peripheral

As with similar displays, five bars is the maximal signal strength, while one bar indicates a weak and potentially unstable connection (the solution is to move the Bluetooth device closer to the Mac or to remove any objects that might be obscuring your Mac or the device, especially those that are metal). To get an updated signal reading, repeatedly click the Bluetooth's entry in the list while holding down Option.

The number corresponds directly with the bar display and shows the power ratio (dBmW) of the signal. A smaller number indicates a stronger signal—in my test -40 equated to a strong five-bar signal, while -70 equated to a poor signal strength of one bar.

Quickly Viewing Signal Strength on the Desktop

Another way to view signal strength that doesn't use System Preferences is as follows: hold down Option while clicking the Bluetooth icon at the top right of the screen, before moving the mouse down the menu showing all connected devices (you can release Option after clicking the Bluetooth icon). Here you'll see not only the power ratio figure mentioned earlier but also battery life (in the case of Apple peripherals) and other technical details, such as the MAC address of the Bluetooth device.

Monitoring Signal Strength Over Time

To monitor signal strength over a period of time, which can be useful when diagnosing connection problems, return to the Bluetooth pane of System Preferences, and select the device you want to monitor in the list. Then hold down `Option` before clicking the cog icon beneath the list of Bluetooth devices, and select Monitor Connection RSSI from the menu that appears. This will open a new window showing a graph of connection strength, updated every few seconds continuously until you click the Close button at the bottom right.

Tip 16

Switch to Black Menus in Full-Screen Mode

Here's a small secret tweak that will make the menu bar at the top of the screen turn black whenever you enter full-screen mode with any application. It brings no new functionality other than altering the appearance of the menu.

Open a Terminal window (open Finder, select the Applications list, and then in the list of applications double-click Terminal within the Utilities folder), and type the following:

```
defaults write -g NSFullScreenDarkMenu -bool TRUE
```

Then log out and back in again. Switch any compatible app to full-screen mode (click the arrow at the top right of the window or click View→Enter Full Screen), and then push the mouse against the top of the screen to see the now-blackened menu bar appear.

To switch back to the standard gray tint menu, again open a Terminal window, and type the following:

```
defaults delete -g NSFullScreenDarkMenu
```

Log out and back in again for the changes to take effect.

Tip 17

Create Reminders Ultra-Quickly

Imagine the situation: you receive an email from a friend reminding you to pick up a book for him from the bookstore. Being a Mac OS X user, you know exactly how to handle the situation: you can add an entry in the Reminders app, which will then be shared with your iPhone, iPod touch, and iPad. No more forgetting!

There's just one problem: starting Reminders and then creating the actual entry on the list is a lot of effort and far from the casual single-click we might expect of Apple technology.

There are two solutions to this terrible problem, as follows.

Dragging and Dropping to the Reminders App

If the mail you've received has as its subject line the nature of the reminder (e.g., "Don't forget to pick up the book!"), you can drag and drop the email from the list within Mail to the Reminders icon on the Dock, or you can drag and drop the email on top of the Reminders program window if it's open. This will instantly create a new reminder named after the subject of the mail, and you'll even be provided with a link to the original email within the reminder (click Show in Mail).

If anybody has replied to the original email or if it's part of a series received from the sender, then this trick needs a little modification—click the email in the list so it's visible in the preview pane on the right side of the Mail window. Then move the mouse cursor over the left side of the email preview, near the Subject and Reply-To headings. The cursor will change to a hand grabber. You can then click and drag the mail to the Reminders app, as described earlier.

Adding a "Create Reminder" Entry to Right-Click Menus

As easy as drag and drop is, wouldn't it be handy just to be able to select the text in the email (i.e., "pick up the book from the store"), then right-click, and select a menu option that will instantly create a Reminders entry—even if Reminders isn't running? This function isn't built into OS X but can be easily created and will work in almost any app. The following are the necessary steps, although there are actually two methods—the first will simply add a reminder without prompting you for any details, while the second will pop up a dialog box wherein you can select which Reminders list to use, the reminder's priority, and its due date.

Creating a Simple Reminders Service

Here's how to create the first of the options mentioned earlier—a simple right-click option that will instantly create a new reminder in the default list based on the text you select:

1. Open Automator, which can be found in the Applications view of Finder. If the new file dialog doesn't appear, click File→New. In the Choose a Type For Your Document dialog box, select Service (the cog icon), and then click the Choose button.

2. In the search field above the list of actions within the Automator program window, type New Reminders Item. Click and drag the only item in the list (which will also read New Reminders Item) to the right side of the Automator window, over the text Drag Actions or Files Here to Build Your Workflow.

3. Leave everything blank. All you need to do is click File→Save and then type a name for your new service in the Save Service As dialog box. This is what'll appear in the right-click menu, so something like Create Reminder is fine (there's no need to choose somewhere to save the service because they're automatically saved in the correct location). Then you can quit Automator.

You can try your new service straightaway. Just highlight some text, right-click it, and select Create Reminder (or Services→Create Reminder if there's no Create Reminder option on the menu). If Reminders is running, you'll see the entry has been added, but even if it isn't, the entry is still added, as you'll find when you next start the app.

Creating a Pop-up Dialog Box Service

Here's how to create a service similar to the one earlier except when you select Create Reminder from the right-click menu, a dialog box will pop up each time to let you set options such as which reminder list will be used, its priority, and due date.

1. Follow steps 1 and 2 earlier so that the basic New Reminders Item automator service is in place. However, click the Options link at the bottom of the service.

2. Check the box Show This Action When The Workflow Runs; then check Show Only The Selected Items.

3. You will now see a checkbox alongside each item of the service. Check everything, except the Title field. You should end up with something that looks like Figure 6, *Creating a service to create new reminders*. Now repeat the earlier step 4 to save the new action.

Figure 6—Creating a service to create new reminders

Test our new service by highlighting some text, right-clicking it, and selecting Create Reminder (or Services→Create Reminder if there's no Create Reminder option on the menu). A dialog box should appear letting you set various options, such as which of your Reminders lists to add the new reminder to. Select from them, and click the Continue button. (Note that, on my test Mac, the first time I used this new service, an additional dialog box popped up asking if the app could access my contacts; I assume this is a bug, but agreeing to it will do no harm.)

If Reminders is running, you'll see the entry has been added—complete with the attributes you set—but even if it isn't, the entry is still added, as you'll find when you next start the app.

Removing the Menu Entry

To remove the service, should you want to, open Finder, and then hit Shift + Command + G. In the dialog box that appears, type ~/Library/Services, and hit Return. Then drag the service you created to the trash. Log out and back in again to complete the removal.

Tip 18

Right-Click to Share Anything

OS X Mountain Lion features Share Sheets, which are buttons at the top of certain program windows (including Finder) that allow you to instantly share things via Twitter, email, Facebook, and Messages or to AirDrop what you're viewing or working on (provided accounts for these services are set up within the Mail, Contacts & Calendars component of System Preferences, of course).

However, you can also right-click just about anything to share it in this way —right-click an image file on the desktop, for example, and you can select the Share option on the menu to instantly tweet or post it to your Facebook wall. This works in Finder windows too, where you can share any file via email, AirDrop, and Messages. Highlight some text (and/or images) within TextEdit before right-clicking it, and the same Share option will appear on the menu, allowing you to send just the highlighted text to your Twitter or Facebook accounts (if they Send button is grayed out and you're attempting to tweet something in this way, it might be because you've exceeded the 140-character limit!).

Tip 19

View Safari's Google History

To see a list of your recent searches in Safari, click in the Address and Search bar, delete what's there, then either click the magnifying glass icon at the left of the Address and Search bar or simply hit `Space`. The previous searches will appear in a list beneath, along with some recent history. You can jump between headings in the list using the keyboard by holding down `Command` and pressing the Up/Down cursor keys.

You can also quickly switch to an alternative search engine by selecting it from the bottom of this drop-down list. Your new search engine choice will remain in place until you again select a different choice—even after you restart Safari.

Tip 20

Open a Link Displayed in Terminal

If you see a web or email link within a Terminal window (in a man page, for example), simply hold down `Command` and then double-click it. The link will instantly open in your usual browser or email client, such as Safari or Mail.

For what it's worth, this will work even if you simply type an address into a Terminal window, even if it isn't preceded with http://.

Tip 21

Get Back "Save As"

With Lion, many OS X apps lost the ages-old Save As option on the File menu. After a file has been initially saved, the preferred way to save a new copy with a different filename is to use the Duplicate option on the File menu, which, as its name suggests, produces a copy of the original that you can then manually save with a new filename. Time-consuming, to say the least!

The good news is that Mountain Lion goes some way to restoring the Save As option. Alas, there are a couple of caveats, as follows:

• The Save As option on the file menu is hidden. To see it, activate the File menu by clicking it, and then hold down `Option`. It will appear where the Duplicate option usually is—see Figure 7, *Restoring the Save As entry to an application's menu*, on page 34. There's a keyboard shortcut for Save As that lets you avoid using the File menu, but it's somewhat convoluted —`Shift`+`Option`+`Command`+`S`.

• Mountain Lion's Save As option doesn't work quite the same way as you might be used to because of OS X's autosave and versions feature (see *Exploring OS X: Autosave and Versions*, on page 280). When you use Save As to create a copy of an older document you've edited, a checkbox headed Keep Changes In Original Document will appear at the bottom of the Save As dialog box. If this is checked, when you click the Save button, the changes you made since opening the original file will be saved to the

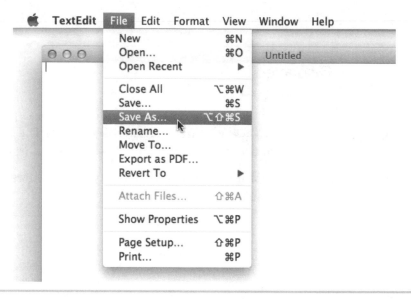

Figure 7—Restoring the Save As entry to an application's menu

old file in addition to the new one you've created. Therefore, you'll want to ensure this box is unchecked whenever you use Save As!

As described next, you can assign the old keyboard shortcut of Shift+Command+S to Save As, which has the added advantage of adding the Save As option permanently to the File menu once again. The Duplicate option will still be listed, but it will lose its shortcut key.

Adding a Save As option to the File menu

Here's what to do:

1. Open System Preferences (Apple menu→System Preferences), and click the Keyboard icon. In the pane that appears, select the Keyboard Shortcuts tab.

2. You'll see two separate panes within the window—the left-showing menu headings and the right-showing keyboard shortcuts. In the left pane, select the Application Shortcuts heading. On the right, click the small plus button beneath the pane.

3. In the dialog box that drops down, ensure All Applications is selected in the Application drop-down list, and in the Menu Title field type Save As.... It's important to type the capital letters at the beginning of each word and the three periods (ellipsis) following.

4. Place the cursor in the Keyboard Shortcut field, then hold down `Shift` plus `Command`, and finally tap the `S` key. This will enter the new shortcut. Then click the Add button and close System Preferences.

The changes should take effect within applications immediately. If not, simply restart the application.

Removing Save As from the Default Menu Options

To remove Save As from the File menu and restore the original key binding, follow these steps:

1. Open System Preferences once again, select the Keyboard option, and ensure the Keyboard Shortcuts tab is visible.

2. Make sure Applications Shortcuts is selected in the menu on the left, and then select your Save As... entry in the list on the right.

3. Hit the small minus key beneath the list. This will delete the entry you created. Then quit System Preferences.

Your changes will take effect immediately.

Tip 22

Quickly Navigate Launchpad

By clicking the little dots representing each page at the bottom of the Launchpad icon listing, you can instantly jump to that particular page, avoiding the need to scroll through each page before it.

If you want to navigate through Launchpad pages using the keyboard, hold down `Command`, and tap the Left/Right cursor keys.

You can move the highlight from icon to icon using the cursor keys on their own (hit `Return` to run an app), and hitting `Command`+`Down` will expand any folder you have highlighted (although hitting `Return` will also expand folders but not close them again if repeated afterward).

Clicking the dots at the bottom of the screen works in Safari's Show All Tabs view too (`Shift`+`Command`+`\` or pinch with two fingers on a trackpad)—just click the small dots at the bottom of the pages display to instantly switch to whichever page you want.

Tip 23

Turn Off Notifications with a Single Click

Should you need to concentrate without being interrupted by desktop notifications, you can quickly turn them off by holding down `Option` and clicking the show/hide notification icon at the top right of the screen. The icon will dim to indicate the notifications will no longer display. Notifications will resume the next day, but you can also repeat the previous step to instantly switch them on again should you want.

Tip 24

Increase Settings in Micro-Increments

You might be used to using the keyboard shortcuts on MacBooks to alter the sound volume, screen backlighting, or keyboard backlighting (if your MacBook features it). But if you've ever thought the jump between each increment in the on-screen bars display was too much, I have some good news for you.

By holding down `Shift` and `Option` before hitting the keys, you'll be able to adjust the sound and backlighting in micro-increments, which are much smaller than the usual range. Give it a try!

Tip 25

Access (and Back Up) All iCloud Documents

iCloud magically stores your data online whenever you choose to save or modify a file there. However, "hard copies" of any documents within iCloud are actually stored on your Mac's hard disk within a hidden directory. These files are automatically updated by the iCloud system service running in the background whenever any changes are made, either on your Mac or on other devices that access the files via iCloud.

Browsing the iCloud Store Folder

To browse to the iCloud store folder, open Finder, and then hit `Shift`+ `Command`+`G`. Then type the following into the dialog box that appears:

`~/Library/Mobile Documents`

Note how the icon at the top of the Finder window changes to show the fact you're browsing iCloud files.

The folder containing documents for each app will be named along the lines of `com~apple~`, followed by the name of the app. For example, the folder containing TextEdit documents is called `com~apple~TextEdit`.

There are two schools of thought when it comes to whether you should edit the files. Some people say that double-clicking the files within the hidden iCloud folder, to edit or view them, is just like accessing them via the app in question's iCloud file browser. However, other people (myself included) advise a more cautious approach because this is, after all, an unauthorized way of accessing the files. I advise treating everything you see as read-only: never delete, edit, or add to the files you see in `~/Library/Mobile Documents` because you might seriously corrupt your iCloud account. Bear in mind that even opening a file can sometimes lead to a new version being instantly saved, so it's best to use Quick Look only if you want to view files (select the file in Finder and hit `Space`).

Adding files to iCloud should be done using the application itself (see Tip 28, *Quickly Get Documents into (and out of) iCloud*, on page 39).

Creating an iCloud-Browsing Shortcut

You can easily create a custom search for Finder's sidebar that, when selected, will automatically list *all* files stored within iCloud—regardless of which application was used to save them. Here's how:

1. Open Finder, hit `Shift`+`Command`+`G`, and then type `~/Library/Mobile Documents` into the dialog box that appears. Then click the Go button.

2. Click in the Search field at the top right of the Finder window, and then hit `Space`. This will clear the list of files within Finder, but don't worry— it'll make sense in a moment.

3. In the Search bar that appears, select `Mobile Documents`. Then click the plus icon at the right side of the line.

4. A new search bar will be added. In the left drop-down list within it, ensure that Kind is selected. In the drop-down alongside, ensure Document is selected. You should now see all your iCloud files listed, regardless of the application used to save them.

5. Click the Save button in the search bar. This will show a dialog box where you can type a name for what will be the Finder sidebar link you'll click in the future. Call it something like iCloud, and click the Save button in the dialog box.

An icon will appear under the Favorites heading on the left of the Finder window. Clicking this will show all iCloud files. To delete it, hold down `Command` and drag the icon out of the Finder window, before releasing. The icon will disappear in a puff of smoke.

Backing Up iCloud Files Independently

By knowing where the files are stored, you can manually back them up using a third-party cloud backup service like SpiderOak (www.spideroak.com), for example. This provides an extra layer of insurance against a fault arising within the iCloud system. Just include the ~/Library/Mobile Documents folder in the list of those to be backed up.

Note that iCloud files are automatically backed up within Time Machine, as explained in Tip 90, *Use Time Machine with iCloud*, on page 94.

Tip 26

Sleep Your Mac with a Remote

If you have an Apple remote control, you can put your MacBook or iMac into sleep mode from a distance away by pointing the remote at the computer and then pressing and holding the central Play/Pause button for three to four seconds. Watch for a series of comic book-style Zs appear on the screen to indicate snoozing—see Figure 8, *Sleeping a MacBook Pro with an Apple remote*, on page 39!

The Mac can be woken from sleep in the normal way—usually by hitting a key on the keyboard or moving the mouse/touching the trackpad—although you can also click the Play button again on the remote.

Figure 8—Sleeping a MacBook Pro with an Apple remote

Tip 27

Restart a Jammed Finder

You can quickly reboot Finder if you see the "beach ball of death" by holding down Option and right-clicking the Finder's icon in the Dock. Then select Relaunch from the menu that appears.

Note that some people report that temporarily switching off Wi-Fi can also recover a crashed Finder. It's not quite clear why this works, but it's probably because Finder has gotten stuck while trying to access a network resource, and turning off the network frees it up. To turn off Wi-Fi, click the Wi-Fi icon at the top right of the screen and select Turn Wi-Fi Off. Then, when Finder has recovered, click the icon again, and this time select Turn Wi-Fi On.

Tip 28

Quickly Get Documents into (and out of) iCloud

While editing a document in apps that are compatible with iCloud, you can quickly move the file to iCloud—even if it has previously been saved on your hard disk. To do so, click the filename in the title bar, and then select the Move to iCloud entry from the menu that appears. Note that when it moves to iCloud, the file will no longer exist on your hard disk—it will disappear. This avoids the confusion of duplicated files.

To move a file *out* of iCloud, repeat the procedure to bring up the menu as described earlier, but this time select Move To. Then select a location on your hard disk from the file-browsing drop-down menu that appears (select Other at the bottom of the menu to specify a location that isn't listed). As discussed earlier, the file will disappear from iCloud as soon as it's saved to your hard disk in order to avoid confusing duplication.

Tip 29

Master Quick Look's Full-Screen Feature

Quick Look lets you select a file and, by hitting `Space`, quickly preview its contents without having to open it in any application. Like many apps on your Mac, it has a full-screen mode, which can be useful when examining things like images. There are quite a few methods of switching to full-screen mode, as follows:

- If you haven't yet activated Quick Look for the file, select it and hit `Option`+`Space` instead of just `Space`, which is the usual Quick Look shortcut key. This will instantly open Quick Look in full-screen mode. A drawback of activating Quick Look in this mode is that hitting `Option`+`Space` again won't close the Quick Look window. Instead, you must hit `Esc` or click the close button on the Quick Look floating toolbar.

- If already viewing a file in Quick Look and your Mac has a trackpad, you can switch to full-screen mode using the pinch-to-expand gesture (that is, placing your finger and thumb together on the trackpad and moving them apart; contracting them again will revert to a standard window). However, regardless of whether you have a trackpad, you can also switch to full-screen mode in an open QuickTime window by clicking the arrow at the top right of the window.

- There's also a secret setting that lets you switch to full-screen mode (and back) in Quick Look when you're viewing a file by rolling up the scroll wheel on a mouse or scrolling up on a trackpad. Scrolling down restores the Quick Look window to normal size.

Although seemingly useful, bear in mind that this tweak will mean you will no longer be able to scroll in any documents you Quick Look, unless you click and drag the scrollbar scroller at the right edge.

To make the change, open a Terminal window (open Finder, select the Applications list, and then in the list of applications double-click Terminal within the Utilities folder), and type the following:

```
defaults write com.apple.finder QLPreviewFakeMagnifyWithScrollwheel -bool
    TRUE;killall Finder
```

The change will take effect immediately, so give it a try.

To deactivate the feature, open a Terminal window, and type the following:

```
defaults delete com.apple.finder QLPreviewFakeMagnifyWithScrollwheel;killall
    Finder
```

Note that if you're Quick Looking an image smaller than your monitor's resolution in Quick Look's full-screen mode, it will be automatically magnified to fill the space. You can temporarily view the image at 100 percent by holding down the Option key.

Tip 30

Put Notes and Sticky Notes on Top

The Notes application in OS X Mountain Lion is very useful, but did you know that you can double-click a note in the list on the left to have it pop out in a window of its own? Not only that, but if you click Window→Float on Top, then all other program windows will appear beneath it so that it's always visible. This can be useful if you're copying and pasting from a number of browser windows into the note, for example. The note will stick around even if you close the main Notes program window (which you can make appear again by clicking Window→Notes or hitting Command + 0).

To switch it back to being a normal note, just close it in the usual way or again click Window→Float on Top.

If you prefer to use OS X's other note-taking app, Stickies, just select any note and click Note→Floating Window. That particular note will then be "always on top," as discussed earlier.

To switch the note back to acting like a standard sticky, which is to say other program windows cover it up, repeat the steps and remove the check from Floating Window on the Note menu.

Tip 31

Don't Delete Files When Copying

If you try to copy two or more files into a folder where files of that name already exist, you'll see a dialog box with buttons offering you the chance to keep both of the files mentioned (in which case, when copied, the file will have copy appended to its name), to stop the entire copying procedure, or to replace the existing file with the one you're copying. However, if you hold down Option, the Keep Both button will change to Skip. If you click it, the file mentioned in the dialog box won't be copied.

Tip 32

Add Your Choice of Search Engine

In its Preferences dialog box, Safari lets you choose between three different search engines that will be used whenever you type anything into the Address and Search bar: Google, Yahoo, or Microsoft's Bing. Other popular search engines are available, such as Duck Duck Go (www.duckduckgo.com), but Safari offers no way to utilize them via the Address and Search bar.

It's possible to force Safari to use a search engine like Duck Duck Go, but it involves a systemwide hack that essentially redirects *all* traffic for one of the existing search engines, such as Bing, to a replacement you specify. The changes you make will affect all software installed on your system, not just web browsers, and all user accounts too. This usually isn't problematic, however, and if you're sure other users of the system will never, ever use the search engine that you intend to replace, then it's a good change to make.

Adding Your Own Search Engine

Here are the necessary steps. These steps make fundamental changes to a system file, and while this is generally safe to do, you should follow the steps and ensure you type the commands exactly as specified.

1. For the purposes of these steps, we're going to use Duck Duck Go as the replacement search engine, and we're going to replace Bing. Start by getting the IP address of the search engine you want to use—open a Terminal window (open Finder, select the Applications list, and then in the list of applications double-click Terminal within the Utilities folder), and type ping followed by the address of the search engine. For example, for Duck Duck Go I'd type the following:

   ```
   ping www.duckduckgo.com
   ```

2. Don't worry about all the results, but simply look at the first line, which will read something like PING duckduckgo.com (46.51.197.88). You're interested in the numbers—46.51.197.88—so make a note of them.

3. At the Terminal, hit Control+C to kill the ping command, and type the following, which will open the hosts system file in the nano text editor (type your login password when prompted):

   ```
   sudo nano /private/etc/hosts
   ```

4. In the file that you open, add the following line to the very bottom on a line of its own, ensuring you hit a carriage return at the end of the line:

   ```
   46.51.197.88 www.bing.com
   ```

   Obviously, you should replace the IP address (the series of four numbers separated by periods) with the one you wrote down earlier, although don't change anything else in the line—for an example from my test Mac, see Figure 9, *Adding a new search engine for Safari*, on page 44.

5. Hit Control+O to save the file, and tap Return to confirm you want to save it. Then hit Control+X to quit Nano, and then close the Terminal window.

6. Open Safari, and hit Command+, (comma) to access its preferences. Select the General tab, and on the Default Search Engine drop-down list, select Bing.

The changes should take effect from the next time you use Safari, but if not, reboot the computer.

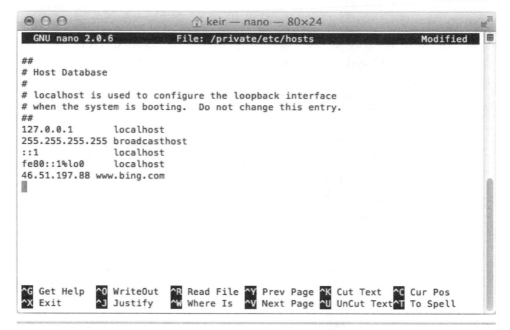

Figure 9—Adding a new search engine for Safari

Note that Safari might still display "Bing Search" in the Address and Search bar, but in fact, anything you type will be sent to your choice of search engine.

Reversing the Changes

To reverse the procedure and restore the ability to use Bing as a search engine, repeat the previous steps to edit the /private/etc/hosts file and remove the line you added (you can do this by using the cursor keys to position the cursor at the end of the line and then using the Delete key). Then save the file, as explained earlier, and quit Nano. You might need to reboot if, when using Safari, the changes don't take effect immediately.

Tip 33

Forward Only a Mail's Attachment

If you receive a mail message with an attachment, you might want to forward only the attachment and not the corresponding mail message. The solution is simple: select click the attachment once within the email so it's highlighted and then hit the forward icon (or hit `Shift`+`Command`+`F`). This will create a new message with just the attachment.

Note that this same trick works if you want to forward only part of a message: click and drag to highlight only the text you want to send to the recipient, and then click the forward icon or hit `Shift`+`Command`+`F`.

Tip 34

Quickly Add to Safari's Reading List

You can instantly add a web page to Safari's Reading List by `Shift`+clicking any link. You'll see the link fly to the Reading List icon on the bookmarks bar, if it's visible.

Tip 35

Get Complex Multiple-Display Setups

If you have three or more displays or projectors attached to your Mac, you might want to selectively mirror the content of one display on another yet use the others as independent monitors with their own desktops. Although there's a Mirrors Displays checkbox in the Displays pane of System Preferences when the Arrangement tab is selected, it's not designed for a setup this complicated.

Setting Up Mirroring

The solution is surprisingly simple. Open System Preferences (Apple menu→ System Preferences), switch to the Displays pane, and select the Arrangement tab. Then turn off display mirroring completely, as described earlier, so that each screen has its own desktop. Then hold down `Option` and drag and drop the first of the screens onto the screen representing the display or projector you'd like to mirror it (note how the border of the screen or projector you want to mirror the display upon will have a red border, making it easy to see what's what).

You should then find that those two displays are mirrored. This can be repeated for any other displays you'd like to mirror.

Deactivating Mirroring

To return each display to its own discrete desktop, again hold down Option and drag the displays so they no longer appear to be on top of each other and are lined up separately side-by-side.

Incidentally, to make any particular monitor or projector the default, which is to say the one that shows the Dock and menu bar, click and drag the white strip shown at the top of one of the blue screen previews within the Arrangement tab to whichever device you like. This will then become the default display whenever it's attached.

Tip 36

Turn a Movie Into a TV Show

If you've manually downloaded an episode of a TV show and imported it into iTunes, you might find that iTunes thinks it's a movie and files it away under the Movies heading.

If you want it to be correctly filed under the TV Shows heading, select it in the Movies listing and hit Command+I. In the dialog box that appears, click the Options tab and select TV Show from the Media Kind drop-down list. You might optionally want to select the Video tab and fill in details of the show, such as its episode and season number.

Once you click OK in the dialog box, the file will jump into the TV Shows listing, where it'll show as an unwatched show waiting to be viewed.

Multiple files can be selected at once and their Media Kind altered in this way.

Tip 37

See Where You're Browsing in Terminal

When using Terminal, you might know of the pwd (print working directory) command, which returns the current directory you're browsing. It's useful if, like me, you get lost while browsing through folders! Well, under OS X Lion and Mountain Lion, there's no need to use the command because the name of the directory appears in the title bar—just like in Finder. For example, if you're browsing the Music directory in your user directory, you'll see something like Music -- bash -- 80x24 (the last two details being the shell you're using and the size of the Terminal window in characters).

Right-clicking the directory in the title bar will also display the folder hierarchy up to that point. Clicking any of the folders in the list will open a Finder window displaying the contents of that folder.

Tip 38

Ultra-Quickly See an App's Open Files

This is a tip for those with a multitouch trackpad. By hovering the mouse cursor over any Dock icon and using two fingers to double-tap (tap, not click!), you will switch to Application Windows mode of Mission Control. In other words, this will show the currently open program windows of that particular app. You might also see a list of recently opened files along the bottom of the screen, although not all apps are compatible with this. If the app you double-tap isn't currently running or has no currently open program windows, you'll just see the list of recently opened apps (or, in the case of an incompatible app, a blank screen!).

If you find this tip doesn't work, open System Preferences (Apple menu→ System Preferences), and click the Trackpad icon, before selecting the Scroll & Zoom tab. Then check the box Smart Zoom. Note that this will also allow you to zoom into web pages in Safari by double-tapping with two fingers in the same way (double-tap again to zoom out).

Tip 39

Use Half-Star Ratings in iTunes

iTunes lets you rate songs, movies, and TV shows with between zero and five stars. This can be done by right-clicking the file within iTunes and selecting from Rating on the menu that appears or by clicking under the Rating heading to the right of the filename if you have Column view activated.

You can use the star ratings you've applied to arrange the order of your song collections by clicking the Rating heading, which will list all your favorite media files first. The information is also used by iTunes to divine your favorite music for playlists.

But if you're a truly discerning music critic, you might not think five stars is enough. One song might be worth only four-and-a-half stars, for example. Well, using a secret setting, you can activate half-star increments within ratings.

Activating and Using Half-Star Ratings

Quit iTunes, open a Terminal window (open Finder, select the Applications list, and then in the list of applications double-click Terminal within the Utilities folder), and type the following:

```
defaults write com.apple.iTunes allow-half-stars -bool TRUE
```

When you restart iTunes, you can apply half-star settings to your media by switching to List view (hit Option + Command + 3) and then clicking and dragging right and left within under the Ratings heading of a song's entry within the list. You have to be subtle when dragging, however, because the half-star ratings are only a nudge away from the full-star ratings.

Alternatively, you can select the file, hit Command + I, and in the dialog box that appears select the Options tab. Then click and drag in the Rating box, as described earlier.

Deactivating Half-Star Ratings

If in the future you'd like to return to full-star ratings only, again quit iTunes and open a Terminal window, before typing the following:

```
defaults delete com.apple.iTunes allow-half-stars
```

When you restart iTunes, you should find that any items you previously gave half-star ratings to are now rounded down to the nearest full-star rating.

Tip 40

Switch Locations in Terminal via Drag and Drop

By clicking and dragging a file or folder onto the Terminal window while holding down `Command`, you'll instantly switch to either the folder that you're dragging or the folder that the file you're dragging is within. In other words, Terminal will automatically type cd for you and then fill in the path, before hitting `Return` on your behalf. Give it a try to see what happens, but remember to hold down `Command` before releasing the mouse button—if you don't, OS X will simply type within Terminal the entire path to the file or the folder, something that can be useful in itself!

Tip 41

Timestamp Zip Filenames

This is one of those tips a handful of people will find useful but is worth sharing nonetheless. Those who use OS X on server computers might find it particularly useful.

The following command will cause any new archives (zip files) you create to automatically have the 24-hour time appended to the filename. For example, creating an archive from the folder Pictures at 2:13 p.m. will result in an archive with the filename Pictures 14.13.27.zip (with the last two digits representing the second count).

To activate this feature, open a Terminal window (open Finder, select the Applications list, and then in the list of applications double-click Terminal within the Utilities folder), and type the following:

```
defaults write com.apple.finder ArchiveTimestamp -bool TRUE;killall Finder
```

To deactivate it at a future date, type the following into a Terminal window:

```
defaults delete com.apple.finder ArchiveTimestamp;killall Finder
```

Copy Better in Mail

Here's a simple solution to an irritating problem: if you copy an email address in Mail by right-clicking it and selecting Copy Address, you'll probably find that not only do you get the email address, but you also copy the person's name—hit Paste, and you'll see something like Keir Thomas <keir@example.com>.

The solution for pasting just the email address (that is, simply keir@example.com) is to activate a secret setting, as follows, that will cause only the email address to be copied and pasted.

Quit Mail, open a Terminal window (open Finder, select the Applications list, and then in the list of applications double-click Terminal within the Utilities folder), and type the following:

```
defaults write com.apple.mail AddressesIncludeNameOnPasteboard -bool false
```

When you open Mail again, you should find that email addresses copy in their more useful, stripped-down format.

To revert to the default settings, again close Mail, open a Terminal window, and type the following:

```
defaults delete com.apple.mail AddressesIncludeNameOnPasteboard
```

Instantly Rename Safari Bookmarks

Click and hold a bookmark in Safari's bookmarks toolbar, and you'll be able to instantly rename it by overtyping the existing name, in a similar way to renaming a file within Finder. This won't affect the actual address of the bookmark.

Tip 44

Spruce Up Terminal

Hitting `Command`+`I` while using Terminal will bring up the Inspector window. Ensure that the Info tab is selected within the window, and enter alternative values within the Columns and Rows fields to alter the dimensions of the Terminal window (you can also click and drag the edges of the window, of course, but this method allows a degree more accuracy in your size choices).

Click the Settings tab, and you can also change the Terminal window's theme (that is, its color scheme and font). Just select an option from the list. This selection lasts only as long as the current Terminal window is open.

To make permanent changes to size and color scheme, hit `Command`+`,` (comma) to open the Terminal window's preferences. Then click the Settings button at the top of the dialog box that appears, and make the changes beneath. When done, click the Default button beneath the list of themes at the left of the dialog box.

Tip 45

Turn Off Trash Sound Effects

The OS X trash is noisy. Add a file to it, and you'll hear a "tish" sound, designed to indicate a piece of paper being thrown into the trash can. Whenever you empty the trash, you'll hear the sound of paper being scrunched up (which is odd because should you empty the trash in real life, that's not at all what you'd hear!). However, the sounds can be annoying if you're playing music or in the middle of a voice/FaceTime call. To turn it off, open a Finder window, and type the following:

```
defaults write com.apple.finder FinderSounds -bool FALSE;killall Finder
```

To turn the sound on again at a future time, again open a Terminal window, and type the following:

```
defaults delete com.apple.finder FinderSounds;killall Finder
```

Once you know the location of Photo Stream photos, you can also add it to the backup list of any third-party backup solutions you might use.

1. Open Finder, and hit `Shift`+`Command`+`G`. In the dialog box that appears, type ~/Library/Application Support/iLifeAssetManagement/assets/sub/, and hit `Return`.

2. In the Search field at the top right of the Finder window, type kind:image. Then click "sub" alongside the Search heading on the thin toolbar above the file listing. You should now see all your Photo Stream images in the Finder window. But we're not finished yet!

3. Click the Save button at the top of the Finder window. In the dialog box that appears, type Photo Stream in the Save As field, and select Desktop from the Where drop-down list. Then click Save. A new icon should appear on your desktop.

From now on, double-clicking the Photo Stream desktop icon will open a Finder window displaying your Photo Stream images. Note: Only ever look at the images or copy them to a new location. Never edit the images or even open them in an image editor. Use only Preview and Quick Look to view them. Never add any files to the folder either. All these actions could damage your iCloud configuration.

Tip 48

Avoid Notifications

If your MacBook has a multitouch trackpad or you have a Magic Trackpad, you can dismiss or "snooze" any notification dialog that appears by moving the mouse cursor over it and swiping with two fingers to the right if you have a MacBook or with one finger if you have a Magic Trackpad. If the notification relates to a calendar entry and features a snooze button, this is simply the equivalent of clicking the Snooze button on the dialog. If the notification has no button (it's telling you about a new email, for example), swiping will simply dismiss the dialog box.

You can also click and drag any notification to the left to temporarily move it out of the way if you need to see something behind it. It will snap back into place when you release the mouse button.

Tip 49

Use Fancy Text in Mail Signatures

If you've tried to add a signature in Mail (select Mail→Preferences, and then click the Signatures tab), it might seem as if it's impossible to add text formatting to signatures.

In fact, it's entirely possible to use different fonts or colors. All you need to do while typing your signature is hit `Command+T` to open the Fonts palette. Here you can select any fonts, colors, and type styles. Hitting `Shift+Command+C` will open the Colors palette to give you an even greater choice of colors. See Tip 46, *Get Handy When Formatting Text*, on page 52 too.

Bear in mind, however, that Windows or Linux computers that might be used to read your emails probably won't have the same selection of fonts as your Mac, so it's perhaps best to stick to "web-safe" fonts such as Arial, Times New Roman, Georgia, Verdana, and Courier.[2]

Ensure the checkbox Always Match My Default Message Font is empty.

Tip 50

Install Any App Without Being Blocked

OS X Mountain Lion and newer releases of OS X feature Gatekeeper, a security measure designed to make it impossible for illicit software to be installed on your Mac. It does this by blocking any program you download that isn't digitally signed with Apple's permission.

You can disable Gatekeeper in the Security & Privacy pane of System Preferences (Apple menu→System Preferences; look under the General tab and the Allow Applications Downloaded From heading), which can be useful if you download a program you know to be safe but that hasn't been digitally signed (although you should ensure it's enabled again afterward). However, a much quicker method of installing or running a single unsigned app is to right-click

---

2. For a more complete list of what are considered web-safe fonts, see http://www.ampsoft.net/webdesign-l/WindowsMacFonts.html.

it and select Open from the menu that appears. You'll still be warned that the app might be a security issue, but you won't be blocked from running it. OS X will remember this decision too, so you won't be blocked in the future either.

Tip 51

Browse Back via the Keyboard in Safari

Here's a simple hidden tweak that allows you to hit the `Delete` key (top right of the keyboard above the `Return` key; sometimes called Backspace on PC keyboards) to go back to the previous page in Safari—the equivalent of hitting the back button on the main toolbar. Once the tweak is activated, you can also hit `Shift`+`Delete` to go forward in your browser history (that is, the equivalent of clicking the forward toolbar button).

For those who like to keep their hands on the keyboard rather than the mouse, this is a very useful tweak and was a default choice in releases of OS X up until Mountain Lion, where it was deactivated because of the risk of accidentally hitting it while filling in web forms.

To activate the feature, simply quit Safari, open Terminal, and type the following line, noting that it's a single command line:

```
defaults write com.apple.Safari
        com.apple.Safari.ContentPageGroupIdentifier.WebKit2BackspaceKeyNavigation
        Enabled -bool TRUE
```

Restart Safari, and you will now find that hitting `Delete` will do exactly the same thing as hitting the back button on the Safari toolbar (although be aware that pressing and holding `Delete` will very rapidly move back through your browsing history).

To deactivate this function, again quit Safari, open a Terminal window, and type the following:

```
defaults delete com.apple.Safari
        com.apple.Safari.ContentPageGroupIdentifier.WebKit2BackspaceKeyNavigation
        Enabled
```

Restart Safari, and `Delete` will return to its default function of doing nothing within Safari.

Tip 52

Quickly Switch Audio Output (Including AirPlay)

Smaller MacBooks come with a single 3.5mm audio jack, which has the dual purpose of being a line-in audio port and a headphone socket. You can switch between the two modes using the Sound component within System Preferences (Apple menu→System Preferences)—select whichever entry you want from the drop-down menu alongside Use Audio Port For. However, a quicker way to switch is to hold down the `Option` key and click the volume control icon at the top right of the screen. Then select either Input or Output from the menu that appears.

Note that you can switch modes only if there's nothing plugged into the socket at the time, such as a pair of headphones.

This same trick lets you instantly select AirPlay as an audio output, provided your Mac is compatible with AirPlay[3] and you're within Wi-Fi range of an Apple TV device or a recent model AirPort Express wireless hub that's attached to a speaker system.

Just select the AirPlay device from the list under the Output Device heading in the menu that appears when you hold down `Option` and click the volume icon at the top right of the screen (see Figure 11, *Selecting an AirPlay device for audio output*, on page 57).

Figure 11—Selecting an AirPlay device for audio output

---

3.   For a list of Macs compatible with AirPlay, see http://www.apple.com/osx/specs/.

Tip 53

Stop Apps from Auto-Quitting

You might have noticed an odd thing while using OS X: if you haven't used it for a while and it has no open files, an app might seem to quit in the background without asking you. If actual fact, the app enters a quasi-sleep mode: as far as the user is concerned, it appears to have stopped running but is still held in memory.

Sometimes apps quit themselves almost instantly: if I close the Messages window, for example, the program usually quits shortly afterward.

Apple calls this feature *automatic termination*[4] if you find it annoying by issuing a secret command. Open a Terminal window (open Finder, select the Applications list, and then in the list of applications double-click Terminal within the Utilities folder) and type the following:

```
defaults write -g NSDisableAutomaticTermination -bool TRUE
```

Then log out and back in again for the changes to take effect.

To reactivate automatic pruning of inactive applications later, again open a Terminal window, and type the following, before logging out and back in again for the changes to take effect:

```
defaults delete -g NSDisableAutomaticTermination
```

Tip 54

Turn Off "Smooth Scrolling"

You might not have noticed, but when you click the scrollbar to move down or up a page in an application or hit the Page Up / Page Down key on full-sized keyboards, the scroll to the new page is animated. This might seem a little slow, laggy, or not quite as responsive as you'd like—it's something that

---

4.   Apple explains the reasoning behind automatic termination of apps here: https://developer.apple.com/library/mac/#documentation/General/Conceptual/MOSXAppProgrammingGuide/CoreAppDesign/CoreAppDesign.html.

reportedly happens on older Macs and first-generation Macs featuring a Retina (high-definition) display.

The technology behind this is called *smooth scrolling*, and to turn it off, you should open a Terminal window (open Finder, select the Applications list, and then in the list of applications double-click Terminal within the Utilities folder), and type the following:

```
defaults write -g NSScrollAnimationEnabled -bool NO
```

Log out and back in again to see the changes.

You can reactivate Smooth Scrolling using the following command, again issued in Terminal and followed by logging out and back in again:

```
defaults delete -g NSScrollAnimationEnabled
```

Tip 55

Save Safari Tabs When Quitting

Each time Safari starts, it shows the home page (or whatever option you selected under the General tab within Preferences).

However, there's another start-up mode, and I find it very useful indeed. It will automatically open the tabs (or web page if no tabs are in use) that were active the last time Safari quit. You can do this manually without changing any settings by clicking History→Reopen All Windows From Last Session, and Safari automatically does this should it restart after crashing, but changing the following secret setting makes this an automatic choice upon every start-up of Safari.

Enabling Tab Memory Across Sessions

Quit Safari, open a Terminal window (open Finder, select the Applications list, and then in the list of applications double-click Terminal within the Utilities folder), and type the following:

```
defaults write com.apple.safari NSQuitAlwaysKeepsWindows -bool TRUE
```

Restart Safari, then quit it, and then restart it. From this point on, all tabs will be remembered across restarts.

6. End the line, type </string>. In other words, if I wanted to have a b c d e f appear in the pop-up menu, the line would read as follows:

```
<string>a b c d e f</string>
```

7. Again, create a new line beneath, and type <key>Strings</key>; then beneath that, create another new line, and then copy and paste into it the whole of the line you typed earlier, featuring the characters you want to insert. In my example earlier, this line was <string>a b c d e f</string>.

8. Finally, on a new line, type </dict>. You should end up with something like the following, which again features my example of wanting a b c d e f to appear in the pop-up list (see also Figure 13, *How the Keyboard-en.plist file should look after additions (highlighted)*, on page 63):

```
<key>Roman-Accent-q</key>
<dict>
<key>Direction</key>
<string>right</string>
<key>Keycaps</key>
<string>a b c d e f</string>
<key>Strings</key>
<string>a b c d e f</string>
</dict>
```

9. Save the file, close TextEdit, and then drag and drop it over the Finder window you opened earlier, showing the Resources folder. You'll be asked to authenticate, so type your password when prompted. You'll also have to click the Replace button when the dialog box appears offering the option.

The changes will take effect immediately, so test it by opening a new document in TextEdit and then pressing q and holding it until the pop-up menu appears. Remember that you can select any of the characters quickly by typing the number listed beneath each character in the pop-up.

Removing the New Character Menu

To remove your new menu, you just need to restore the backup you made earlier, as follows:

1. Navigate to where the backup keyboard-en.plist file is stored, select it, and hit Command+C to copy it.

2. Follow steps 1 to 3 to open the PressAndHold package so the Resources folder is displayed.

3. Tap Command+V to paste the original keyboard-en.plist file back into place. Again, you'll be asked to confirm you want to overwrite the original and also asked to authenticate by providing your password. As before, the changes should take effect immediately. Once you're sure things are working correctly, you can then delete the backup of the keyboard-en.plist file.

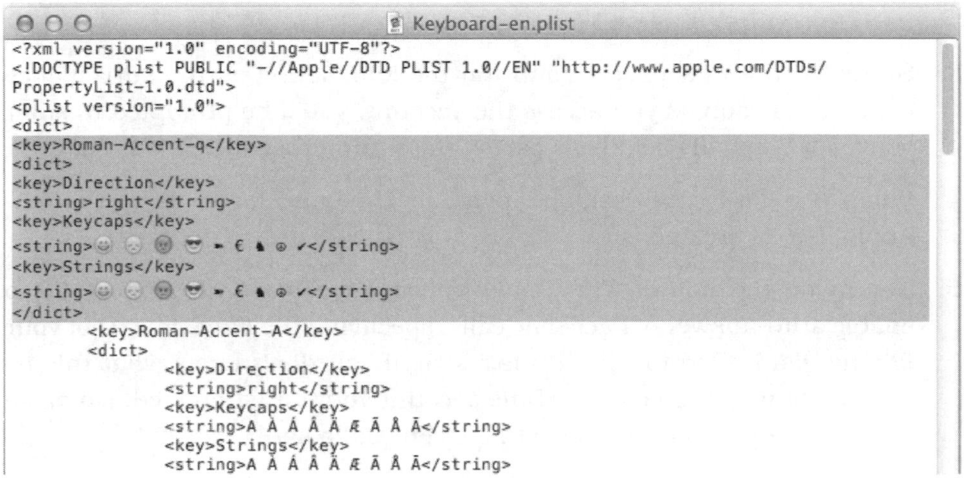
Keyboard-en.plist

```
<?xml version="1.0" encoding="UTF-8"?>
<!DOCTYPE plist PUBLIC "-//Apple//DTD PLIST 1.0//EN" "http://www.apple.com/DTDs/
PropertyList-1.0.dtd">
<plist version="1.0">
<dict>
<key>Roman-Accent-q</key>
<dict>
<key>Direction</key>
<string>right</string>
<key>Keycaps</key>
<string>😃 😞 😡 😎 ➨ € ♞ ☮ ✓</string>
<key>Strings</key>
<string>😃 😞 😡 😎 ➨ € ♞ ☮ ✓</string>
</dict>
        <key>Roman-Accent-A</key>
        <dict>
                <key>Direction</key>
                <string>right</string>
                <key>Keycaps</key>
                <string>A À Á Â Ä Æ Ã Å Ā</string>
                <key>Strings</key>
                <string>A À Á Â Ä Æ Ã Å Ā</string>
```

Figure 13—How the Keyboard-en.plist file should look after additions (highlighted)

Tip 58

Turn Your Mac Into a Surveillance Camera

As mentioned in Tip 7, *Auto-answer FaceTime Calls*, on page 20, FaceTime can automatically answer incoming calls from contacts you specify. Another use for this trick is to dial into a Mac at any time, anywhere, from your iPhone, iPad, or iPod touch, thus creating a simple surveillance camera setup. Because FaceTime will automatically start upon receiving a call and then auto-answer the call, you'll instantly see what's happening in front of your Mac.

Setting Up a Mac as a Surveillance Camera

Here are the steps required. Some of them are concise because it's assumed you already know the basic procedures referenced, such as how to create a new user account.

1. Create a new account using the Users & Groups element of System Preferences (Apple menu→System Preferences). It doesn't matter what you call the new account, but for safety reasons you might want to make it a Standard account type (i.e., limited). This will stop anybody who might physically access the computer in your absence doing any damage.

2. Then create a new Apple ID at the following site: https://appleid.apple.com. You'll need a spare email address to assign the account to, which will be used to confirm it as well.

3. Switch to the new user account on the Mac acting as the surveillance camera. As soon as you access the account, you'll be prompted to enter your new Apple ID details as part of the setup procedure, so do so.

4. When you get to the desktop, open FaceTime and log in using the new Apple ID you created.

5. Now follow the steps in Tip 7, *Auto-answer FaceTime Calls*, on page 20 to enable auto-answer of FaceTime calls, specifying the FaceTime ID of your iPhone, iPad, iPod touch, or other Mac. If you don't know what this is, try dialing into the new FaceTime account you've just created. Doing so will show your FaceTime ID in the Recent Calls list.

Finally, test your new setup by dialing in from an iPhone, iPad, iPod touch, or other Mac and ensuring that the Mac auto-answers and then displays what will essentially be surveillance camera footage of what's in front of it. Bear in mind you'll need to alter the power saving settings of your Mac so that it doesn't enter sleep mode, although it's OK for the screen to be turned off. Also, remember that FaceTime doesn't need to be running all the time and will automatically start itself whenever you call into the Apple ID you entered during setup.

Deactivating the Security Camera

To permanently deactivate the security camera, simply delete the account you created for it within the Users & Groups element of System Preferences.

Tip 59

Modify Messages' Look and Feel

By right-clicking the message bubbles within Messages (ensuring you don't right-click any text) or selecting View→Messages, you can select a different look and feel for conversations. You can select to have "boxy" messages, for example, or "compact" and can also select to show people's names in addition to (or in place of) their picture. Experiment to see which works best for you!

Fonts and colors can be changed on the Messages tab of the Preferences dialog box (click the application menu→Preferences, or hit `Command+,` [comma]).

Tip 60

Use Your Own Choice of Notes Font

Many OS X apps try to look like real-life equivalents. For this reason the Notes app defaults to a font called Noteworthy, intended to look like handwriting, but which many people find irritatingly hard to read. There are two ways to change the typeface, depending on your needs.

- While writing a note, you can switch to any font you'd like by hitting `Command+T`, which will open the Fonts palette, where you can also choose bold and italic text if need be. This will affect only the note you're currently writing.

- To change the default font used to display all notes that have had no text formatting applied, which will be nearly all of them, you can click Format →Font→Default Font and choose from three choices: Noteworthy, Marker Felt (a similar handwriting style font), and Helvetica.

If you find the default choice of fonts to be not to your tastes, you can personalize them by tweaking a configuration file, as outlined next. This allows any font to be used as the default within Notes. The steps modify system files, and this tip therefore affects all users of the computer. Ensure you have an up-to-date Time Machine backup. Like all tips that involve hacking system files, you might find your changes reverted to the defaults if you install a major operating system update. The solution is simply to repeat the steps.

Changing the Default Display Font

Here's how to alter the choice of default fonts. Start by quitting Notes if it's open, and then follow these steps:

1. Open Finder, and then hit `Shift`+`Command`+`G`. In the dialog that appears, type the following before clicking the Go button:

    ```
    /Applications/Notes.app/Contents/Resources/en.lproj/
    ```

    In the list of files you see, hold `Command`, and then click and drag Default-Fonts.plist to the desktop to create a copy of it.

2. Create a separate, second backup copy of the DefaultFonts.plist file somewhere safe on your hard disk. We'll revert to this file should anything go wrong or if we want to restore default settings later.

3. Then double-click the DefaultFonts.plist file on the desktop, which should open it in TextEdit.

4. The file looks complicated, but don't worry about it. We're going to swap one of the three default choices mentioned earlier for a choice of our own. I assume you're reading this tip because you'd like to swap out the default Noteworthy font, so that's the one we'll change! Therefore, move the cursor to the eighth line from the top, which reads as follows:

    ```
    <string>Noteworthy-Light</string>
    ```

    And over-type the font of your choice, although you should type the font name without any spaces between the words. For example, should you want to use the American Typewriter font, you should change the line so it reads as follows:

    ```
    <string>AmericanTypewriter</string>
    ```

    You can hit `Command`+`T` to open the Fonts palette, which will list all the fonts by name (although don't attempt to change the font of the file you're editing!). See Figure 14, *Editing a config file to change the default Notes font*, on page 67 for a completed example from my system, where I've specified the Lucida Grande font (that is, the same font used by OS X for its icons and menus).

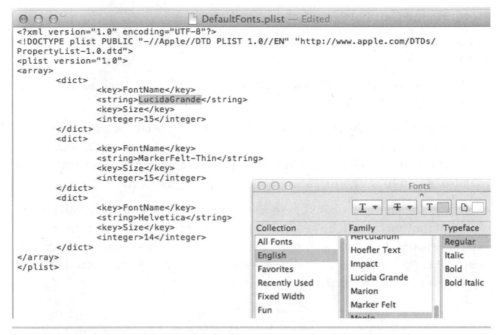

Figure 14—Editing a config file to change the default Notes font

5. If you want, you can also alter the point size mentioned two lines beneath this in the <integer> field. A replacement value of 20 will make the font slightly larger.

6. You can also alter the style of the font to bold or italics, assuming the font includes such a character set (most do). Just type either Bold or Italic after the font name, separated by a dash (if the font offers choices like Narrow or Condensed, you can specify these too in the same way). For example, if I wanted to change the font to Bold Arial Narrow, I'd change the line to read <string>ArialNarrow-Bold</string>.

7. Save the file, close TextEdit, and then drag and drop it over the Finder window you opened earlier, showing the en.lproj folder. You'll be asked to authenticate, so type your password when prompted. You'll also have to select to replace the original file when the dialog box appears offering the option.

Start the Notes app, and the changes should take effect immediately. Remember that you can still switch between fonts using the Format→Font→ Default Font option, although the choice of Noteworthy will now be replaced by your personalized choice.

Restoring the Original Font Choice

The default font choices can be restored by quitting Notes and following these steps:

1. Navigate to where the backup DefaultFonts.plist file is stored, select it, and hit `Command`+`C` to copy it.

2. Follow step 1 in the earlier instructions to open the en.lproj folder, and then tap `Command`+`V` to paste the original DefaultFonts.plist file back into place. Again, you'll be asked to confirm you want to overwrite the original and also asked to authenticate by providing your password.

As before, the changes should take effect immediately, so restart Notes. Your choice of font might still be visible, but you can finish restoring things to the default settings by selecting Noteworthy from the Format→Font→Default Font menu. Once you're sure things are working correctly, you can then delete the backup of the DefaultFonts.plist file.

Tip 61

Duplicate a File with One Click

To quickly create a duplicate of a file within the same folder (or on the desktop), click and drag the file to a new blank spot and hold down `Option` before releasing the mouse button. This is the equivalent of right-clicking the file and selecting Duplicate from the menu that appears.

Tip 62

Share Google Links

Safari in OS X Mountain Lion lets you query Google by typing a search term into the address bar. This works very well but raises an issue: what if you want to send somebody the link to a search you've done? You can't copy and paste the address from the address bar because you never get to see the search address—the search query takes its place.

The solution is simple: click and drag the small magnifying glass symbol at the very left of the address bar to where you want to insert the link within your document or email. This will insert the URL for the search straight into your document.

Master Notification Center

In a default installation of OS X, Notification Center can be activated in two ways, as follows:

- Swiping from right to left with two fingers on a trackpad, if your computer has one; start the swipe gesture from the very right edge of the trackpad. This can take some practice to get right!

- Clicking the Notification Center icon at the top right of the screen.

However, you can add two quicker and substantially more intuitive ways to activate Notification Center, as follows.

Using Hot Corners to Activate Notification Center

OS X lets you configure *hot corners* to activate certain desktop functions, which is to say you can push the mouse cursor into any of the four corners of the screen to activate things like Mission Control or Notification Center. Because the Notification Center icon is at the top right, it makes significant sense to configure the top-right Hot Corner to activate it.

To do so, open System Preferences (Apple menu→System Preferences), click the Mission Control icon, and then click the Hot Corners button at the bottom left of the program window. In the drop-down dialog box that appears, click the drop-down list at the top right—the one relating to the top right of the screen preview—and select Notification Center. Then click OK and close System Preferences.

The changes take effect immediately, so give it a try—push the mouse cursor into the top-right corner, and the Notification Center will appear. Click anywhere outside of Notification Center to dismiss it.

To turn off the Hot Corner, repeat the previous steps, but in the drop-down list for the choice of what function to activate for the top-right Hot Corner, select the hyphen at the bottom of the list.

Assigning a Keyboard Shortcut to Open Notification Center

You can also (or alternatively) assign a keyboard shortcut to open and close Notification Center. For some reason Apple doesn't include this in a default install.

To do so, open System Preferences and click the Keyboard icon. Then click the Keyboard Shortcut tab, and in the list on the left select Mission Control. On the right of the window, check Show Notification Center. You'll immediately be prompted to type the keyboard shortcut you want to use. The choice is up to you, but I find that Option+Commmand+Tab works well and isn't already assigned to a function in OS X. I hold down Option+Commmand with my left thumb while tapping Tab with a finger.

To remove the keyboard shortcut, repeat the previous steps, but this time remove the check alongside Show Notification Center in the list.

Tip 64

Switch Time Machine Disks

Once upon a time, Time Machine worked with just one destination—be that a removable disk drive you attached to your computer or a Time Capsule. However, with Mountain Lion and newer versions of OS X, you can seamlessly back up to multiple destinations. Each will contain a full Time Machine backup, with the most recently attached disk containing the most recent backup. If you have two or more backup devices attached at the same time, Time Machine will back up to each device in sequence (that is, if you have two backup disks attached, Time Machine will hypothetically back up to disk 1 at 1 p.m., disk 2 at 2 p.m., disk 1 at 3 p.m., disk 2 at 4 p.m., and so on, although the hourly time of backup will depend on when the disks are attached).

To set up additional backup destinations, attach the disk (or get within Wi-Fi range of the Time Capsule), open System Preferences (Apple menu→System Preferences), and select the Time Machine option. Click the Select Disk button, and then select the new hardware from the list in the dialog box that appears. Remember that it can take hours if not days before the first backup has completed on a new backup device.

There are a number of advantages of having more than one backup destination, as follows:

- If you have a portable Mac, you can set up a Time Machine backup device at home and one at work. Your Mac will seamlessly back up to whichever one it's attached to without any need for you to select it. You could use a removable disk drive at work, for example, and a Time Capsule at home.

- You can "rotate" disks by setting up two or more removable storage devices for use within Time Machine and then attaching each daily (that is, disk 1 on Monday, disk 2 on Tuesday, and so on). This helps avoid wear on any particular disk, reducing the risk of failure, but also lets you store the currently out-of-sequence backup disks in a different physical location to avoid all the backups being destroyed by a disaster such as a fire.

Tip 65

Share Reminders and Calendars

Within the Reminders app, you can share a reminder list with one or more people, allowing them to create or delete entries in the list or check off tasks. This can be useful if you're working on group projects or perhaps if you simply want to share a shopping list with a family member.

You can also share a calendar within the Calendar app, which again can be useful if you're working within a group. You could even create a special calendar for a particular project and then share it with others. Others will be able to view and create/modify/delete entries within the calendar, or you can share it as read-only so people can only view the calendar's contents.

There are some caveats. The people to whom you want to share the reminder list or calendar must be updated to the latest OS X Mountain Lion release, must have an Apple ID (the login email address of which you'll need to specify), and also must have iCloud activated within their Apple ID.

Sharing a Reminders List

To share a reminder list, click any reminder list and keep the mouse in position until a new icon appears at the right of the entry within the list—an icon of a transmission signal (see Figure 15, *Sharing a reminder list with others*). Click the icon, and a pop-out dialog box will appear, inviting you to type the email address of the individual(s) you'd like to share the list with. Hit Tab after each email address you type.

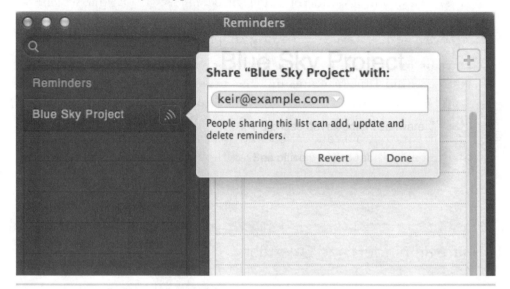

Figure 15—Sharing a reminder list with others

Once you click the Done button, the individual(s) will be sent an email link so they can subscribe to your reminder list. Once they subscribe, you'll be notified by a notification pop-up. Additionally, the reminder entry in the list will always display the sharing icon mentioned earlier. To see who the list is shared with, just click the icon. A tick alongside the email address means they have subscribed. A question mark alongside their email address means they've yet to respond to the invitation.

Sharing a Calendar

To share a calendar, open the Calendar app and click the Calendars button at the top left so you can see a list of all your calendars in the left side pane. Right-click the calendar you'd like to share (note: you can always create a new calendar specifically for sharing), and then select the Sharing Settings entry on the menu that appears. Following this, the steps are the same as with sharing a reminder list, although you can check the box to make the calendar read-only, in which case people will be able to view the calendar but not create, remove, or edit entries.

Unlike with sharing a reminder list, there's no obvious sign the calendar is shared unless you right-click the calendar's entry in the list and again select Sharing Settings to view the pop-out dialog box.

Sharing via iCloud.com

By visiting the iCloud website[5] and logging in with your Apple ID, you can share your reminder lists and calendars in a virtually identical way to that described earlier—select either the Reminders or Calendar icon on the iCloud home screen, and then select whichever reminder list or calendar you'd like to share. Finally, click the share icon.

Sharing a calendar is slightly different when using iCloud.com because in the pop-out dialog box that appears you'll be asked if you want to share the calendar privately—that is, with people whose emails you type into the dialog —or share it as a public calendar, in which case absolutely anybody using Calendar on their Mac can view the calendar in read-only mode if they sub- scribe to it using the URL provided, which you'll need to manually send to people via email/instant messaging.

Rescinding Sharing

To deactivate sharing for one or more people or to remove the offer of sharing if they've yet to respond, follow the previous steps to open the sharing pop- out alongside the entry in the list in either the Reminders or Calendar app (or within iCloud). Then simply select the email address in the list and hit the Delete key, or click the email address and select Remove Person. In the case of public calendars shared via iCloud, uncheck the Public Calendar box.

The changes should take effect immediately—access to the list or calendar for the individuals will be rescinded completely, and they will be notified by email and also via a pop-up notification on their computer.

---

5.   http://icloud.com

Tip 66

Update Your Profile Pic

You can change your login account profile picture by opening System Preferences, clicking the Users & Groups icon, and then clicking your existing profile picture when the Password tab is selected.

A pop-out window will let you select from the built-in (default) images or iPhoto images (assuming you have iPhoto installed). You can also select the Camera option to take a new photo using the iSight/FaceTime camera built into your Mac.

But how do you use a picture you've downloaded from a website or happen to have on your disk but that hasn't been imported into iPhoto?

The solution is simple—just find the photo within Finder and then drag and drop it on top of the pop-out window. It will then instantly become your profile picture, and you can resize it using the slider at the bottom of the pop-out window and apply effects in the same way as described in Tip 195, *Enhance Your Login Picture with Visual Effects*, on page 218.

Tip 67

See Your Mac's Serial Number

To quickly view your computer's unique serial number, as well as the build version of OS X (that is, the internal code used by Apple to track software releases), click the Apple menu, and then select About This Mac. In the window that appears, click Version several times (beneath the large "OS X") to cycle through the available information.

You will almost certainly need your serial number if you phone Apple for technical support.

Tip 68

Use a VIP Mailbox

Mail features a way of prioritizing email from certain people who you value above others—a feature Apple calls the *VIP mailbox* (short for Very Important People, of course).

The feature isn't activated by default and can't be found on any menu but is actually easy to set up.

Configuring VIP Mail

To activate the feature, you must first mark at least one person who sends you email as a VIP. To do this, select any email from the individual, and then click the empty star alongside their name in the mail, or right-click their name in the From field of an email and select Add to VIPs.

Once you do this, a new VIP mailbox will appear in the mailbox list sidebar and Favorites toolbar (if you have either visible—you can select to view either from the View menu). Selecting the new mailbox will cause your mail to be filtered so that only VIPs are visible, although you can also further filter the list of mails by selecting individual VIPs in the list that appears beneath.

Be Notified Only of VIP Mail

You can configure Mail so that you're notified within Notification Center only of new VIP mail. To do so, open Mail's Preferences dialog box (Mail→Preferences), and ensure the General tab is selected. Then select VIPs from the New Message Notifications drop-down list.

To return to being notified of all mail at a future date, repeat this step, but select Inbox Only from the drop-down list.

Deactivate the VIP Mailbox

To remove somebody from the VIP list, simply click once more the star alongside their name in an email, or right-click their name and click Remove from VIPs. To completely deactivate the VIP function, remove all VIPs in this way, and then quit and restart Mail.

Tip 69

Supertip: Get the Most from Reminders

The Reminders app lets you create lists of tasks and attach alerts to them. Used correctly, it's an app that can revolutionize your workflow. It also works seamlessly with the identical apps on the iPhone, iPad, and iPod touch—any reminders you create on these devices will be instantly shared with your Mac, and vice versa.

Here are some tips for getting the most of the Reminders app, although you might also want to see Tip 17, *Create Reminders Ultra-Quickly*, on page 29 and Tip 65, *Share Reminders and Calendars*, on page 71.

Quickly Create Reminders Alerts

Each entry in the Reminders app can have its own alert to remind you of the task as a particular time or based on your physical location.

In a similar way to the Calendar app, the Reminders app is somewhat intelligent in interpreting what you type. For example, if you create a new reminder and type as its body "Pick up dry cleaning at 5 p.m. on Tuesday," a reminder will be created called "Pick up dry cleaning" with an alert automatically set to sound at 5 p.m. on Tuesday.

See All Reminders Due on a Particular Day

Want to see all the reminders for which you've set an alert that'll chime on a particular day? Open the calendar view in Reminders by clicking the icon at the bottom left of the program window (the middle of the three buttons), and then click the date in question from the calendar that pops up. Double-click the date to cause a new window to appear listing the reminders due on that day.

To return to the list of reminders, just select from the reminder lists in the list at the top left of the program window.

View All Your Reminders at Once

By default Reminders has just one list that can contain individual reminders, but you can create others by clicking the plus icon at the bottom left of the Reminders window. You could create two reminders, for example Home and

Work. You can delete lists by selecting them and hitting `Delete` (or right-clicking any and selecting the Delete option on the menu that appears).

However, using multiple lists raises an issue: How does one see *all* upcoming reminders at once, without having to click through each separate list?

Just hold down `Command` and select each one of the lists. Just like when selecting files, you'll be able to select multiple items, and any reminders contained within them will be shown on the right in a unified task list. Or you can select the first task list, then hold down `Shift`, and select the last, which will select all the reminder lists in between.

In fact, the Reminders list works in a very similar way to a file list in Finder. You can slow double-click to rename a list, for example, just like you would a file, or you can click a list and then hit `Return` in order to rename it.

Another way to view all your reminder lists at once is to double-click each in turn in the list. This will cause the list to pop out into its own window, allowing you to see the contents of all lists at once.

Be Reminded When You Arrive (Or Leave) Somewhere

Here's a tip for those with MacBook computers. Reminders is location-aware, which is to say you can set a reminder alert to pop up whenever your computer senses you've arrived at a particular location or—conversely—when you're no longer at a location (that is to say, upon leaving).

For example, you could create a reminder to buy some milk but be reminded of it only once you've left your house. Or you could add a reminder to speak to a colleague and be prompted about it only when you enter your workplace. If your Mac is powered-down, as it almost certainly will be if you're traveling, then you'll be reminded as soon as it powers back up again, although the alerts will pop up on any iPhone, iPod touch, or iPad that you have with you and that is signed into the same iCloud account as your Mac.

What You Need to Know About Location Alerts

There are a couple of caveats related to location alerts, as follows:

- For reminders to work on your Mac, Location Services needs to be enabled; if you didn't enable this while installing OS X, you can do so in the Security & Privacy pane of System Preferences (Apple menu→System Preferences) by selecting the option on the Privacy tab. When you first set a location alert in Reminders, you'll be asked to confirm that you want the app to use the location service.

Tip 70

Turn Off Java

Java doesn't come as an out-of-the-box install on OS X Mountain Lion, but it will be installed automatically when an app needs it. Any app you install that needs Java will therefore install it the first time it runs, but this raises an issue: Java has persistently been proven to be a serious security risk.

One solution is to simply turn off Java unless you need it. To do this, open Java Preferences, which is in the Utilities folder of the Applications list of Finder, and then remove the check alongside Enable Apple Plug-In and Web Start Applications. Then remove the checks under the On heading in the list of Java SE engines installed on your system.

Should an app start that needs Java, you'll be shown an error to the effect that Java isn't installed. Simply repeat the previous steps in reverse and enable Java—but don't forget to disable it again afterward!

You might also want to disable access to Java within Safari, bearing in mind this is a typical attack vector for malware. To do so, start Safari, start System Preferences (application menu→Preferences), and select the Security tab. Then remove the check alongside Enable Java.

Tip 71

Notify from the Command Line

There's no official way of making a notification pop-up appear from the command line. This would be useful to send a message that a certain command has completed, for example. The good news is that you can use a Ruby gem called terminal-notifier to do so (gems are extensions to the Ruby programming language that's included with OS X).

To install terminal-notifier, open a Terminal window in the usual way, and type the following:

```
sudo gem install terminal-notifier
```

Type your password when prompted. Installation should take seconds.

Using terminal-notifier is easy. Just use the -message command option to specify the message, which should appear within quotation marks (or be escaped in the usual way), and use the -title option to specify the title of the notification dialog. Here's an example:

```
terminal-notifier -message "Mac Kung Fu goes places other books don't dare"
          -title "Mac Kung Fu"
```

You can also specify things to happen when the notification dialog is clicked: using -open, you can specify a URL (which must include its http:// component), for example. You can find more information at the GitHub site for terminal-notifier.[6]

Tip 72

Stop the Dock from Getting Broken

It's very easy to accidentally resize the Dock when using a Mac or delete icons from it. All it takes is a misclick of the mouse. The following two commands typed into a Terminal window will "freeze" the Dock, making it impossible to resize it or to remove/rearrange/add icons:

```
defaults write com.apple.dock size-immutable -bool TRUE
defaults write com.apple.dock contents-immutable -bool TRUE;killall Dock
```

To "unfreeze" the Dock so you can resize it and add/remove/rearrange icons, issue the following two commands in a Terminal window:

```
defaults delete com.apple.dock size-immutable
defaults delete com.apple.dock contents-immutable;killall Dock
```

Tip 73

Control QuickTime Player Using Keys

The following keyboard shortcuts let you control QuickTime Player without touching the mouse:

---

6.   https://github.com/alloy/terminal-notifier.

- `Space`: Start playback, or stop it if it's already playing.

- `Up`/`Down` cursor keys: Increase/decrease playback volume.

- `Option`+`Up`/`Down` cursor key: Maximize/mute playback volume.

- `Left`/`Right` cursor keys: Hold down to cue in slow-motion back and forward. Tap to advance frame by frame.

- `Command`+`Left`/`Right` cursor keys: Start cueing backward and forward; `Space` restores playback to normal (repeated presses of the cursor keys while still holding `Command` will speed up cueing).

- `Option`+`Left`/`Right` cursor keys: Move to beginning or end of movie file.

- `Command`+`+`/`-`: Increase/decrease the size of the playback window (`Command`+`1` restores it to its actual pixel dimensions).

Tip 74

Let OS X Create Passwords

If you're looking for a memorable yet secure password (that is, one involving numbers, capital letters, and symbols), you can let OS X do the hard work, as follows:

1. Open Keychain Access, which is the application in OS X that handles password and certificate security. You'll find it in the Utilities folder of the Applications view in Finder.

2. Once the app has started, click File→New Password Item. Don't worry— we're not actually going to create a new item for the keychain. Instead, we're simply going to make use of its password tool.

3. In the dialog box that slides into view, click the small key icon alongside the Password textbox. This will open the Password Assistant, which is what we're interested in.

4. In the Password Assistant dialog box, ensure the Type drop-down list is set to Memorable. Then look in the suggestion box for the password that's been created for you. To generate another, once again select Memorable from the drop-down list.

5. The Length slider lets you create longer passwords, and it's wise to slide this a little to the right. The green Quality bar shows how secure the password is, which is to say how theoretically easy it is to crack. However, a password of twelve letters is normally considered extremely strong within the wider security community, even if it means the green bar doesn't entirely fill.

Once you're happy, you should attempt to learn the password. This can be done by saying it out loud ten to twenty times or by typing it into a blank document the same number of times so that you learn it by rote.

You can close Password Assistant and then click the Cancel button to close the Keychain Access dialog box. You can then quit Keychain Access.

Tip 75

Prefer Plain-Text Emails

Once upon a time all email was sent in plain text, but nowadays HTML emails —that feature alternative fonts, colors, and images—have become the norm. Yet most of these emails come with a plain-text version hidden inside them. This is included for those who might have email clients that can't display HTML.

While the Mail app in OS X is fully compatible with HTML email, you can hit Option+Command+P to switch the email currently being viewed to a plain-text rendition, sans any kind of formatting.

This is only temporary, however. Just select another email in your email list, and then select the original email again to view it with its formatting intact.

Setting Plain-Text View

To always view emails in plain text, you can change a secret setting that makes it prefer the plain-text component of emails, if they're included in the message (and they nearly always are). This will mean you should never see another HTML email!

To activate the setting, shut down Mail, open a Terminal window (open Finder, select the Applications list, and then in the list of applications double-click Terminal within the Utilities folder), and type the following:

```
defaults write com.apple.mail PreferPlainText -bool TRUE
```

Restart Mail, and you'll see that any HTML mails are now shown as plain text. Should you subsequently want to view the full HTML-formatted email, you'll see that most messages include a link at the top that lets you view the email at the sender's website.

Restoring Default Settings

To return to Mail's automatic displaying of HTML emails, again close Mail, open a Terminal window, and type the following:

```
defaults delete com.apple.mail PreferPlainText
```

Restart Mail for the changes to take effect.

Tip 76

See a Big Long List of Your Contacts

Here's a tip that lets you view all your contacts in a long list, alongside which you'll be able to see each contact's email address or their telephone number(s). It uses a debug setting within the Contacts app.

1. Close the Contacts app if it's open, open a Terminal window (open Finder, select the Applications list, and then in the list of applications double-click Terminal within the Utilities folder), and type the following:

   ```
   defaults write com.apple.AddressBook ABShowDebugMenu -bool true
   ```

2. Open Contacts, and you should see a new Debug menu option. Select the Show People Picker Panel option. This will open a new window showing all your contacts in one long list with their email addresses alongside.

3. Click the Email heading to switch to show telephone numbers alongside the list of contacts.

Note that the same list showing only email addresses is also available within Mail; just click Window→Address Panel.

From either list you can click, hold, and drag to create .vcf files by which contacts details can be exported to another computer—see Tip 142, *Share Your Contacts with Others*, on page 165.

Close the window when you're finished. To deactivate the Debug menu option, again close Contacts, and open a Terminal window, typing the following:

```
defaults delete com.apple.AddressBook ABShowDebugMenu
```

Tip 77

Type into PDFs

If you open a PDF form within Preview, you might find you can simply click in any boxes or on any files and start typing—even if the PDF hasn't been created or designed for you to type into. This is because Preview detects fields intended for you to write in and automatically turns them into text fields.

Whatever you type can usually be dragged and dropped out of the boxes and onto any location on the page, if you want.

Tip 78

Play Ripped DVD Backups

By downloading and installing the libdvdcss system file,[7] you can create backups of any DVD movie discs you own by dragging and dropping from Finder the VIDEO_TS folders on the disc to your Mac's hard disk (you can ignore any other files or folders on the DVD). Unlike apps that rip movies to your hard disk, copying the VIDEO_TS folder makes a 100 percent faithful copy of the movie, including its menu and chapter system.

However, playing the movie from within the backup folder is difficult: you must start the DVD Player app (ensuring no movie DVD disc is in the drive), click File→Open DVD Media, and select the folder.

There's an easy way around this: rename the VIDEO_TS folder after the name of the movie (i.e., Star Wars), and then give the folder a .dvdbundle extension (so the full folder name becomes something like Star Wars.dvdbundle).

---

7. Download the libdvdcss installation package from http://download.videolan.org/libdvdcss/last/macosx/. You'll need to temporarily bypass Gatekeeper to install it—see Tip 50, *Install Any App Without Being Blocked*, on page 55.

Once you do this, a miraculous thing will happen: the folder's icon will change to indicate it's a DVD movie, and suddenly double-clicking the folder will cause the movie to start playing in DVD Player as if you've just inserted it as a DVD movie disc.

Should you want to browse the backup folder at any point, right-click the new .dvdbundle package, and select Show Package Contents from the menu that appears.

Removing the .dvdbundle extension will return the folder to its ordinary status as simply containing files.

Tip 79

Link to Emails in Notes/Stickies/Docs

If you drag and drop an email from the list within Mail onto a Notes window, sticky note, or TextEdit window, it'll automatically create a text link that—when clicked—will open the email for viewing.

However, bear in mind that, when doing this, you're merely creating a link. You aren't copying the mail's contents into the document, sticky note, or note. Therefore, if you send the document to another person, the link will be useless and will result in a nasty error message when that person clicks it.

Tip 80

When Did I Make That Sticky?

You can find the Stickies app in the Applications list within Finder. The app borrows from the real-life sticky notes, and you can stick virtual notes anywhere on the desktop. Whatever you type on them is automatically saved across reboots.

However, here's a cool tip: hovering your mouse over a sticky note will show a tooltip telling you when the sticky note was created and when it was last modified.

Tip 81

Use Facebook Chat

The Messages app can be configured as a Facebook chat client, which is to say you'll be able to chat to your Facebook friends from within Messages, and the messages will appear for them when they're logged into Facebook. This is possible because Facebook chat uses the Jabber protocol, which is a feature offered within Messages.

Setting up Facebook chat can be done whether or not you've configured Facebook within the Mail, Contacts & Calendars section of System Preferences.

Adding Facebook Chat to Messages

Here's how to set it up:

1. Before starting, you must find out your Facebook username. Often this is the latter part of the web address you see when you view your own profile in Facebook (for example, http://facebook.com/*john.smith*).[8]

2. Open Messages, and then open its Preferences dialog box (Messages→ Preferences). Select the Accounts tab in the Preferences dialog box.

3. Click the plus icon at the bottom left of the dialog box. In the new dialog box that slides down, select Jabber from the Account Type drop-down list.

4. In the Account Name field, type the Facebook username you discovered, followed by @chat.facebook.com. In other words, if my username were john.smith, I would type john.smith@chat.facebook.com.

5. In the password field, type your Facebook password, and then click the Done button (there's no need to fill in any of the Server Options fields—these fields are automatically detected).

And that's all that's needed! You'll be logged into Facebook chat immediately. To see a list of your Facebook friends who are online and have chat activated, click Window→Buddies. To chat to any of them, double-click their entries within the list.

---

8. See also https://www.facebook.com/help/usernames/general.

Removing Facebook Chat from Messages

To remove Facebook Chat from Messages, again open Messages' Preferences dialog box and ensure that the Accounts tab is activated. Then select the chat.facebook.com option in the list, and click the minus button directly beneath the list of chat servers.

Exploring OS X: Folder Actions

Wouldn't it be useful if you could make something happen automatically whenever a file was added to a folder? Or even if somebody simply accessed the folder?

The Folder Actions feature of OS X fulfills this need. It lets you attach one or more AppleScripts or Automator actions to a folder, which can be run whenever the folder is opened, closed, moved, resized, has things added, or has things removed.[a]

For example, you could have a folder action convert to JPEG any image file added to a folder, regardless of its original format. You could have a folder pop up an alert box to the user whenever it's accessed, explaining what the folder contains. A folder could automatically print any file added to it.

Any folder in your User folder can have a folder action attached—just right-click it and select Folder Actions Setup. Several example AppleScripts are provided by Apple and are listed when you configure a folder action, but many more are freely available online, created by third-party developers, and they're often geared toward specific tasks such as processing music files for iTunes. Just search Google. Some are provided within the Mac App Store too—again, all you need to do is search. Any you download should be placed in /Library/Scripts/Folder Action Scripts/.

---

a.   For a guide to creating AppleScripts for Folder Actions, see:
https://developer.apple.com/library/mac/#documentation/applescript/Conceptual/ApplescriptLangGuide/
reference/ASLR_folder_actions.html.

Tip 82

Preview Widgets

If you download new Dashboard widgets, you have to install them to your Dashboard before you can run them. This is counterintuitive because it might transpire that the widget isn't much use, in which case you have to go through the work of uninstalling it.

However, if you double-click a downloaded widget to open it and then hold down `Option`+`Command` when the installation dialog box appears, you'll see that the Install button changes to Run. Clicking this button will then run the widget from its current location in your Downloads folder, without actually installing it.

After trying the widget in Dashboard using this technique—regardless of whether you want to keep it—you must close the widget by holding down `Option` and clicking the close button at the top left of the widget. Then, if you want to install the widget, you can do so in the usual way by double-clicking it and choosing the Install option. If you decide you don't want the widget, drag it to the trash like you would any other file you want to delete.

Tip 83

Create a "Drives" Stack

Here's a neat little trick that will add a new stack to the Dock that, when clicked, will display any storage attached to your computer (things like USB memory sticks, FireWire/Thunderbolt drives, and SD cards). As an added bonus, it will also show any installation .dmg files you currently have mounted.

Setting Up the Stack

Here are the steps needed to add the stack to the Dock:

1. Follow the instructions under the "Viewing Hidden Files" section of Tip 156, *Hide Files*, on page 178, specifically for using the secret command that shows hidden files within Finder. This will let you view the entire filesystem hierarchy, which is necessary for the following steps.

2. Open a Finder window, and hold down `Shift`+`Command`+`G`. In the dialog box that appears, simply type / (forward slash). Then click Go.

3. This will show the entire OS X filesystem. Scroll down until you can see the Volumes folder. Click and drag this to the stacks area on the right of the Dock. The other stacks will slide out of the way to make room for it. Don't worry—you're not copying the folder. You're just creating a shortcut.

4. Go back to the tip mentioned in step 1, and disable the viewing of hidden files in Finder.

Give the new stack a try. Clicking any entries in the list will open that storage device in Finder. Note that the stack will always contain a link to your hard disk, and as with any stack, the icon is always that of the item last added, which in this case will be the last drive attached to your computer.

Removing the Stack

You can remove the new stack in the same way you remove any Dock icon—click and drag it to just above the middle of the screen. The icon will change to a puff of smoke, which is your cue to release the mouse button and finish the deletion.

Tip 84

Calculate All File Sizes

If you view files and folders in Finder using List view and look under the Size column, you'll see that although you see the sizes of files, you aren't told the amount of disk space folders take up. Instead, you see two dashes. To change this, hit Command+J to bring up the View window, and then check Calculate All Sizes. You'll see the Finder window update instantly, and you can then close the View window.

Note that this is a per-folder setting. To make it a systemwide default, again open the View window, and click the Use as Defaults button.

Tip 85

Quickly Switch Calculator Modes

You can quickly cycle through the three modes of the Calculator app (basic, scientific, and programmer) by holding down Command and tapping 1 (basic), 2 (scientific), or 3 (programmer).

Tip 86

Add Your Contacts' Websites to Safari

If you're in the habit of noting the home pages for your contacts in the Contacts app, you can configure Safari to automatically show a drop-down list of these addresses in the bookmarks toolbar, alongside the name of each contact.

Just open Safari's Preferences dialog box (Command+, [comma]), select the Bookmarks tab, and check Include Contacts under the Bookmarks Bar/Bookmarks Menu heading.

Tip 87

Import Twitter or Facebook Contacts

If you have your Twitter and/or Facebook accounts configured within OS X (that is, within the Mail, Contacts & Calendars component of System Preferences), you can automatically add the Twitter or Facebook details of any of your contacts to your address book. OS X does this by querying the Twitter and Facebook databases using the email addresses or phone numbers of your contacts.

Profile photographs will also be imported into your address book for each contact who doesn't already have a photo.

Once done, you'll find that each contact "card" within the Contacts app will have Twitter and/or Facebook fields for those who have such accounts, regardless of whether you've friended them on Facebook or are following them on Twitter. Clicking these fields will show a submenu allowing you to do the following:

- Facebook: Clicking the Facebook heading will let you view the individual's profile or photos on the Facebook website (assuming you've friended them on Facebook or they've set their profile or photos to be visible to the public).

- Twitter: Clicking the Twitter heading will let you either create a tweet automatically addressed to the individual or view their recent tweets on their Twitter web page.

Importing Twitter and/or Facebook Contact Details

Importing Twitter or Facebook details for your contacts is very easy, as follows:

1. Open System Preferences (Apple menu→System Preferences), and click the Mail, Contacts & Calendars icon. Select either the Twitter or Facebook account entry on the left of the System Preferences window.

2. Click the Update Contacts button at the bottom right of the program window. In the dialog box that pops up, click Update Contacts, after reading the short description of what will happen when you do.

3. OS X will now query Twitter or Facebook, and you'll see a progress pie chart at the middle bottom of the window. When it's finished, you'll see there a summary of how many contacts' details were updated.

It's a good idea to repeat this procedure periodically to import details for any new contacts you add to your address book and to update details that might change among your existing contacts.

Tip 88

Email Web Pages in a Simple Layout

The Safari web browser features a Reader feature, which can reformat article-based web pages to make them simpler and easier to read. Only certain pages are compatible, but you'll know those that are because the blue Reader button will appear in the address bar at the top of Safari's program window. Clicking it will activate Reader mode.

A useful byproduct of Reader is that it will also simplify a page if you want to email it to somebody, reducing the risk that the page will display incorrectly when they open the email. Just switch to Reader view, and then click the Email this Page link in the Share Sheet drop-down menu (the first button to the left of the address bar).

Tip 89

Quickly Send Files to an iPhone or iPad

Getting things like pictures and music files from your computer to an iPhone and iPad can be a struggle. However, if all you want to do is quickly transfer something like an image, office document, or song, then you can use the Messages app to—essentially—send the file to yourself.

You can then open the file on an iPhone, iPad, or iPod touch by looking within the Messages app.

What You Can Do with Files Once Transferred

What you can do with the file on your iPhone, iPod touch, or iPad varies, as follows:

- Image or video files: Once these files are received on the iPhone or iPad, you'll be able to add the image or video files into your camera roll. Just open the file for viewing by tapping it, and then select the icon at the top right or bottom left.

- Office documents: If you send a word processor document, spreadsheet, or presentation file, you'll be able to view it by tapping it and, if you have a compatible app installed (like Pages, Numbers or Keynote), import it into that app's iCloud filestore for editing. Just click the icon at the top right of the display.

- PDF files: These can be viewed by tapping them and imported into the iBooks app for later viewing, if you have iBooks (free within the App Store) or any other PDF reader installed.

- Alas, if you send a music file like an MP3, all you can do is listen to it in a preview application. You won't be able to import it into your iPhone's or iPad's music collection.

How to Transfer Files

First make sure that the iPhone or iPad you want to transfer the file to is logged in with the same Apple ID as your Mac. Then open Messages on your Mac and start a new conversation, but type your own iMessage contact details into the To field, essentially starting a conversation with yourself. Following this, drag and drop the file you want to transfer onto the Messages text field and hit Return to send the message. The file will then be sent to your iPhone, iPad, or iPod touch. In fact, it will also appear as a new message within Messages on all these devices and will also appear as a new message on the Mac used to send it! However, this can be ignored.

Figure 16—Delving into iCloud's Time Machine file history

Tip 90

Use Time Machine with iCloud

Apps that utilize iCloud, like TextEdit and Preview, are fully compatible with Time Machine. This means you can go back in a file's history to retrieve an earlier version, for example, or retrieve a deleted file.

Simply start the app and open the file browser showing iCloud—usually this can be done by clicking File→Open and selecting the iCloud tab at the top left of the file-browsing window.

Then click the Time Machine button at the top right of the desktop, and select Enter Time Machine from the drop-down menu. This will show the iCloud file-browsing dialog box within Time Machine, and you can "go back in time" in the usual way by selecting from the timeline on the right of the screen. See Figure 16, *Delving into iCloud's Time Machine file history*, on page 94.

Note that this works only if the iCloud view is selected in the file-browsing window. If a standard file-browsing dialog is open and showing files on your hard disk, selecting to use Time Machine will cause OS X to switch to an open Finder window to display files.

Find Docs by Zooming

Quick Look offers a fantastic way to preview documents (see *Exploring OS X: Quick Look*, on page 103), but there's an even faster way to look inside many documents at once using Finder and its Icon view feature. This can be very useful if you're trying to locate a file based on its contents. Here's how it's done:

1. Use Finder to browse the directory where the files are located, then switch to Icon view (select View→as Icons, or hold down `Command` and tap `1`).

2. Activate the Finder status bar by clicking View→Status bar.

3. Drag the slider at the bottom right of the Finder window to its right extremity. This will make the file icons as big as they can be and also—crucially—provide readable previews of their contents. Make the Finder window bigger by dragging its edges if you can't see all of each icon.

4. Click View→Arrange by→Kind. This will sort the files into horizontal "shelves" according to their file type (pictures, PDFs, Word files, and so on).

5. Scroll up and down through the shelves and left and right through the icons to view each file's contents (if you're using a standard PC mouse without a horizontal scrolling feature, you can use the cursor keys to highlight each file and navigate through them in that way). You should see enough of the file's contents (albeit with small text) to know what's in each file. PDF files and Word document icons will have two arrows on them at the bottom of their icons to advance forward/backward in the pages of the documents (sadly, spreadsheets and presentations don't feature this!).

To restore to Finder the default view settings without huge icons, open the View properties dialog box (View→Show View Options or `Command`+`J`); then when the dialog box appears, hold down `Option`. This will change the button at the bottom to Restore to Defaults. Click it. Close the View dialog, and then click View→Arrange by→Name.

Tip 92

Share via Twitter or Facebook with a Keystroke

In apps that have Share Sheet buttons, you can opt to tweet or send to Facebook whatever interests you (see Tip 18, *Right-Click to Share Anything*, on page 32). Perhaps surprisingly, there's no keyboard shortcut setup for this purpose.

Adding Shortcuts

However, you can add your own keyboard shortcuts easily, as follows:

1. Open System Preferences (Apple menu→System Preferences), and then click the Keyboard icon.

2. Click the Keyboard Shortcuts tab and then, in the list on the left of the window, select Application Shortcuts (this might be truncated to "Application Shor...").

3. Click the plus button beneath the list on the right. In the dialog box that appears, ensure All Applications is visible in the Application drop-down list.

4. In the Menu Title field, type either Twitter or Facebook, ensuring that you type them exactly as printed here.

5. Click in the Keyboard Shortcut box, and then type the actual keyboard shortcut you'd like to use to activate Twitter or Facebook. Because different apps have used up nearly all the obvious keyboard shortcut combinations, it's best if you use all three modifier keys (`Control`, `Option`, and `Command`) plus either `T` for Twitter or `F` for Facebook. So, for a Twitter shortcut, you would press `Control`+`Option`+`Command`+`T`. For Facebook, you'd press `Control`+`Option`+`Command`+`F`.

6. You can create other shortcuts for options on the Share Sheet menus. If you have a Flickr account set up on your system, for example, you could follow the earlier steps, and in the Menu Title field, type Flickr. You must type the exact text that appears for the option when you click the Share Sheet button, including taking note of capitalization (or lack of).

Once the shortcuts are created, you can close System Preferences and then test them in any application that supports sharing in this way—try opening an image in Preview and then hitting Control+Option+Command+T to tweet it to the world!

Note that if you have any bookmarks within Safari that are called "Facebook" or "Twitter," you'll need to rename them, or the keyboard shortcuts you've created will apply to them too.

Removing Keyboard Shortcuts

To remove the shortcuts you created, repeat the earlier steps so the keyboard shortcuts are listed in System Preferences. Then select the new shortcut in the list and click the minus button beneath the list.

Tip 93

Stop iCloud from Being the Default

Assuming you have the Documents & Data option activated in iCloud, you'll find that any iCloud-enabled app like TextEdit will always automatically choose iCloud in Save dialog boxes. You can manually select your hard disk if you want to save files there, but it's something of a chore!

A secret command will switch Save dialogs to default to your hard disk as the destination for new files.

Open a Terminal window (open Finder, select the Applications list, and then in the list of applications double-click Terminal within the Utilities folder), and type the following:

```
defaults write -g NSDocumentSaveNewDocumentsToCloud -bool FALSE
```

Then close all open apps, and log out and back in again for the changes to take effect.

Give it a try in an app like TextEdit—create a new file, and then hit File→Save to see the old-style dialog box showing folders on your hard disk. You're still be able to select iCloud as a destination, although you'll have to switch to the "rolled-up" dialog box by hitting Command+= and then clicking the Where drop-down list to select iCloud as an option.

To restore iCloud as the default Save As location for new files, again open a Terminal window, and type the following:

```
defaults delete -g NSDocumentSaveNewDocumentsToCloud
```

Again, close all apps and log out and back in again for the changes to take effect.

Note that if this tip has left you wondering whether there's a similar setting for Open file dialog boxes, then there's no need to worry—if you switch to browsing your hard disk in an Open file dialog box, the app will remember your choice for next time. You won't see iCloud again unless you specifically select it.

Tip 94

Export in More Formats via Preview

When you open an image or PDF in Preview, you can convert it to a different format by clicking File→Export and selecting from the Format drop-down list in the dialog box that appears. By holding down Option before clicking it, however, you'll find the drop-down list contains significantly more file format options for you to choose from.

Note that if you open a Word document in Preview, you can use this trick to quickly export it as a PDF.

Tip 95

Supertip: Get the Most from QuickTime Player

Here are a handful of secret tweaks that can be made to QuickTime Player in order to potentially make it more useful and user friendly.

Each is to be typed into a Terminal window after you've first quit QuickTime Player.

Make the Playback Window Square

By default the corners of the QuickTime Player window are rounded a little to create a pleasing look, but for those who like to see everything that's going on in each frame of a movie, this can be annoying.

The following command will make the playback window fully square:

```
defaults write com.apple.QuickTimePlayerX
     MGCinematicWindowDebugForceNoRoundedCorners -bool TRUE
```

To restore rounded edges later, use the following command:

```
defaults delete com.apple.QuickTimePlayerX
     MGCinematicWindowDebugForceNoRoundedCorners
```

Automatically Start Playing Upon Opening a Movie

By default QuickTime Player won't start playing a movie you open until you click the Play button on the controller bar. The following setting will cause movies to start playing automatically:

```
defaults write com.apple.QuickTimePlayerX MGPlayMovieOnOpen -bool TRUE
```

...and the following will turn off the autoplay feature:

```
defaults delete com.apple.QuickTimePlayerX MGPlayMovieOnOpen
```

Hide the Controller Bar and Title Bar

QuickTime Player hides the controller bar and title bar whenever the mouse leaves the program window, but as soon as the cursor enters again, both become visible. The following setting hides them permanently, although they'll still be visible when QuickTime Player first starts. The first time you move the cursor outside the program window, they'll permanently disappear. Essentially this turns QuickTime Player into nothing more than a borderless movie frame, without even a progress display, and you'll have to start/stop the movie using keyboard shortcuts, as described in Tip 73, *Control QuickTime Player Using Keys*, on page 81.

The command to activate this feature is as follows:

```
defaults write com.apple.QuickTimePlayerX MGUIVisibilityNeverAutoshow -bool
     TRUE
```

To restore the controller bar/title bar later, again open a Terminal window, and type the following:

```
defaults delete com.apple.QuickTimePlayerX MGUIVisibilityNeverAutoshow
```

Stop the Controls from Hiding So Quickly

As mentioned previously, the controller bar appears when the mouse cursor is in the QuickTime Player window but disappears instantly when it leaves. The following tweak will cause the controller bar to stick around a few seconds longer when the mouse cursor leaves the QuickTime window:

```
defaults write com.apple.QuickTimePlayerX MGUIVisibilityNeverAutohide -bool
    TRUE
```

The following will disable this feature:

```
defaults delete com.apple.QuickTimePlayerX MGUIVisibilityNeverAutohide
```

Automatically Show Subtitles/Closed Captioning

If the movies you play in QuickTime Player have subtitle/closed captioning (CC) files, the following tweak will cause movies to automatically show their subtitles, negating the need to select the option from the View→Subtitles menu:

```
defaults write com.apple.QuickTimePlayerX MGEnableCCAndSubtitlesOnOpen -bool
    TRUE
```

Note that subtitle/CC files need to be placed in the same directory as the movie file and also have the same filename; for example, if the movie is called JourneyToTheMoon.mpg, then the subtitle/CC file should be renamed to JourneyToThe-Moon.srt (assuming it's an .srt file).

The following will deactivate automatic displaying of subtitles:

```
defaults delete com.apple.QuickTimePlayerX MGEnableCCAndSubtitlesOnOpen
```

Tip 96

Subscribe to Useful Calendars

Sites like http://icalshare.com provide links to calendars that you can subscribe to (that is, incorporate) within the Calendar app. These are known as *iCal subscriptions*.

The available calendars list events such as public holidays for particular countries, or the timetable of particular sporting events, and are usually updated by enthusiasts so you can easily keep up-to-date in a hassle-free way (the calendars aren't actually stored on your computer). Indeed, there are hundreds of calendars for just about any need—from listing the fictional birthdays of computer game characters to pointing out the phases of the moon.

All you need to do is click the link for the calendar on the site, and the Calendar app will ask if you want to subscribe to it. Just click the Subscribe button in the dialog box that appears.

Removing a calendar (that is, unsubscribing) is as easy as starting Calendar, clicking the Calendar button at the top left so the list of calendar subscriptions is visible, right-clicking the one you no longer want, and selecting Delete from the menu that appears.

Note that you can even create your own calendars to share with others—see Tip 65, *Share Reminders and Calendars*, on page 71.

Tip 97

Turn Off Annoying Special Effects

Call me a cynic, but it feels like OS X is a little showy with its visual effects. Dialog boxes and some program windows pop onto the screen from nowhere. This design mirrors the iPod and iPad user experience. On a larger screen, however, the effect can be unsettling.

Wouldn't it be nice if they just appeared on-screen with no fuss, like they did in the good old days?

Here's how you can turn off the majority of OS X's visual effects.

Pop-Up Windows and Dialogs

To turn off dialog boxes and windows that spring out from the middle of the screen, open a Terminal window (open Finder, select the Applications list, and then in the list of applications double-click Terminal within the Utilities folder), and type the following:

```
defaults write -g NSAutomaticWindowAnimationsEnabled -bool FALSE
```

Then log out and back in again for the changes to take effect.

To restore the effect, open a Terminal window, and type the following, logging out and back in again afterward to make the changes take effect:

```
defaults delete -g NSAutomaticWindowAnimationsEnabled
```

Quick Look

Quick Look windows appear when you select a file and hit Space . They show a preview of the file's contents. You can stop Quick Look windows from springing up from the file in question by typing the following into a Terminal window (this change will also remove the effect of the Quick Look window shrinking back into the file):

```
defaults write com.apple.finder QLPanelAnimationDuration -int 0;killall
        Finder
```

The change will take effect immediately. To restore the effect, open a Terminal window, and type the following (again, the change will take effect immediately):

```
defaults delete com.apple.finder QLPanelAnimationDuration;killall Finder
```

Mission Control

To turn off the Mission Control zoom effects that appear whenever it's activated and deactivated, open a Terminal window, and type the following:

```
defaults write com.apple.dock expose-animation-duration -int 0;killall Dock
```

The changes take effect immediately. Note that this also removes the animated effect of windows zooming out of the way when Show Desktop is activated (usually via the "finger spread" trackpad gesture).

To revert to the default animated Mission Control effects, open a Terminal window, and type the following:

```
defaults delete com.apple.dock expose-animation-duration;killall Dock
```

File and Print Dialog Boxes

To stop the Save and Print dialog boxes from sliding out and down from the title bar of each application, open a Terminal window, and type the following:

```
defaults write -g NSWindowResizeTime -float 0.01
```

You'll need to log out and in again for the changes to take effect. If you want to reintroduce the visual effects later, type the following, logging out and back in again afterward for the changes to take effect:

```
defaults delete -g NSWindowResizeTime
```

Exploring OS X: Quick Look

Quick Look is a simple feature that lets you instantly preview the contents of files without having to open them in an application. To use Quick Look, just select a file in a Finder window or on the desktop and hit Space (or right-click the file and select Quick Look from the menu that appears). Its contents will be instantly viewable in a pop-up window that will disappear if you hit Space again (or Esc) or click the close button.

Quick Look understands most commonly used files, including Microsoft Office and iWork documents, images, and movies. The document formatting within Office documents isn't always great, but you can at least get an idea of the file's contents.

Quick Look works almost everywhere within OS X, and not just Finder windows. For example, select an attachment in Mail and hit Space to instantly view it. Select a file sent to you in Message, and then hit Space to do the same thing. Looking at files in the print queue? Just select one and hit Space to see its contents.

You can also select several files at once and take a look at them as described earlier (hit Space or right-click and select Quick Look). The first of the files will be previewed, but you can move through the rest you highlighted using the left/right buttons at the top left. If you click the gallery button to the right of the left/right buttons, the files will be arranged in a gallery within the Quick Look window, so you can rapidly glance through their contents. Selecting one will enlarge it within the Quick Look window, and clicking the gallery button again will let you return to viewing all the files.

Launchpad

A hidden setting can be tweaked to make Launchpad appear and disappear instantly. To activate it, open a Terminal window (open Finder, select the Applications list, then in the list of applications double-click Terminal within the Utilities folder). Type the following two lines, hitting Return after each:

```
defaults write com.apple.dock springboard-show-duration -int 0
defaults write com.apple.dock springboard-hide-duration -int 0;killall Dock
```

The changes take effect instantly. To revert to the previous animated effect, open a Terminal window again, and type the following two lines:

```
defaults delete com.apple.dock springboard-show-duration
defaults delete com.apple.dock springboard-hide-duration;killall Dock
```

You can also reduce the amount of time pages of apps within Launchpad take to scroll in and out. Open a Terminal window, and type the following if you want the pages to slide in and out instantly:

```
defaults write com.apple.dock springboard-page-duration -int 0;killall Dock
```

The changes take effect immediately. To revert to the default, open a Terminal window, and type the following:

```
defaults delete com.apple.dock springboard-page-duration;killall Dock
```

Dock

The Dock can be hidden so that it slides off the screen when not being used. This saves a little screen space. Nudging the cursor against the edge of the screen where the Dock is normally positioned will make it slide back into view again. To turn this feature on or off, right-click the dashed lines between the main Dock icons and the stacks, and select Turn Hiding On or Turn Hiding Off.

To make the Dock instantly leap back into view when it's needed (which is to say, when your mouse touches the bottom of the screen), rather than slide, open a Terminal window, and type the following two lines:

```
defaults write com.apple.dock autohide-delay -float 0
defaults write com.apple.dock autohide-time-modifier -int 0;killall Dock
```

To revert to the default sliding effect, open a Terminal window, and type the following two lines:

```
defaults delete com.apple.dock autohide-delay
defaults delete com.apple.dock autohide-time-modifier;killall Dock
```

Tip 98

Start Apps Without the Mouse

A quick way to start an app that you don't have in the Dock is to hit Command+Space and begin typing its name. Command+Space activates the Spotlight search tool, and this will autocomplete the program name after just a few letters, selecting it automatically. All you need to do is hit Return to run the app. I often use this to start programs I already have in the Dock if I don't want to take my hands off the keyboard.

You can open Launchpad instead of Spotlight and do the same thing—as soon as you open Launchpad, the cursor is placed in its search field where you can start to type the name of an app, before hitting Return to open it.

However, Launchpad isn't assigned a keyboard shortcut by default, unlike Spotlight.

If the app's name consists of several words, such as QuickTime Player, in either Spotlight or Launchpad you simply type the initials: for QuickTime Player you could simply type qt, for example, while for Photo Booth you could type pb. This works because Spotlight spots that you're typing the capital letters in the app name (qt for QuickTime, for example). Because of this, this trick won't work for an app like Dropbox,[9] where the b for "box" is lowercase.

Tip 99

Select Text In Quick Look

If you use Quick Look to view any files that feature text—such as PDFs or Word documents—you'll notice that you can't click and drag to highlight text. Clicking anywhere on the Quick Look window simply moves it around.

However, a secret setting will let you click and drag as usual to highlight text, and you can use the standard key combination of Command+C to copy text. The Quick Look window can still be moved around the screen by clicking and dragging its title bar, as with any other program window.

To activate the setting, open a Terminal window (open Finder, select the Applications list, and then in the list of applications double-click Terminal within the Utilities folder), and type the following:

```
defaults write com.apple.finder QLEnableTextSelection -bool TRUE;killall
    Finder
```

The changes take effect immediately. To deactivate the setting, open a Terminal window, and type the following:

```
defaults delete com.apple.finder QLEnableTextSelection;killall Finder
```

---

9. http://dropbox.com

Tip 100

Resize Windows Easily

You can resize any program window by hovering the mouse cursor over any of its borders until it changes to an arrow cursor and then clicking and dragging. However, it can be very difficult to get the mouse cursor in exactly the right spot.

Tweaking the following secret setting will increase the area in which the resizing cursor will activate. Open a Terminal window (open Finder, select the Applications list, and then in the list of applications double-click Terminal within the Utilities folder), and type the following:

```
defaults write -g AppleEdgeResizeExteriorSize 10
```

Then log out and back in again for the changes to take effect. You should now find that the cursor changes to the resize cursor when it's close to the outside edge of a window and no longer has to be precisely placed on the very edge.

You can increase the number in the previous command from 10 to perhaps 15 or 20 to make an even larger area in which the resize cursor takes effect.

To revert to the default setting, open a Terminal window, and then type the following:

```
defaults delete -g AppleEdgeResizeExteriorSize
```

Log out and back in again for the changes to take effect.

For easier resizing of windows, you can also hold down either `Option` or `Shift` (or both) as you click and drag any edge. The latter causes windows to contract vertically at both sides as you click and drag (a concertina effect), while the former shrinks the entire window—the equivalent of clicking and dragging a corner. Used together, they cause the window to shrink into or out of its center point.

Tip 101

Get to the Dock in a Full-Screen App

Many Mac apps, such as Safari and Mail, can run in full-screen mode, in which case they occupy a Mission Control space all their own. Switching an app to full-screen mode is usually done by clicking the small icon at the top-right corner of the program window. Full-screen mode hides the menu bar at the top of the screen, along with the Dock. You can make the menu bar appear again by pushing your mouse cursor against the top edge of the screen and waiting for a second, but the same doesn't work with the Dock. Push it against the Dock's usual location on the screen, and it resolutely refuses to appear.

In fact, it will appear, but you have to perform an odd little trick—push the mouse cursor against the edge of the screen where the Dock is normally positioned, and then pause for a second before pushing again. This will cause the Dock to move into view. It takes a little bit of practice, so give it a go!

If you'd like the Dock to slide into view as soon as the mouse touches the bottom of the screen, like it does normally if the Dock is hidden, the following secret setting will do the trick. If any apps are set to run full-screen, temporarily exit full-screen mode, open a Terminal window, and type the following:

```
defaults write com.apple.dock autohide-fullscreen-delayed -bool FALSE;
        killall Dock
```

The changes will take effect immediately, so try switching an app to full-screen to see what happens.

To restore the default behavior of the Dock in full-screen mode, again temporarily exit full-screen mode in any open apps, open a Terminal window, and type the following:

```
defaults delete com.apple.dock autohide-fullscreen-delayed;killall Dock
```

Tip 102

Play Sounds When Certain Mail Arrives

Not all mails are equal, and sometimes you might want to be notified if a mail arrives from a particular individual or if the subject line or mail body contains a certain phrase (perhaps something like "The money has been wired to your account").

Setting up this feature in Mail is easy and can be done via mail rules, as follows:

1. Open Mail's Preferences dialog box (application menu→Preferences), and then select the Rules tab. Then click the Add Rule button.

2. A drop-down dialog box will appear. In the Description field, type a name for your new rule; something like "Mail from John" is good. This is only for your own reference later.

3. Below the line If Any of the Following Conditions Are Met, click the Any Recipient drop-down list, and choose an option from the list. If you want a sound to play when the mail is received from a certain person, click From. If you want a sound to play when the mail contains a certain phrase or word, select Message Content.

4. Leave the Contains drop-down list as it is, but in the text field next to this, type either the email address of the recipient—if you've selected to be alerted when mail arrives from them—or the word or phrase within the email that you'd like to be alerted about.

5. Click the Move Message drop-down list directly beneath the Perform The Following Actions heading, and select Play Sound. Note that you can also select to do other things too, such as bounce the Mail icon in the Dock (it will bounce until you click it).

6. In the drop-down list that appears, select one of the system sounds, or click the Add/Remove entry at the bottom of the list. In the Sounds dialog box that appears, click the Add button, and then navigate to what sound file you'd like to use. Note that sound files can be downloaded from a number of websites, and you can choose .mp3 files or .wav files, although be aware that once a sound has started playing, there's no way to stop it, so selecting a four-minute MP3 tune might not be a great idea. Note

that sound files are copied to Mail's own private store of sound files so can be deleted if you want once you've added them.

7. When you add the sound, you'll be treated to a preview of it.

8. Click Done in the Sounds dialog box, and then select the new sound from the drop-down list of sound effects. When you do this, you'll hear a preview of the sound.

9. Click OK to close the Rules dialog box. You'll be asked whether you want to apply the rule to messages in selected mailboxes. There's no need to do this, so click Don't Apply.

Your new rule is in place. It's now just a matter of waiting until a mail arrives that matches the criteria you set! Note that the rule will be applied only to new mail you receive.

To remove the rule later, again open Mail's Preferences dialog box, and click the Rules tab. Then select the rule in the list, and click the Remove button.

Tip 103

Migrate from Outlook to Calendar

Calendar in Lion and Mountain Lion has impressive features and might prompt you to make the move from Microsoft Outlook or Entourage for your appointment needs. If you decide to make the switch, you can drag and drop an existing calendar event from Outlook or Entourage onto an open Calendar app window to immediately import it.

Tip 104

Stop iTunes from Adding Track Numbers

Most people are happy to let iTunes entirely manage their collection of music files, but some choose to delve into the iTunes filestore in order to make copies of any files that have been ripped from CDs. I do this to play the files on my car's stereo, into which I can insert memory cards full of music files.

Any ripped files are usually stored in the Music/iTunes/iTunes Media/Music folder, within a series of folders named first after the artist (i.e., The Beatles) and then after the name of the album (i.e., Revolver). If you look at the files, however, you'll notice a slight problem—each file is named after the song but has the track number inserted before it in the filename. I'd prefer that this didn't happen because track numbers are meaningless to my car stereo and seeing 01 Love Me Do scroll past on the stereo's display can be confusing!

The solution is to issue a command to deactivate track numbering within files. Quit iTunes, open a Terminal window, and type the following:

```
defaults write com.apple.iTunes create-filenames-with-tracknumber -bool FALSE
```

Then restart iTunes. Any tracks you rip from CD will now be named after the song and will contain no other information. Sadly, this trick won't go through already ripped tracks and remove the track numbers from filenames.

Note that you can still view the files in track order within a Finder window; just select View→Arrange by→Date Created.

Should you decide to reverse the procedure and reintroduce track numbering, again quit iTunes before opening a Terminal window and typing the following:

```
defaults delete com.apple.iTunes create-filenames-with-tracknumber
```

Tip 105

Switch Desktop Space Ultra-Quickly

Here are two tips to speed up how you use desktop spaces.

Nudging from Space to Space Instantly

If you use more than one desktop space, you might already know that if you click and drag program windows to the far right (or left) side of a screen, you can "nudge" the window into the next desktop space. To do this, drag the window so that the mouse cursor cannot move any further against the screen edge.

There's a one- or two-second delay before OS X switches to the neighboring desktop space, and you can speed this up using a hidden setting, as follows:

```
defaults write com.apple.dock workspaces-edge-delay -float 0;killall Dock
```

The desktop space will now change as soon as you touch the edge of the screen. I find this useful, but if you'd like a split-second delay before the desktop space switches, try the following:

```
defaults write com.apple.dock workspaces-edge-delay -float 0.15;killall Dock
```

To revert to the default second or two delay later, open a Terminal window, and type the following:

```
defaults delete com.apple.dock workspaces-edge-delay;killall Dock
```

Using Keyboard Shortcuts

Another way of very quickly switching program windows between desktops is to use keyboard shortcuts. This isn't quite as quick as the secret setting described earlier, but it's worth investigating.

First you must enable keyboard shortcuts for each of your desktop spaces. This can be done by opening System Preferences (Apple menu→System Preferences), selecting the Keyboard icon, then clicking the Keyboard Shortcuts tab. Select Mission Control in the list on the left of the window, and then check the entries on the right that read Switch To Desktop 1, Switch To Desktop 2, and so on, for all the desktop spaces you have configured.

From then on, moving a program window from one space to another is a matter of clicking and holding its title bar and then hitting the keyboard shortcut for that space, which will be a combination of Control plus 1, 2, 3, and so on, relating to the number of the desktop space.

Tip 106

Protect USB Memory Sticks

Lots of people use USB memory sticks to transfer data from one computer to another or just to keep their files with them at all times.

OS X lets you format a USB memory stick so that its contents are encrypted. You'll need to enter a password whenever it's inserted.

Essentially this turns any USB stick into a ultra-secure portable file storage device, of the type often sold at a premium. However, there are a number of caveats, as follows:

- The memory stick must be Mac-formatted, which is to say it must use the GUID Partition Table (GPT) system. Out of the box, most memory sticks are formatted as Windows-compatible FAT32/FAT32X, which your Mac can read and write to but cannot encrypt. Therefore, the first step is usually to reformat a memory stick to GPT format.

- The memory stick will work only on Macs running OS X Lion or Mountain Lion and not on Macs running earlier versions of OS X or on PCs running Windows or Linux. To those operating systems, the memory stick will appear to be unformatted or corrupted. For a way of creating a cross-platform encrypted archive that you can store on a USB memory stick, see Tip 209, *Create Encrypted Archives for All Computers*, on page 234.

Therefore, there are two potential paths from this point: formatting and encrypting the memory stick with GPT format or simply encrypting the disk if it's already GPT formatted. The following instructions explain all you need to know, although you should note that they apply equally well to any kind of removable storage device, including FireWire, Thunderbolt, and USB external drives.

Converting a Memory Stick to GPT and Encrypting It

The following steps detail how to first format a memory stick in Mac-compatible GPT format and also encrypt it at the same time. Theoretically, these two steps can be done separately, but it makes sense to do them at the same time.

Be aware that files already on the stick will be deleted during the formatting process, so you should temporarily copy them to a safe location and then copy them back once the following procedure is finished.

1. Start by opening Disk Utility (open Finder, select the Applications list, and then double-click Disk Utility in the Utilities folder), and then insert the USB memory stick you intend to use.

2. Look for the memory stick's entry in the list of disks on the left side of the Disk Utility window. It will probably be identified by its size. Select the entry, but make sure you select the disk itself and *not* the partition(s), which will be listed below and indented slightly.

3. Click the Erase tab in the Disk Utility window. In the Format drop-down menu, select Mac OS Extended (Journaled, Encrypted). In the Name field, type whatever you want to call the memory stick. This name will appear in Finder's sidebar whenever you insert the stick in the future.

4. Click the Erase button. You'll be prompted to enter a password and verify it by typing it again immediately below. It's important that you don't forget this password! If you do, there is absolutely no way of recovering the contents of the memory stick—they're lost forever. However, you will be able to reformat the memory stick so you can keep using it. Because of the risk, it's a good idea to type something in the Hint field that might provide a clue to what the password is—the hint will appear in the future should you get stuck when entering the password. For an example, see Figure 17, *Encrypting a removable storage device like a USB stick*, on page 113.

5. When you are done, click the Erase button in the dialog box. Erasing, partitioning, and encrypting will take a minute or two depending on the size of the memory stick. Once you're done, the new memory stick will be ready for use. You can copy files to it by selecting its entry in the sidebar of Finder. You can also close Disk Utility.

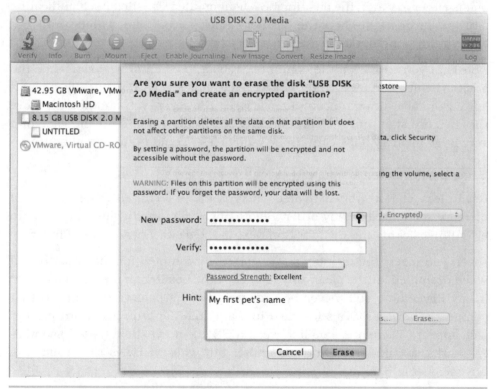

Figure 17—Encrypting a removable storage device like a USB stick

Encrypting a USB Memory Stick Already Formatted for Macs

Encrypting a USB memory stick already Mac-formatted is easy—just right-click the memory stick's entry on the left of a Finder window under the Devices heading, and select the Encrypt option. This is possible because encryption can be done "on the fly," which is to say it can be done invisibly and in the background, without destroying the existing contents of the memory stick and while you're still using the memory stick to save and retrieve files.

You'll be prompted to enter a password and verify it by typing it again, so do so. You'll also be prompted to enter a password hint in case you forget your password.

Once you've done both, click the Encrypt Disk button, and the encryption process will begin. The memory stick will be unmounted and then mounted again a minute later, after which the background encryption process will begin. You'll see no progress display, and, in fact, the only way you'll be aware of it is either to watch the flashing LED light on the USB stick itself, indicating activity, or to right-click the memory stick's icon and watch until the Encrypting menu option ceases to be grayed out.

Note that you can sleep the computer, reboot, or even shut down while the stick is being encrypted, and the process will pick up automatically where it left off the next time the computer is used. However, you shouldn't remove the memory stick until encryption has completed, which—in the case of a very large memory stick containing many files—could take several hours.

Using the Protected Memory Stick

Regardless of how you activated encryption, you can use the encrypted memory stick just like any other. Before physically unplugging it, be sure to eject it by clicking the Eject button next to the disk's entry within Finder.

When you insert the memory stick, you'll be prompted for the password. If when prompted for the password you check the box Remember the Password in My Keychain, you'll never be prompted for the password again on that computer. However, if it's inserted into another Mac, the password prompt will appear. Therefore, you'll have a USB memory stick that—essentially—works seamlessly on your computer but whose data is inaccessible to anyone else.

Tip 107

Find Out Where Your Wallpaper Lives

This is a quirky but potentially useful tip that will make your Mac tell you the file location of the wallpaper you're currently using.

Open a Terminal window (open Finder, select the Applications list, and then in the list of applications double-click Terminal within the Utilities folder), and type the following:

```
defaults write com.apple.dock desktop-picture-show-debug-text -bool TRUE;
        killall Dock
```

You should now find the filename and path of the wallpaper across the middle of the desktop—even when you access Mission Control and Dashboard.

To revert to having no filename and path displayed, open a Terminal window, and type the following:

```
defaults delete com.apple.dock desktop-picture-show-debug-text;killall Dock
```

Tip 108

Summarize Any Document

Some word processors include text-summarizing tools that can take salient points from several paragraphs (or even pages) and present them in a single paragraph or series of paragraphs. The summary is often a bit hit-and-miss, but it can be a good place to start if you lack the time to do the full job yourself. Your Mac includes a built-in tool to do this.

Setting Up the Service

Some initial setup is needed before you can make regular use of this tool. Open System Preferences (Apple menu→System Preferences), click the Keyboard icon, and ensure the Keyboard Shortcuts tab is activated. In the list on the left, select Services. Then check Summarize under the Text heading in the list on the right. Close System Preferences.

Summarizing Text

From now on, to summarize text, just highlight the text in the program window and either right-click it and select Summarize from the menu that appears or click the application menu, followed by Services, and then the Summarize entry. Not all apps are compatible with Services and therefore won't offer this feature—Microsoft Word 2011 is OK, but Word 2008 is a particularly annoying offender. However, it works fine in built-in OS X apps as well as in most Adobe apps that deal with text, like InDesign.

To use the Summary tool, which appears as an app window of its own (complete with Dock icon), click the Sentences or Paragraphs radio button to choose between summarizing text as a series of discrete sentences or as a series of paragraphs. The Summary Size slider adjusts the length of the summary; that is, it adjusts how much of the original text remains within the summary.

Once done, highlight the text in the Summarize program window and copy and paste it into a new destination, or click File→Save As to save the text as a plain-text file on your hard disk (sadly, the Summarize app is unable to save files to iCloud).

Tip 109

Activate Stacks and Mission Control by a Gesture

This is a neat little hack that lets you activate stacks within the Dock by hovering the mouse cursor over each stack's icon and making the scroll gesture on a multitouch trackpad or Magic Mouse or by rolling the scroll wheel on a mouse.

Do the same trick while hovering the mouse cursor over an app icon in the Dock, and Application Windows mode of Mission Control will activate—you will see open program windows for that particular app and, with compatible apps, the app's document history.

However, in each case, once you've activated the secret setting, you need to scroll up to activate it (that is, to make the stack expand) and then scroll down to deactivate it (to make the stack hide again). You'll need to scroll a substantial amount to activate the feature so that OS X knows you're doing it on purpose and not accidentally. In other words, you'll need to flick the scroll wheel up rather than just rotate it a few clicks.

To activate this hidden feature, open a Terminal window (open Finder, select the Applications list, and then in the list of applications double-click Terminal within the Utilities folder), and type the following:

```
defaults write com.apple.dock scroll-to-open -bool TRUE;killall Dock
```

The changes take effect immediately. To deactivate this feature, open a Terminal window, and type the following:

```
defaults delete com.apple.dock scroll-to-open;killall Dock
```

Tip 110

Quickly Create a List of Files

Need to quickly create a text list of files and folders contained within a directory? Open the directory in Finder and select all (Command+A); then copy to the clipboard (Command+C). Then open TextEdit, switch to plain-text mode (Format→Make Plain Text, or Shift+Command+T), and hit Command+V to paste. Don't worry—you won't paste the actual files into the document. Instead, you'll see a text list of the files and folders. This will work in any text-mode editor as well as in some word processors, such as Microsoft Word.

Tip 111

Supertip: Take Control of Scrolling

Here's a series of tips designed to give you more control over scrolling within Finder windows or when scrolling through documents and web pages.

Turning Off Inverted Scrolling

Compared to other operating systems, OS X inverts scrolling when you turn the mouse wheel or use the two-finger scroll gesture on a multitouch trackpad or Magic Mouse. It's entirely possible to get used to this, and if you have an iPad or iPhone, it might not seem strange, but here's how to turn it off, listed by pointing device:

- Apple Magic Mouse: Open System Preferences (Apple menu→System Preferences), click the Mouse icon, and then select the Point & Click tab. Remove the check next to Scroll Direction: Natural. The changes will take effect immediately.

- Other mice (including the Apple mouse): Open System Preferences (Apple menu→System Preferences), click the Mouse icon, and remove the check next to Scroll Direction: Natural. The changes will take effect immediately.

- Trackpad: Open System Preferences (Apple menu→System Preferences), click the Trackpad icon, and then select the Scroll & Zoom tab. Remove the check next to Scroll Direction: Natural. The changes will take effect immediately.

Always Showing Scrollbars

OS X hides scrollbars when they're not in use. To always show them, open System Preferences (Apple menu→System Preferences), click the General icon, and then click the radio button alongside the Always entry next to Show Scroll Bars. See also Tip 3, *Stop Scrollbars from Disappearing*, on page 12.

Turning Off Inertia Scrolling

OS X tries to mirror the experience of using an iPad or iPhone, and this includes inertia scrolling, where the page scrolls rapidly should you flick two fingers across a multitouch trackpad or Magic Mouse surface. What's actually happening is that the trackpad or mouse is sensing any acceleration in the finger gesture before you lift your finger from the surface. As such, it's not perfect, and you might see acceleration occurring accidentally. Additionally, I find inertia scrolling gives me slight motion sickness on bigger screens.

It's possible to turn off inertia scrolling within System Preferences, but it's buried within the Accessibility pane. Start System Preferences (Apple menu →System Preferences), and click the Accessibility icon. Then click the Mouse & Trackpad icon in the list on the left, and select the Trackpad Options button. In the dialog box that appears, select Without Inertia from the drop-down list next to the Scrolling checkbox.

Should you find that intertia scrolling is still occurring within certain apps or pointing mice you attach to your computer, try this trick: open Terminal (open Finder, select the Applications list, and then in the list of applications double-click Terminal within the Utilities folder), and type the following:

```
defaults write -g AppleMomentumScrollSupported -bool FALSE
```

Log out and back in again for the change to take effect.

To reenable inertia scrolling, either repeat the previous steps to activate it within System Preferences or—if you've disabled it using the secret command described earlier—open a Terminal window and type the following, logging out and back in again for the change to take effect:

```
defaults delete -g AppleMomentumScrollSupported
```

Scrolling Horizontally Using PC Mice

Newer Apple mice have special scrollballs or small trackpads that allow both vertical and horizontal scrolling. Most standard PC mice simply have a scroll wheel that allows only vertical scrolling. However, to scroll horizontally using any mouse, just hold down Shift while turning the wheel.

Jumping to a New Location Using the Scrollbars

You can scroll up or down a page in the document or website you're viewing by clicking the area above or below the scroller in the scrollbar. Usually this will cause the application to scroll page by page. Sometimes, however, you might want to simply jump to a new location in the document without having to scroll one page at a time. To do so, move the cursor to where you want to jump on the scrollbar, hold down Option, and click the mouse button. This will cause the slider to jump instantly to that spot.

This can be very useful if you want to jump to the beginning or end of a document—just hold down Option and click at the top or bottom of the scrollbar range.

Slowing Down Scrolling

Holding down Option while you click and drag the scroller (the little bar that shows your position within a document in the scrollbar) will slow down scrolling. It's best shown in practice, so give it a try—grab the scroller in any open window displaying a large file, and then hold Option and drag. You see that as well as slowing down, scrolling becomes more fluid, making it easier to read the window contents as they scroll by.

Tip 112

Turn a Small Keyboard into a Big One

Modern Mac portables and the Apple wireless keyboard have a `Delete` key, which will delete characters behind the cursor. However, by holding down the `Fn` key (bottom left of the keyboard), you can turn the `Delete` key into a forward delete key, which, just like on a full-sized keyboard, will delete characters in front of the cursor.

While we're on the subject, pressing the `Fn` key at the same time as the Up/Down cursor keys will turn them into `Page Up`/`Page Down` keys. Holding `Fn` while hitting the Left/Right cursor keys transforms them into `Home` and `End` keys, respectively, which will either scroll to the beginning/end of the document or move the cursor to the beginning/end of the line, depending on which application you're using.

Tip 113

Fix Ugly Fonts

If you attach a non-Apple external display, you might find fonts look a little faint or gritty because the font antialiasing hasn't been correctly set. The fix is easy—open a Terminal window (open Finder, select the Applications list, and then in the list of applications double-click Terminal within the Utilities folder), and type the following, logging out and back in afterward for the changes to take effect:

```
defaults -currentHost write -g AppleFontSmoothing -int 2
```

Should this method not work for you or if you're unhappy with the results, open a Terminal window, and type the following, logging out and back in again for the changes to take effect:

```
defaults -currentHost delete -g AppleFontSmoothing
```

Tip 114

Type Symbols and Diacritical Characters

Here's how to insert commonly used symbols and characters into your text documents, as shown in Figure 18, *Inserting various symbols via keyboard combinations*, on page 121. Note that this tip assumes you are using a U.S. English keyboard.

Figure 18—Inserting various symbols via keyboard combinations

Apple Symbol

Hit Shift+Option+K to insert an Apple logo () into your text. Bear in mind that the symbol probably won't appear in documents or emails opened on other operating systems, such as Windows or Linux. Instead, these systems will probably display a square, indicating a missing character. Some Linux systems might display a symbol representing an apple but not the Apple logo.

Copyright

Hit Option+G to insert a copyright symbol (©) into your text. Typing (c) will achieve the same result in most applications (you'll need to hit Space after typing for the symbol to appear).

Currency

The dollar sign is typed by hitting `Shift`+`4`, as marked on the key. Here's how to type other common currency symbols:

- Cent (¢): `Option`+`4`
- Pound sterling (£): `Option`+`3`
- Japanese Yen (¥): `Option`+`Y`
- Euro (€): `Shift`+`Option`+`2`.

Dashes and Ellipses

To type an en dash, hit `Option`+`-` (hyphen). To insert the longer em dash, hit `Shift`+`Option`+`-` (hyphen).

To type an ellipsis character, that is, three periods in a row that indicate an omission, hit `Option`+`;`.

Math Symbols

Many mathematical symbols are easily accessible via marked keys (to insert a less-than symbol, for example, hit `Shift`+`,`). However, to insert other mathematical symbols, you'll need to hit the following key combos:

- Approximately (≈): `Option`+`X`
- Degree (°): `Shift`+`Option`+`8`
- Division (÷): `Option`+`/`
- Infinity (∞): `Option`+`5`
- Less than or equal to (≤) and greater than or equal to (≥): `Option`+`,` and `Option`+`.`, respectively.
- Not equals (≠): `Option`+`=`
- Pi (π): `Option`+`P`.
- Plus/minus (±): `Shift`+`Option`+`=`
- Square root (√): `Option`+`V`
- Sum (Σ): `Option`+`W`

Trademark

`Option`+`2` will produce the trademark symbol (™). Typing tm followed by a space will do the same thing in most apps. `Option`+`R` inserts the registered trademark symbol (®). Typing (r) will also insert the symbol within most apps.

Type Diacritical Characters

Here are a variety of ways to type the occasional non-English language character or symbol into text using the majority of word processors and editors. Note that this tip assumes a U.S. English keyboard is being used.

Using the Characters Palette

In most text-editing applications, you can click Edit→Special Characters (or hit `Option`+`Command`+`T`) to bring up the Characters palette, from which you can choose non-English letters or symbols by selecting the Latin entry from the list on the left (in Microsoft Word, click Insert→Symbol, or Insert→Symbol→ Symbol Browser in Word 2011). Double-click the letter to insert it into the text.

Pressing and Holding

Another technique that works with some built-in Mac apps, like TextEdit and Mail, is to simply hold down the standard English version of the key for a few seconds. Doing this will cause a pop-out menu of accented variations to appear, and you can use the Left/Right cursor keys to move the selection highlight between them, hitting `Return` or the Down cursor key to insert the one you need. You can also simply type the number that appears beneath the character in the pop-out window to insert it immediately.

To insert é, for example, just press and hold `E`, and then select é from the pop-out menu. For uppercase variations, just hold `Shift` plus the key in question.

Typing Manually

However, you can also type the more commonly encountered foreign-language characters on standard English Mac keyboards as follows (the following should work in virtually all Mac apps):

- Acute accent: Hit `Option`+`E` and then type the letter. For example, for café, type c, a, f, `Option`+`E`, e. Hold `Shift` when typing the letter to add accents to uppercase letters.

- Cedilla: `Option`+`C`. For example, for façade, type f, a, `Option`+`C`, a, d, e. For an uppercase version, hold `Shift`.

- Common ligatures: For œ, hit `Option`+`Q`. For æ, type `Option`+`'` (that is, the apostrophe key). In both cases, hold `Shift` for uppercase versions. For example, to type œvere, type `Option`+`Q`, v, e, r, e.

- Circumflex: `Option`+`I` (I as in India), followed by the letter. For example, for the word rôle, type r, `Option`+`I`, o, l, e. Hold `Shift` when typing the letter for uppercase versions.

- Eszett: `Option`+`S`. For example, to type weiße, type w, e, i, `Option`+`S`, e.

- Grave: Hit `Option`+`‘` (backtick; the key above `Tab` on U.S. English keyboards, and left of the Z key on other English keyboards); then type the letter. For example, for città, you'd type c, i, t, t, `Option`+`‘`, a. Hold `Shift` when typing the letter for uppercase versions.

- Inverted punctuation: For an inverted question mark, hit `Option`+`?` (that is, `Option`+`Shift`+`?`). For an inverted exclamation mark, hit `Option`+`1`—there's no need to hold `Shift`.

- Ringed A: For å, hit `Option`+`A`. Hold `Shift` for the uppercase version.

- Stroked O: `Option`+`O`. For example, for the name Jørgensen, type J, `Option`+`O`, r, g, e, n, s, e, n. Hold `Shift` for the uppercase version.

- Tilde: `Option`+`N`, followed by the letter. For example, to type España, type E, s, p, a, `Option`+`N`, n, a. Hold `Shift` when typing the letter for uppercase versions.

- Umlaut: `Option`+`U`, followed by the letter. For example, to type über, type `Option`+`U`, u, b, e, r. Hold `Shift` when typing the letter for the uppercase version.

Tip 115

Rename Hundreds of Photos

Digital cameras seem to like filenames such as DSCF0407.JPG. I don't know about you, but I prefer names such as Disneyland Vacation 023.jpg. Renaming each and every file can be somewhat annoying, but a quick and easy solution is to create a simple app to do it for you, and that's just the kind of thing Automator is for (to learn what Automator is, see *Exploring OS X: Automator*, on page 347).

Creating an Automator Renaming Tool

Here are the steps required to create the Automator tool:

1. Create the folder to store the photos. This can be anywhere and called anything you choose. Then copy the image files into it. Make sure you only copy and don't move the files—keep the originals safe until you're sure the renaming has worked correctly!

2. Start the Automator program. It's among the first programs listed in the Applications view of Finder; its icon is a robot.

3. In the Choose a Type for Your Document dialog that appears, click the Application icon (again, the icon that's a robot), and then click the Choose button. If the Choose a Type dialog doesn't appear, click File→New.

4. The Automator program window is a little daunting, but you can ignore most of it. In the Library list at the left of the Automator program window, select Files & Folders, and then in the list to the right, select Rename Finder Items. Click and drag this menu entry to the right of the program window and release over the spot that reads Drag Actions or Files Here to Build Your Workflow.

5. In the dialog box that appears, you'll be asked whether you want to add an additional action to copy the renamed files. You don't need to do this, so click the Don't Add button.

6. You'll see a new element on-screen, Replace Text. There, click the drop-down Add Date or Time, and select Replace Text.

7. Click the Options heading at the bottom of the Replace Text "bubble," and check Show This Action When The Workflow Runs. For an example of how it should look at this stage, see Figure 19, *Renaming files automatically using Automator*, on page 126.

8. And that's all you need to do! Click File→Save and then give your new Automator Action a name. Anything will do, such as Rename Pictures. Choose somewhere to save it to, such as the desktop.

9. Once saved, you can quit the Automator program. There's no need to click the Run button or test anything.

Your new Automator action icon will be where you saved it, and you can identify it by the same robot icon as the Automator application itself. Essentially you've created a small app dedicated to the purpose of renaming files, and you can drag and drop files onto it to make it work.

2. Click the file whose icon you want to replace, and hit `Command+I` to view the file's info. In the window that appears, click the icon preview at the top left. This will highlight the icon. Hit `Command+V` to paste in the new icon image. The change should take place instantly.

To restore the original icon, repeat the step to open the file's info window and again select the icon so it's highlighted, but this time hit the `Delete` key.

Using Icons from Other Files

You can also copy and paste icons from one file to another. Just open the info panel for each file, as described earlier, and then highlight the icon in the first file by clicking it. Hit `Command+C` to copy the icon. Click to highlight the icon in the other info window that you want to replace, and then hit `Command+V`.

Using this tip, you can personalize the entire OS X interface. You can find icon replacements online at a variety of sources.[10] Usually, replacement icons can simply be dragged and dropped onto the icon preview at the top left in the info window, without the need to open and copy them first in Preview.

Tip 117

Bring Widgets to the Desktop

Unlike some versions of Microsoft Windows, OS X uses the Dashboard space to present applets to the user (known as *widgets* in Mac-speak). However, with a little hacking you can also put widgets on the desktop. It's not quite like Windows because the widgets stay on top of every other window, rather than on just the desktop, but for those with large monitors it's an excellent way of keeping useful widgets such as the time and date visible at all times.

Setting Up

To get Dashboard widgets on your desktop, it's first necessary to turn off the Dashboard being managed by Mission Control. To do this, open System Preferences (Apple menu→System Preferences), and then click the Mission Control icon. Remove the check next to Show Dashboard as a Space. Note that in the future to bring up the Dashboard you'll need to use the keyboard

---

10. http://interfacelift.com/icons, for example

hotkey, if your keyboard features it, or hit F12 (Fn+F12 if you're using a portable Mac or Mac aluminum keyboard).

To activate desktop widgets, open a Terminal window (open Finder, select the Applications list, and then in the list of applications double-click Terminal within the Utilities folder), and then type the following at the command prompt:

```
defaults write com.apple.dashboard devmode -bool TRUE;killall Dock
```

The Dock will temporarily slide out of view and the wallpaper might vanish for a second or two, but don't worry; they'll come back within seconds.

Using Desktop Widgets

To bring a Dashboard widget to the desktop, access the Dashboard by hitting the keyboard hotkey or F12 (Fn+F12 on MacBooks or Mac aluminum keyboards). For various reasons, this works only with new widgets you add, so open the widget chooser (click the plus icon at the bottom left), double-click a widget to add it to the Dashboard, and then click and hold the widget as if you're going to move it to a new position. Then, while still holding the mouse button down, hit F12 again (or Fn+F12) and, hey, presto—you have a Dashboard icon on the desktop.

To put the widget back on the Dashboard, simply repeat the procedure in reverse—click and hold the widget on the desktop, hit F12 (or Fn+F12) to start the Dashboard, and then release the mouse button.

If any widgets don't appear after you drag them to the desktop, open a Terminal window, and type killall Dock. This should make them visible.

To delete an individual widget, hold down Option, and then move the mouse cursor over it. The small X icon will appear in the top left and, when clicked, will cause the widget to vanish, just like when you're using widgets within Dashboard normally.

Deactivating

To turn off desktop Dashboard icons later, open a Terminal window, and type the following:

```
defaults delete com.apple.dashboard devmode;killall Dock
```

Note that after making this change, any widgets left on your desktop will stick around until you manually move them back to the Dashboard, in the inverse of the procedure described previously—click and hold the widget that's on the desktop, and then activate Dashboard and release the mouse button. However, it will be impossible to move any new widgets to the desktop.

Don't forget to reactivate Mission Control's management of the Dashboard, as described earlier.

Tip 118

Discover Software Version Numbers

If you want to check the version of an application, you can start it up and click the application's menu; then click About. Another, quicker way is to select the application in the Applications list in Finder and hit `Command+I` to bring up the info window. It will be listed under the Version heading, which will be under the General heading.

Tip 119

Use a Screensaver as a Desktop Background

This is a fun hack that lets you use the currently selected screensaver as a desktop backdrop in place of the regular wallpaper.

Setting Up

To give it a try, follow these steps:

1. Open a Terminal window (open Finder, select the Applications list, and then in the list of applications double-click Terminal within the Utilities folder), and carefully type the following line of code, replacing XX with the name of the screensaver you noted earlier—if the screensaver name includes a space, type a backslash before the space (that is, Sliding Panels would be typed as Sliding\ Panels):

```
nohup /System/Library/Frameworks/ScreenSaver.framework/Resources/
        ScreenSaverEngine.app/Contents/MacOS/ScreenSaverEngine -background &
```

You'll see the screensaver start to play in the background.

2. You can now close the Terminal window, and the screensaver will continue to play in the background after a momentary delay. Ignore the warning that appears about terminating an application.

3. If you get tired of the screensaver, open a Terminal window, and type the following:

```
killall ScreenSaverEngine
```

Note that this tip isn't ideal for regular use on portable Macs because it places a small additional drain on the battery. However, desktop Macs or portable Macs connected to power sources shouldn't see any downside.

Tip 120

Add Folders of Wallpaper Images

Here's a tip if you're a fan of downloading lots of wallpaper from online sources.

Copy your downloaded wallpaper images to their permanent location on your computer (that is, within your Pictures folder, for example), and then open System Preferences (Apple menu→System Preferences) and the Desktop & Screen Saver panel. Select the Desktop tab; then just click and drag the folder onto the left pane of the window, under the iPhoto heading. This will instantly add the files to the list of available wallpapers, and this can be repeated with any other folder containing images.

To remove the folder later, again open the Desktop & Screen Saver pane within System Preferences, select the folder in the list, and click the minus symbol button at the bottom of the list.

Incidentally, if you're choosing a new wallpaper in the Desktop & Screen Saver pane of System Preferences, you can make the thumbnail previews bigger by placing the mouse cursor over the thumbnail previews of the wallpapers and using the pinch-and-expand gesture—placing a finger and thumb on the trackpad and moving them slowly apart (if your Mac uses a multitouch trackpad, of course!).

Tip 121

Put Notebooks in Deep Sleep

Mac notebooks use magnetic case closing mechanisms to keep the lid shut, rather than physical clasps. This makes opening them much more convenient, but it also means they can open themselves sometimes, while in a travel bag, for example. Once open, they can switch themselves on and thus waste battery life. They might even create a hazard during a flight if the wireless hardware activates.

If this is a problem for you, you can set your MacBook to hibernate to disk when the lid is closed, rather than simply go into sleep mode. This turns the computer off completely, rather than keeping the memory alive with a trickle of battery power.

Note that this is arguably not a good choice for Macs with a solid-state hard disk (SSD), such as MacBook Air computers. It will mean that every time the computer powers down, a multigigabyte hibernation file is saved to the hard disk, usually slightly larger than the size of your computer's RAM (that is, 4GB or 8GB). In theory, this can wear out SSD more quickly.

Setting Up

This tip changes a firmware setting for the entire computer, so it will affect all users.

Open a Terminal window, and type the following:

```
sudo pmset -a hibernatemode 25
```

You'll need to enter your login password when prompted. The changes should take effect right away.

Putting to Sleep and Waking

Give your changes a try by closing the lid and waiting a minute or two for it to hibernate. Then wake your computer (remember, you'll now need to press the power button each time). Waking a hibernated computer takes a few seconds longer as the RAM contents are read in from disk, but it's still fast enough for everyday use.

Putting Desktop Macs to Sleep

For what it's worth, it isn't just portable Macs that hibernate—desktop Macs support it too. Once you've changed the setting as described earlier, click Apple menu→Sleep to hibernate. After a minute or so, the computer will completely power down. To wake the computer from hibernation, depress the power button as usual.

For desktop Macs that take a long time to boot from cold, hibernating can save a few seconds each time you boot.

Restoring the Original Setting

To return to the standard sleep mode later, open a Terminal window, and type the following:

```
sudo pmset -a hibernatemode 3
```

Tip 122

Fix a Slow Boot

If you find there's a huge delay after the desktop first appears until the computer becomes usable, try cleaning up your desktop by removing as many files, folders, and aliases as you can without impeding your workflow. Either create folders and file things away in them or put things where they're supposed to go in your Documents, Movies, and so on, folders. Try to have as few icons on your desktop as possible, and definitely try to avoid any that might be automatically turned into thumbnail previews, such as movies and pictures, because this adds to OS X's workload when it's already busy loading the system at boot time.

You can try turning off icon thumbnailing by right-clicking a blank spot on the desktop and selecting Show View Options. In the dialog that appears, remove the check from Show Icon Preview. Close the dialog box. The changes take effect immediately.

Also consider pruning the number of programs that start when you boot—see Tip 134, *Control Start-up Apps*, on page 153.

Tip 123

Know Exactly Where You Are

There are a variety of ways of seeing at a glance where you are in Finder, as follows.

Using a Better Path Bar

Finder can show the path to the currently browsed folder (that is, something like Macintosh HD→Users→John→Music→MP3 collection). Just click View →Show Path Bar. However, there's a slight problem—the path is listed from the root of the hard disk up to the current directory. If all you ever do is browse your home directory, then this information isn't much use, and the display can get bunched up very quickly. Luckily, there's a secret setting you can use to cause the path bar to relate everything it shows to your home folder. In other words, should you browse your Pictures folder, the path bar will read something like John→Pictures, rather than Macintosh HD→Users →John→Pictures.

Open a Terminal window (open Finder, select the Applications list, and then in the list of applications double-click Terminal within the Utilities folder), and type the following:

```
defaults write com.apple.finder PathBarRootAtHome -bool TRUE;killall Finder
```

The changes will take effect immediately. See Figure 20, *Improving the Finder path bar: before and after*. Should you want later to revert to the default path bar, open a Terminal window, and type the following:

```
defaults delete com.apple.finder PathBarRootAtHome;killall Finder
```

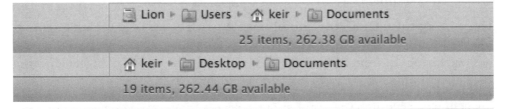

Figure 20—Improving the Finder path bar: before and after

Bonus tip: Files can be dragged and dropped onto any entry within the path bar to move the file to that location (hold `Option` before releasing the mouse button to copy the file instead, or hold `Option`+`Command` to create an alias).

Show Full Paths in the Title Bar of Finder

By default the title bar of every Finder window displays the name of the current folder you're browsing or its current mode (that is, if you're using AirDrop, for example). To switch it to show the full path of the directory (that is, /Users/keir/Documents rather than just Documents), open a Terminal window (open Finder, select the Applications list, and then in the list of applications double-click Terminal within the Utilities folder), and type the following:

```
defaults write com.apple.finder _FXShowPosixPathInTitle -bool TRUE; killall
        Finder
```

Bear in mind that if you switch to the All My Files view in Finder, you'll see a long path pointing toward /System/Library/CoreServices/Finder.app. This is simply where the All My Files function is stored and can be ignored.

To revert to showing just the folder name, open a Terminal window, and type the following:

```
defaults delete com.apple.finder _FXShowPosixPathInTitle;killall Finder
```

Tip 124

Tweak Launchpad Visual Effects

Here are some subtle yet useful tweaks to alter Launchpad's look and feel.

Changing the Background Effect

Launchpad uses the desktop wallpaper as a backdrop but blurs it slightly. You can change it to a variety of different settings using a secret command. Open a Terminal window (open Finder, select the Applications list, and then in the list of applications double-click Terminal within the Utilities folder), and type the following:

```
defaults write com.apple.dock springboard-background-filter -int 0;killall
        Dock
```

This will turn off the background blurring entirely, simply showing the wallpaper as you see it normally on the desktop.

The number used after -int specifies the nature of the background effect. Typing 1 sets the default blur, 2 makes the background black and white but not blurry, while 3 makes it both black and white as well as blurry. For example, the following command makes the background both black and white as well as blurry:

```
defaults write com.apple.dock springboard-background-filter -int 3;killall
        Dock
```

To revert to the default settings, just type the following:

```
defaults delete com.apple.dock springboard-background-filter;killall Dock
```

Altering the Background Blurring

You can also alter the degree to which the background blurs, provided you haven't used the previous commands to switch to a nonblur background. Adjusting the blur can create a more subtle effect than the default. To do so, open a Terminal window, and type the following, this time replacing X after the -int part of the line with any number between 0 and 255 (0 is no blur, while 255 is maximum blur):

```
defaults write com.apple.dock springboard-blur-radius -int X;killall Dock
```

Experiment a little with different settings. Generally speaking, values between 1 and 10 produce the most subtle effects, while something like 150 will turn the background into a colorful haze where it's impossible to see detail. To revert to the default degree of blur at any point, open a Finder window and type the following:

```
defaults delete com.apple.dock springboard-blur-radius;killall Dock
```

Tip 125

Create "Crazy" Emails

Here's a fun trick that can be used to send entertaining emails to people on special occasions, such as birthdays.

Open a Finder window, hit Shift+Command+G, and then type /Library/Scripts/Mail Scripts/Crazy Message Text.scpt. Double-click the file that's highlighted in the Finder window. This will open AppleScript Editor, but you can ignore it and simply press the Run button on the AppleScript Editor toolbar. Then follow the prompts in the dialog boxes that appear (click the Set Prefs button if you'd like more control over things like font sizes). Eventually you should end up with something similar to Figure 21, *Creating "crazy text" emails*.

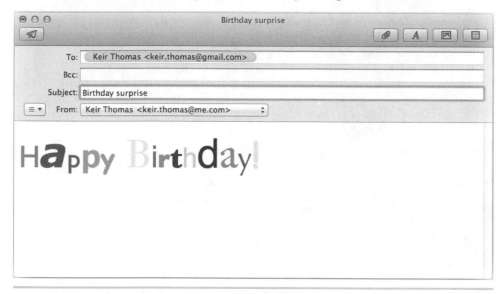

Figure 21—Creating "crazy text" emails

You can quit AppleScript Editor once the program has finished. Be sure to check out the other scripts in the /Library/Scripts/Mail Scripts folder. Although they're intended primarily to show AppleScript's potential integration with the Mail app, many are very useful in their own right. You can use each the same way—double-click them and click the Run button in the AppleScript Editor window that appears.

Tip 126

Secure All Your Files Against Hackers

Encrypting data is a good idea if you use a portable Mac because it'll mean that even if a thief or hacker gets ahold of the data, they won't be able to do anything with it. The type of encryption offered by OS X as described next is theoretically unbreakable, although you might also read Tip 209, *Create Encrypted Archives for All Computers*, on page 234.

Exploring OS X: Spotlight

Spotlight is OS X's instant search tool, but it goes far beyond mere files. It indexes emails you receive, for example, and web pages you've recently visited. Instant message chats are cataloged. In fact, Spotlight's goal is to index all information you interact with on your Mac. To see the type of things that are indexed, click the Spotlight icon within System Preferences (Apple menu→System Preferences) and select the Search Results tab. Here you can also tell Spotlight not to index certain types of files by removing the check alongside their entries in the list. Clicking and dragging any entry within the list will affect the order in which files of that type will appear in Spotlight's list of results—if you wanted photos to be the first result listed in Spotlight, for example, then just click and drag Images to the top of the list.

Spotlight also indexes the contents of documents, as well as any other information about them. This means you can search for documents that contain a particular term, such as the name of a project you're working on. Any documents that contain text are indexed—word processing documents, spreadsheets, and so on.

To access Spotlight, click the magnifying glass icon at the top right of the screen, or hit Command+Space. Type the search query and then look through the list of results for what you want.

Pause the selection highlight or mouse cursor over an entry in the list, and a Quick Look window will pop out the side of the list, showing a preview of the document.

To open any document, just highlight it and hit Return.

Using FileVault

Perhaps the most comprehensive solution is to enable FileVault full-disk encryption in the FileVault & Privacy pane of System Preferences (Apple menu →System Preferences), which ensures that all data on your hard disk is encrypted. However, this can result in marginally slower disk access compared to an unencrypted disk—it's not enough to notice during everyday use, but it might affect periods of prolonged disk access, such as when you're booting up. However, if your Mac uses a solid-state hard disk (SSD), then this slow-down will be practically unnoticeable.

Encrypted Archives

As an alternative to FileVault, you can create an encrypted archive. This is like a container file that you can save files into, a little like a USB memory stick except it's just a file. You can *mount* and *unmount* the file whenever you want to add, remove, or view files within it, which is like plugging in and removing a USB stick. Mounting is done by simply double-clicking the file and entering the password when prompted. To unmount it, just click the Eject icon next to its entry in the sidebar of Finder, under the Devices heading—just like you eject a USB memory stick when you've finished with it.

Because it's just a file, the encrypted archive can be transferred to a USB memory stick and should be compatible with other Mac computers (including those running recent versions of OS X, from Snow Leopard 10.6 upward). Once the encrypted archive is created, you can rest safe in the knowledge that—without the password—absolutely nobody will be able to access the data inside it.

Creating an Encrypted Archive: Step-by-Step

Here are the steps required to create a password-protected archive:

1. Start Disk Utility, which you can find in the Utilities folder within the Applications view of Finder.

2. On the Disk Utility toolbar, click the New Image button.

3. In the dialog box, type a filename for the archive into the Save As field, and beneath that choose a location where you want to save the archive. Type the same name in the Name field below—this is what'll appear in Finder to identify your filestore whenever you mount your new archive.

4. In the Format drop-down list, select MS-DOS (FAT). This gives you the ability to create smaller archive containers compared to using Mac disk formats. Don't worry if this sounds less than perfect—FAT is the same disk format used on USB memory sticks and photographic memory cards. Your Mac is 100 percent compatible with it.

5. In the Size drop-down, select an archive size. Even if they're empty, OS X archives are still full size. In other words, a 2.5MB archive will always be 2.5MB, even if there's only a tiny 10KB file in it, and they don't expand and contract to fit their contents. Choose a size that fits your needs.

6. In the Encryption drop-down list, select 256-Bit AES Encryption. This is an extremely secure form of encryption that's as strong and unbreakable as you could need. It's a little slower if you're saving massive files to archives, so if you intend to encrypt huge video files and are also impatient, you might like to select the 128-Bit AES Encryption option. This choice is also extremely secure.

7. Leave the other fields as they are, and click the Create button to begin making the archive.

8.   Soon after this, you'll be prompted to create the password for the archive. You'll need to type it again in the Verify field to make sure you haven't made a typo the first time around. Don't forget this password! If you do, you'll *never* be able to access its contents again. The form of encryption used by OS X is unbreakable.

9.   By checking Remember Password in My Keychain, you can avoid being prompted for the password each time you mount the archive. However, this will mean anybody with access to your computer (for example, somebody walking past) can also mount the archive without being prompted for a password. Once you're done, click the OK button.

10. The archive will now be created.

When the create process has finished, your new encrypted filestore will be automatically mounted. It'll appear as a volume in Finder and will be listed under the Devices heading in exactly the same way as if you had inserted a memory stick or a digital camera, and you can drag/drop files into it. Don't forget to click the Eject button alongside it when you've finished with it.

In the future, to remount the filestore, double-click the archive image file and enter the password when prompted.

Creating Aliases

You can create aliases to any file within the archive, which, when double-clicked, will automatically mount the archive, prompt you for a password (if it's not in the keychain), and load the file. To do so, drag and drop a file from the archive to the desktop, but before releasing the mouse button, press and hold `Option`+`Command`. When you release the mouse button, an alias to the file will be created. However, don't forget to eject the archive when you've finished working on the file!

Tip 127

See Every Wi-Fi Detail

Once you've joined a wireless network, hold down the `Option` key and click the Wi-Fi icon at the top right of the screen. Along with the usual options of switching networks, you'll be shown a list of interesting technical details about the connection.

Checking Signal Strength

For information about signal strength, pay particular attention to the line labeled RSSI (for received signal strength indication), about halfway down the list. It'll probably be a minus figure, like -40 or -73. The closer this figure is to 0, the stronger the signal. So, -30 is better than -50. The scale is from -100 to 0. My experience is that networks beyond -80 are impossible to connect to, but your mileage may vary. See Figure 22, *Viewing the technical details of a Wi-Fi connection.*

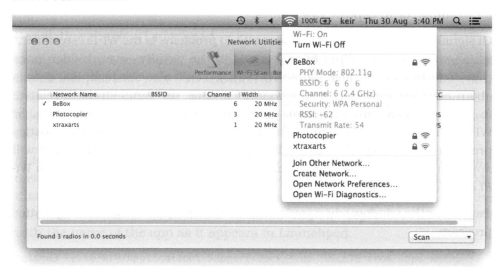

Figure 22—Viewing the technical details of a Wi-Fi connection

Checking Data Transfer Speeds

The transmit rate figure is also worth paying attention to. It tells you the maximum data speed possible with the connection. For example, at the moment, my MacBook Pro's transmit rate figure reads 54, indicating a 54Mb/sec connection speed and also indicating I'm connected to the Wi-Fi base station using 802.11g—the older but still widely used Wi-Fi standard. Using a more modern 802.11n router over a good connection, the transmit rate figure will read anything up to 300, indicating speeds of up to 300Mb/sec.

Performing a Wi-Fi Diagnostic

OS X has a hidden Wi-Fi diagnostics tool that lets you monitor the performance of the connection, among other things. It's primarily for those who understand the technical details of how Wi-Fi works, however. To access it,

in the list on the left of the window. Check Show Launchpad in the list on the right, and then type the keyboard shortcut you want to use. A good choice is `Command`+`Esc`.

Close System Preferences, and then try your new shortcut by hitting the key combination.

To remove the shortcut in the future, repeat the previous steps to set a shortcut, but simply select Show Launchpad in the list and click the Restore Defaults button at the bottom.

Reverting to the Default Launcher

If at any point in the future you want to revert to a default Launchpad setup showing all your apps, just open a Terminal window, and type the following to rebuild the Launchpad from scratch:

```
defaults write com.apple.dock ResetLaunchPad -bool TRUE;killall Dock
```

You might have to give the system a few seconds to rebuild the list of apps from scratch, but you'll see a progress display when you activate Launchpad. Note that unlike other defaults write commands in this book, there's no need to undo or remove this configuration tweak—that's done automatically by the Launchpad reset procedure.

Tip 129

Supertip: Get the Most from Spotlight

Spotlight is one the highlight features of OS X and is something I would severely miss if it wasn't present. Here are some useful tips for getting the most from it.

Opening Spotlight Results in Alternative Apps

Any entry in Spotlight's list of results can be clicked and dragged onto a Dock icon in order to open it in that particular application. For example, you could drag a word processing document in the list of results onto TextEdit's Dock icon to stop it from automatically opening in Microsoft Word.

You can also drag and drop files from Spotlight's list of results to the desktop or to any open Finder window to instantly create a copy. Hold down `Option`+ `Command`, and you'll create an alias to the original file instead.

Where Do Files Found by Spotlight Live?

One slight irritation when searching for a file via Spotlight is that there's no clear indication of where each file is located on your hard disk. However, if you hold `Option`+`Command` for a few seconds after the pop-out file preview appears, the file's location will appear at the bottom of the preview pop-out.

Hold down `Command` on its own, and you'll see either the date the file was last opened or when it was modified. If it's a file whose contents Spotlight indexes (that is, files such as Microsoft Word documents or PDFs), you'll see a very brief extract from the file showing the search term in situ. Wait a second more, still holding down `Command`, and the path to the file will slide into view too.

Reveal the Locations of Files in Spotlight

Spotlight lets you find files in an instant and open them for editing or viewing. But what if you can remember the name of a file but not that of others you know are in the same folder, and it's the other files you're looking for? Wouldn't it be useful to just instantly open the folder containing a file in the Spotlight list of results?

You can! In the list returned by Spotlight, hold down `Command` when clicking the file or folder. This will open a Finder window at the file or folder's location, with the file or folder highlighted. You can also highlight an entry in the list using the cursor keys and hit `Command`+`R` or `Command`+`Return` to reveal the file in Finder.

Incidentally, this works on the Dock too, although with a slight twist: holding down `Option`+`Command` and clicking any icon in the Dock will open a Finder window browsing its location. This can be very useful if you want to quickly open a Finder window showing Documents or Downloads—just hold `Command` and click the Documents or Downloads stack.

Useful Keyboard Shortcuts

In addition to `Command`+`R` to reveal the location of a Spotlight result in a Finder window, the following keyboard shortcuts can be used when the list of Spotlight results appears:

- `Command`+`T`: Open the first result in the Spotlight list (even if a different result is currently highlighted).

- `Command`+`B`: Search the Web for the search term using the default browser.

- `Command`+`D`: Open the Dictionary app and look up the search term (provided the search term is one that ordinarily can be found within the Dictionary app—if it can't be, then this shortcut won't work).

- `Command`+`K`: Open the Dictionary app and look up the search term within Wikipedia.

- `Command`+`L`: Show a dictionary definition of the search term in a pop-out window (if the search term is one that can be found within the Dictionary app—if it can't be, then this shortcut won't work).

- `Command`+`C`: Copy the full path and filename of the currently highlighted item to the clipboard for pasting elsewhere.

- `Command`+`C`: Show the same File Info window that appears if you select a file within Finder or on the desktop.

Save Spotlight Searches for Reuse

To save a search for reuse later, click the Show All in Finder entry at the top of the Spotlight search results. This will open a Finder search window. Directly beneath the search box at the top right, a Save button will appear, which when clicked will let you save the search as a *Smart Folder*—a pseudo-folder that contains links to files returned by the search term. It'll be saved to the Saved Searches folder within the Library folder of your home directory, but if you check Add to Sidebar when saving the search, the Smart Folder will always be visible in the left pane of every Finder window. You can simply click the saved search to run it again.

By navigating manually to the Saved Search folder (open a Finder window, hit `Shift`+`Command`+`G`, and type ~/Library/Saved Searches/), you can double-click the searches to run them or create aliases on the desktop to be able to run them very quickly (to create an alias, hold `Option` and `Command` together and drag the saved search to where you'd like the alias to live).

Do Instant Math

The Spotlight search tool also includes a simple calculator. Simply activate Spotlight search and type the math expression (for example, 2+2 or 15-4). You'll see the response immediately underneath in the form of a search result for the Calculator app. For multiplication and division, use * and /, respectively.

Constants such as pi are understood (just type pi), and for square roots type sqrt followed by the number in parentheses, such as sqrt(9). cos, sin, and tan also work as you'd expect (for example, type cos(90)).

By hovering your mouse over the result so that it's highlighted, you can copy the math into the clipboard using `Command`+`C` and then paste it into any application with `Command`+`V` (or by clicking Edit→Paste on the application's menu). Ensure that the Spotlight search term isn't highlighted, or you'll end up copying that instead (clicking in the middle of it should remove the selection highlight).

Spotlight's math function is actually an extension of the math abilities built into the command line of OS X. To learn more about what commands you can use, open a Terminal window (open Finder, select the Applications list, and then in the list of applications double-click Terminal within the Utilities folder), type man math, and then look under the List of Functions heading.

Jump Between Categories in Spotlight

When searching via Spotlight, you'll usually see results categorized according to what they are: files, dictionary definitions, website results, and so on. You can move up and down the list of results using the Up/Down cursor keys, but to quickly jump between the categories, hold down `Command` and hit the down or up arrow keys.

Tip 130

View a Quick Calendar

Although OS X has a built-in calendar application in the form of Calendar, I sometimes find myself simply wanting a calendar view of forthcoming months so I can see what day a certain date falls on. There are two ways of quickly getting this on OS X.

Using Dashboard

If you switch to the Dashboard, you can use the Calendar widget to view the current month. This is a default widget that should already be set to Show, but it can also be chosen from the widget selection—click the plus icon at the bottom left, and then double-click the Calendar widget to add it to the Dashboard.

Creating at the Command Line

I also make use of an old Unix command-line tool called cal that's included by default with OS X. Open a Terminal window (open Finder, select the Applications list, and then in the list of applications double-click Terminal within the Utilities folder), and simply type cal at the command prompt to see the current month in a calendar view. To see another month, type the short version of its name along with the year. For example, to see June 2013, I'd type cal jun 2013. To see an entire year, just type cal 2013.

The ncal command is almost identical but switches the axes: days are listed as a column at the left side, rather than as a row along the top. Add the -w switch, and you'll also be told week numbers: ncal -w 2014 will show dates for 2014 and also the week numbers.

Tip 131

Add Magical Links for Email, Messages, Web, and More

You might be used to inserting web hyperlinks into documents or when composing emails (click Edit→Add Link and type the address). Whenever anybody clicks the link, they'll visit the site you specified, just like in a web page.

In addition to links to websites, OS X lets you create app-specific links. For example, you could include a link in a mail message that, when clicked, will start within the Messages app an instant messaging conversation with somebody. You could create a link in a document that, when clicked, looked up a particular word in the Dictionary app.

To create a link in a TextEdit document or new mail window, highlight the text you want to serve as the link, and click Edit→Add Link, or hit Command + K.

Then look to the following list for what to type into the Create Link dialog box. (Of course, you could simply paste or type a web address too.)

- http://—You can insert links to web pages by simply typing the address, including the http:// component. For example, typing http://keirthomas.com will create a link to that site.

- imessage://—This will start a Messages conversation within the Messages app. For example, typing imessage://55512398765 will open Messages and attempt to start an iMessage conversation with that cell phone number. You can also specify IM handles: if you have a Yahoo buddy whose handle is johnsmith, you could create the following link: imessage://johnsmith. This assumes you've configured Messages to log onto your Yahoo account, of course.

- facetime://—This will start a FaceTime conversation within the FaceTime app. For example, facetime://keir@example.com will attempt to start a FaceTime conversation with the individual whose FaceTime account is registered to that address. Apple IDs and cell phone numbers can also be specified, although as with iMessage, the cell phone number should be typed without any spaces or symbols in it.

- dict://—This will cause the Dictionary app to start and look up a particular word. For example, dict://epicurean will open Dictionary with the word definition for *Epicurean* displayed, as if it had been typed into the search field.

- vnc://—This will open a screen-sharing session with whatever address is specified, although the user will still have to click the Connect button in a dialog box that appears when the Screen Sharing software starts. vnc://macbook will attempt to start a screen-sharing session with the computer whose network name is macbook.

- x-man-page://—This will open the man page for the specified term within a Terminal window. For example, x-man-page://sharing will open the man page for the sharing command.

When used without any specified address (that is, if you simply type imessage:// or facetime:// in the link dialog box), the apps will be activated when the link is clicked, as if the user has clicked their app icon in the Dock.

It's also possible to insert other, typical URLs that are used in web pages, such as mailto://, ssh://, and telnet://.

For the sake of completeness, it should be mentioned that OS X understands many other app-specific URLs, but many require specific and complicated

URL structures: itms:// lets you create links for the iTunes Store, for example, although a URL would take the form of something similar to this:[11]

itms://phobos.apple.com/WebObjects/MZSearch.woa/wa/advancedSearchResults?artistTerm=Beatles&albumTerm=Revolver

The addressbook:// URL again requires a complicated URL following it, relating to the user ID (in hexadecimal) of a contact, which is difficult to discover, but when specified on its own as a link, addressbook:// will open the Contacts app when the user clicks it. Other URLs that can be used this way are reminders://, which will start the Reminders app, and ical://, which will start Calendar (by specifying the URL of an online iCal calendar, you can create a link that will subscribe whoever clicks it to that particular calendar—see Tip 96, *Subscribe to Useful Calendars*, on page 100). macappstore:// will open the Mac App Store, although macappstore://showUpdatesPage will open Mac App Store and switch immediately to the Updates page.

Note that any links created within documents can be dragged and dropped to the desktop or a Finder window to create an *inetloc* file—a small file that's little more than a link. When double-clicked, they'll act the same way as within the document.

Tip 132

Stop Notes from Being Yellow

Apple clearly loves yellow legal paper because that's the default look and feel for the Notes app. Unfortunately, there's no way of changing this within Notes' Preferences dialog box. However, by tweaking a system file, you can easily and quickly change the page to white. Note that this hack affects all users of the computer and might also need to be repeated whenever you install a new OS X system update. Because we're editing a system file, as always it's a good idea to create a Time Machine backup before commencing.

Changing the Notes Default Background Color

Here are the steps required:

---

11. See http://nslog.com/2003/04/29/itms_links for a partial explanation of itms: links.

1. Quit Notes if it's running; then open Finder, and hit `Shift`+`Command`+`G`. In the dialog that appears, type the following before clicking the Go button:

   `/Applications/Notes.app/Contents/Resources/`

   In the list of files you see, hold `Command`, and then click and drag the paper.png file to the desktop to create a copy of it. Then repeat this step with the paper@2x.png file too.

2. Create a separate, second backup copy of the paper.png and paper@2x.png files somewhere safe on your hard disk. We'll revert to these files should anything go wrong or if we want to restore default settings later.

3. Double-click the paper.png file on the desktop, which should open it in Preview.

4. Click Tools→Adjust Color; then in the Adjust Color palette that appears, drag the Saturation slider all the way to the left, and drag the Exposure slider all the way to the right.

5. Save the file and close Preview; then repeat the steps 3 and 4 with the paper@2x.png file.

6. Save the file, and then close Preview. Drag and drop the two files over the Finder window you opened earlier, showing the Resources folder. You'll be asked to authenticate, so type your password when prompted. You'll also have to click the Replace button when prompted in the dialog box that appears.

The changes will take effect immediately when you restart the Notes app.

Restoring the Default Yellow Paper Color

The default yellow paper can be restored by quitting Notes and following these steps:

1. Navigate to where the backup paper.png and paper@2x.png files are stored, and then select both by holding down `Command` while clicking them, and hit `Command`+`C` to copy them.

2. Follow step 1 in the earlier instructions to open the /Applications/Notes.app/Contents/Resources/ folder, and then tap `Command`+`V` to paste the original files back into place. Again, you'll be asked to confirm you want to overwrite the originals and also asked to authenticate by providing your password.

As before, the changes should take effect immediately, so restart Notes. Once you're sure things are working correctly, you can then delete the backup of the paper.png and paper@2x.png files.

Replacing the "Torn Paper" Look

You might notice a slight issue with the new white paper background in Notes, in that the thin band of "torn paper" at the top of the Notes window is still colored yellow. To change this to a white/gray color scheme, repeat all the previous steps, but this time edit the paper-torns.png and paper-torns@2x.png files, ensuring you make backups before editing any files. This time around, however, simply drag the Saturation slider all the way to the left, and *don't* drag the Exposure slider. This will make the torn paper gray, matching the new white pages.

Tip 133

Simulate an iPhone or iPad

By downloading the free Xcode from the Mac App Store, you can gain access to a primitive but useful iPhone and iPad emulator called iOS Simulator. It's provided to allow developers to test any apps they create, and as such, the range of built-in apps is limited to Safari, Photos, Contacts, Settings, Game Center, and Newsstand. However, if you create websites on your Mac, you can use the simulator to see how the site looks on the iPad/iPhone version of Safari. You can also just play around a little because the simulator is fun to use!

To access the simulator, start Xcode, click the application menu, and then select Open Developer Tool→iOS Simulator. A simulated iPhone will appear as a floating window. This will work like a standard iPhone, except your mouse cursor replaces your fingertip when tapping the screen (so scrolling within Safari is a matter of clicking and dragging with the mouse cursor).

To switch to emulating an iPad, click Hardware→Device→iPad, although note that unless you have a very high-resolution screen, it's unlikely the iPad will fit properly, and you'll have to use the scrollbars at the side to view the entire iPad surface. This is because the iPad uses a very high-resolution display.

Unfortunately, although you can run any apps you write yourself on the simulator, you can't run any apps you might have downloaded for your actual iPhone or iPad. The simulator runs as an x86/64 application, while the iPhone and iPad use the completely different ARM CPU architecture.

Tip 134

Control Start-up Apps

If you're a convert from Windows, you might be used to periodically pruning the list of programs that start at login by editing the Startup folder.

Editing a Mac's Start-up List

You can find the equivalent function on Macs by opening the Users & Groups component of System Preferences (Apple menu→System Preferences). Unlock System Preferences if necessary by clicking the lock icon at the bottom left (note that only system administrator-level accounts can change start-up items), and then select your account in the list on the left. Then click the Login Items tab on the right. To remove a program from the list, select it and click the minus button beneath the list.

Note that a check alongside an entry in the list has no bearing on whether it starts at login. The checkbox merely controls whether the program starts hidden, that is, whether the program starts with its window invisible (the equivalent of minimized under Windows).

Adding New Start-up Items

There are a variety of different ways to add a program so it starts when you log in:

- Click the plus icon within the Login Items view within System Preferences, as described earlier, and navigate to the program using the File Open dialog box.

- Drag and drop icons from the Applications list within Finder on top of the start-up application list within the Login Items view.

- Right-click the program's Dock icon, and click Options→Open at Login.

Tip 135

Watch CPU Load and Activity

To have a small floating window appear showing CPU activity at the present time, start Activity Monitor (Open Finder, select the Applications list, and then double-click Activity Monitor within the Utilities folder), and click the Window menu. Then select Floating CPU Window, and choose from either horizontal or vertical displays. The floating window will appear at the bottom left of the screen, and you can click and drag to move it around.

On most modern Macs, you'll see two, four, or more charts, representing each of the cores in the processor. If you're using a high-end Mac Pro system, you might have up to sixteen processing cores and therefore sixteen bar charts!

To get rid of the graph, select None from the Floating CPU Window menu.

To see a graph showing the CPU load over time, select the CPU History entry from the Window menu. To get rid of it, just click the Close button on the window.

For examples of the various CPU load graph types, see Figure 23, *Graphing CPU load.*

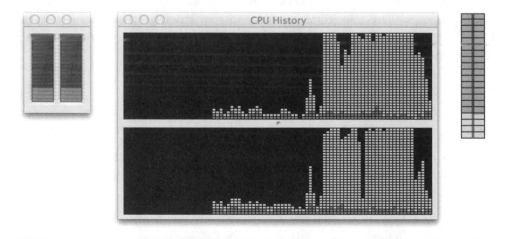

Figure 23—Graphing CPU load

Tip 136

Create Doc Templates and Boilerplate Text

Let's say you've created a form letter that you periodically send out to different people, changing only the name and address details. Some word processors allow you to create document templates. These are master files that, when opened, will create a new file containing the document's contents. But did you know that this feature is built into your Mac, and you can use it with any kind of file in practically any application?

It's also possible to automatically insert boilerplate (that is, stock phrase) text into a document or new email using OS X's Text Substitution feature.

Creating and Using a Template

To create a template, simply create a new file and then save it as usual, or locate an existing file. In either case, you must close the file, locate it using Finder, and select it before hitting Command+I to bring up the File Info dialog box. Then put a check in Stationery Pad, under the General heading near the top of the dialog box.

From now on, whenever anybody double-clicks to open the file, a copy of the file will automatically be created and opened for editing (usually with the filename of the original plus the word copy appended).

To open the original for editing at any stage, click and drag it straight to an application's Dock icon or open it using the File→Open menu option within an application.

To return the file to being an ordinary nontemplate file, just repeat the previous steps, but remove the check from the Stationery Pad box.

Creating and Using Text Substitution Phrases

OS X includes the ability to autocorrect mistypes. For example, type "teh," and it will correct it to "the." This feature is known as *text substitution*, and it can be subverted so you can insert just about any word, sentence, or paragraph—even a series of paragraphs—when you type a particular keyword. Here's how to set it up:

1. Open System Preferences (Apple menu→System Preferences), and then click the Language & Text icon.

2. Click the Text tab, and then in the list of substitutions on the left, click the plus button at the bottom.

3. In the Replace field, type the keyword you want to trigger the substitution. For example, if you wanted to insert a boilerplate paragraph of legalese, you could type legalbp. It's important to choose a keyword that you're not going to type in everyday use.

4. Hit `Tab` to move to the With field. Here's where you should type (or paste in) the word, sentence, or paragraph(s) you want to appear when the keyword is typed (hit `Option`+`Return` for a line break and `Option`+`Tab` to indent the text). Don't worry if the text you type doesn't appear to fit in the small field—it will all be recorded. Hit `Return` when done.

Repeat the previous steps however many times are needed to store all the boilerplate phrases you want.

In any application where you want to use the substitutions, you must select the Text Replacement option on the Edit→Substitutions menu so that it has a check next to it. You need to do this only once. (Remove the check next to the entry to deactivate substitution for that app.)

Note that any substitution won't appear until you hit `Space` after typing the keyword.

To delete a substitution, again open System Preferences, and navigate to the Text tab of the Language & Text pane. Select the entry in the list, and click the minus button. To temporarily deactivate a substitution, simply remove the check next to it.

Tip 137

Create an Event from an Email or Web Page

Here's how to quickly create new Calendar events.

Creating a Calendar Event from an Email

Click and drag an email from the list within Mail onto a day displayed in the Calendar app, and you'll automatically create an event named after the title of the email.

If you drag and drop onto a day shown within Day or Week view, you'll be able to set the time for the event by moving it up and down vertically before releasing the mouse button (the appointment time is automatically set for an hour, which is default).

If Calendar is set to Month view, the time of the event will default to midday when you drop the email onto a particular day, but you can easily change this by clicking the Edit button in the pop-out window that also appears, which will let you edit the event in the usual way.

Note that you'll be prohibited from dropping an email onto a day shown within the Year view of Calendar.

Create a New Calendar Event from a Web Page

Click and drag just about anything from a web page shown in Safari onto a day displayed in Calendar, and you'll automatically create an event named after the text of what you drag. You can drag a web link, for example, or an image (in the case of an image, the new event will be named after the "alt" text, which is the text that appears in a tooltip if you hover the mouse cursor over the image).

If you drag and drop onto a day shown within Day or Week view, you'll be able to set the time for the new event by—before releasing the mouse button—moving the link up and down vertically (the appointment time will be set for an hour, which is default).

If Calendar is set to Month view, the time of the event will default as midday, but you can easily change this by clicking the Edit button in the pop-out window that also appears, which will let you edit the event in the usual way. It's not possible to drop a link if you have Year view selected.

This tip is ideal if, for example, you're browsing the page of a conference you intend to attend that is listing its various events—just drag and drop the link to the event onto the day it's due in Calendar.

Tip 138

Keep Your Mac Wide Awake

If you need to leave your Mac unattended for a while but want to temporarily stop it going into sleep mode, open a Terminal window, and type the following:

```
caffeinate -di
```

For as long as the Terminal window is open and the command is still running, the computer won't go to sleep through inactivity, and nor will the display. Technically you're turning off *idle* sleep mode, which occurs when OS X detects the user hasn't done anything for a while.

To end the wakefulness, switch back to the Terminal window and hit `Control`+`C` or simply close the Terminal window.

Rather than running `caffeinate` indefinitely, you can specify a time limit, although this must be specified in seconds. If you wanted your computer not to sleep for two hours, for example, then you'd first need to work out the number of seconds (2 hours x 60 minutes x 60 seconds = 7200 seconds) and then specify it after the -t command-line option, as follows:

```
caffeinate -dt 7200
```

Again, you can bring this to a premature end by using `Control`+`C` or closing the Terminal window.

Tip 139

Stress Test Your Mac's Memory

Problems with the RAM inside your computer can manifest themselves as the random freezing of your computer or as frequent application crashes, especially when a lot of programs are open.

Most experts agree that testing memory is best done using a third-party application called MemTest86. To run the test, you'll need to burn this to a blank CD-R or CD-RW disc and boot from it as follows (obviously, those with a newer Mac Mini or a MacBook Air will need an external CD-R/RW drive):

1. Head over to http://www.memtest.org and download a prebuilt ISO. At the time of this writing, this was described as Precompiled Bootable ISO, accessed via the Download (Pre-build & ISO) link. Usually the ISO is compressed as a zip file, so double-click to unpack it once it's downloaded.

2. Start Disk Utility (open Finder, select Applications, and then double-click Disk Utility in the Utilities folder), and on the menu, click Images→Burn. In the file browser window, select the ISO image you downloaded (it'll probably be in your Downloads folder), and click the Burn button.

3. Insert a blank CD-R or CD-RW disc as prompted, and click the Burn button in the dialog.

4. Once the burning has finished (it'll take less than a minute), reinsert the disc, and then restart the computer (Apple menu→Restart).

5. Before the Apple logo appears, press and hold down `C`. This will force the computer to boot from the CD rather than from the hard disk.

6. For the basic memory test, which is good enough for all but certain specialized cases, MemTest86 is entirely automated and will start after a few seconds. It's simply a matter of waiting for it to finish, which could take a few hours. Keep an eye on the PASS figure at the top of the screen—for details, see Figure 24, *Testing a Mac's memory*, on page 160. This will slowly creep from 0 percent to 100 percent. Note that when the test has reached 100 percent, the test will automatically restart and will continue to do so until you quit MemTest86. This allows "burn-in" testing to take place, whereby components can be stressed over a long period of time. Once a test run-through is complete, however, the program will display a "Pass complete" message at the bottom of the screen.

7. Keep an eye on the Errors column during testing, in the row in the middle of the screen. This displays a total of any errors that are found. Errors are also reported in the lower half of the screen, highlighted in red, along with details of the exact fault. Anything other than zero errors at the end of the test means that the memory is faulty. Modern computers are very good at tolerating minor RAM faults, and you might even experience years of unhindered computing, but ideally you should consider replacing the RAM as soon as possible.

8. To restart the computer at any time or when the test has finished, hit `Esc` (top left of the keyboard). If this doesn't work, hold down the power key on the computer for five seconds to force the computer to turn off. Press

```
     MemTest86+ v4.20     : Pass   4% #  ◄──────────────
Intel Core 2 2520 MHz     : Test  74% ##############################
L1 Cache:   32K  33163 MB/s : Test #3  [Moving inversions, 8 bit pattern]
L2 Cache: 3072K  12665 MB/s : Testing:    184K - 2048M 2048M
L3 Cache:        None     : Pattern:    fbfbfbfb
Memory  : 2048M   7242 MB/s :----------------------------------------------
Chipset : Intel i440BX


  WallTime   Cached   RsvdMem    MemMap    Cache   ECC   Test   Pass    Errors   ECC Errs
  ───────   ──────   ──────    ──────    ─────   ───   ────   ────    ──────   ────────
   0:01:09    2048M      4K     e820      on    off   Std     0         0


                                                                            ────────────
(ESC)Reboot   (c)configuration   (SP)scroll_lock   (CR)scroll_unlock
```

Figure 24—Testing a Mac's memory

the power button again as usual to start the computer. If you immediately click and hold the mouse button, the disc will be ejected before the computer boots.

Tip 140

Create an Install and Recovery Stick

Recent versions of OS X have been sold primarily through direct download from Apple via the App Store as an upgrade to the version of OS X already installed on your system. The installer is downloaded as an installation package and added to the Applications list.

This creates a problem if your computer is somehow made unbootable: how do you reinstall OS X now that your applications list is inaccessible? Alternatively, what if you simply want to create a clean installation of OS X?

The answer is to create an install and recovery USB stick. To do so, you'll need a USB stick 8GB or larger, and you'll have to wipe it clean as part of the process so it can be used only for the purpose of recovery and reinstallation.

Exploring OS X: AirDrop

AirDrop lets you quickly share files with other Mac users who are nearby. Only certain recent models of Macs are compatible,[a] and they must also be running Mac OS X Mountain Lion or OS X Lion.

AirDrop requires no setup and no password, and it works even if you're not connected to a wireless network. However, your computer's Wi-Fi will have to be switched on for AirDrop to work. To do so, click the Wi-Fi icon at the top right of the desktop and select Turn Wi-Fi On.

How it works is simple. If you switch to browsing AirDrop within Finder, either by clicking the shortcut in the Finder sidebar or by clicking Go→AirDrop, your user account will join the AirDrop network and will be visible to others also browsing Air-Drop from their Macs. Once you stop browsing AirDrop, your computer stops being visible.

All other Mac users running AirDrop in the vicinity will appear on your "radar" (and you on theirs) and will be identified by username, along with their personal login picture. You can transfer files or folders to another Mac by dragging and dropping them onto the other Mac's icon. Recipients will be asked to confirm that they want to receive files. They can do the same to transfer files to you.

Received files appear in the Downloads folder.

---

a.   http://support.apple.com/kb/HT4783

When it comes to making an install and recovery USB stick, there are two options:

- You can create a copy of the recovery system that's already on your hard disk. In addition to reinstalling OS X, this is useful for fixing problems such as disk corruption. However, to reinstall OS X, it requires a working Internet connection via Wi-Fi or Ethernet, because the installation files are downloaded as needed.

- You can create a USB stick that contains all the installation files. This is almost identical to the old DVD installation discs that were once distributed with new Macs—you can use it to install OS X even if the computer is unable to get online. It offers some rescue facilities in the form of being able to repair a damaged filesystem, but not the ability to restore from a Time Machine backup.

Creating a Repair and Reinstall USB Stick

OS X installs a small set of tools on your hard disk that you can boot to should things go wrong. Just hold down the `Option` key when you start your computer, before you hear the chime sound and before the Apple logo appears. Then use the Left/Right cursor keys to select the recovery option from the choices that appear (you can release `Option`) and hit `Return` to boot.

Once the recovery system is running, you can access Disk Utility to scan the disk for errors, restore from a Time Machine backup, and get access to a Terminal window to carry out other repairs. You can even reinstall OS X from scratch, although the files will be downloaded as needed, so you'll need an Internet connection.

You can write this recovery toolkit to a USB memory stick, from which you can boot the computer to get things back on the road should you find yourself not even able to boot the hard disk. Apple has released a free utility that can be used to do just this.[12] Just insert the memory stick, run the program, and follow the step-by-step instructions. You'll need to enter your login password when prompted.

Creating a Full Reinstall USB Stick

Writing the entire installation system and files to a USB stick is perhaps the best guarantee of being able to get your system up and running in the event of a disaster, because no matter what happens you'll be able to create a clean installation of OS X—without the need to install over an older version or download the files.

Creating a full reinstall stick works by writing to the USB stick a hidden file within the OS X installation package. Here's how it's done:

1. Look in Applications within Finder for the Install Mac OS X Mountain Lion entry that appeared when you purchased Mountain Lion from the App Store. If it isn't there, you'll have to download the OS X Mountain Lion installer again—open the Mac App Store, click the Purchases icon at the top, and then click the Download button to the right of the OS X Mountain Lion entry. You'll see a warning that Mountain Lion is already installed, but just click the Continue button to download regardless. Note that once the installer has completed downloading, it'll automatically run, but you can quit it by clicking the entry on the application menu.

---

12. See http://support.apple.com/kb/DL1433.

2. When the download has finished, find it within the Applications list of Finder; then right-click it, and select Show Package Contents. Navigate to the SharedSupport folder, and you'll see a file called InstallESD.dmg. This file is the entire Mountain Lion installation—you can ignore all the other files in the package. Leave the Finder window open showing the file while you perform the next few steps.

3. Insert the USB stick you intend to use to make the installation stick. Remember that this will be blanked during the follow steps, so ensure no valuable files are on it.

4. Open Disk Utility, which you'll find in the Utilities folder of the Applications list within Finder.

5. In the Disk Utility window, locate the USB stick in the list of drives on the left of the window. Select the USB stick itself, and not the partition, which will be slightly indented beneath it.

6. Click the Partition tab in the upper middle of the window. From the Partition Layout drop-down, select 1 Partition. From the Format drop-down, select Mac OS Extended (Journaled). In the Name field, type something like OS X Install—this is what will appear in Finder whenever the USB stick is inserted.

7. Click the Options button. In the dialog box that appears, ensure the GUID Partition Table radio button is selected. This makes the USB stick bootable. Click the OK button when done; then, in the main Disk Utility program window, click the Apply button at the bottom right. Formatting the USB stick will take a few seconds, and you'll see a progress display at the bottom of the program window.

8. When it's finished, click the Restore tab. Return to the Finder window you opened later, which is browsing the installation package, and drag the InstallESD.img file to the Source text field. This will add it as the source from which you're going to write the USB stick.

9. Drag the entry for your USB memory stick from the left of the Disk Utility window to the Destination field. Then select the USB stick's partition (that is, the entry indented beneath the main entry for the stick in the listing on the left of the Disk Utility window), and click the Unmount button on the toolbar.

10. Click the Restore button at the bottom right of the window and then the Erase button on the warning dialog telling you that the USB stick will be

erased. For an example taken from my test machine, see Figure 25, *Creating a bootable OS X install USB stick*, on page 164.

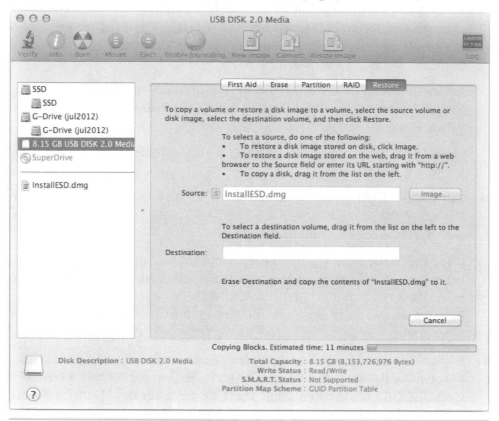

Figure 25—Creating a bootable OS X install USB stick

It'll take up to twenty minutes to write to your USB memory stick. Watch the Copying Blocks progress display in the bottom right of the screen. Once it's finished, quit Disk Utility and eject the memory stick within Finder in the usual way.

To install or attempt recovery via the memory stick in the future, insert it into the computer, and then restart the machine. Hold the Option key when the computer starts; then select the USB stick from the menu that appears using the Left/Right cursor keys (hit Return to boot). Follow the on-screen installation instructions to install. If you want to scan the disk for errors, click the Apple menu, and select Disk Utility.

Tip 141

Recover Crashes and Lock-Ups

I've owned Macs since 2003, and I've only ever had one crash that's rendered the computer completely unresponsive. All I did was press and hold the power button for five seconds. This forces the computer to switch off. As an alternative, however, some people report that holding down Shift+Option+ Command for a few seconds would also cause the computer to power down.

If an application has become unresponsive—that is, the spinning mouse cursor (aka the beach ball of death) has appeared, indicating the computer is busy—but the rest of the system seems to be working fine, many users report that simply starting Activity Monitor somehow fixes things. To start Activity Monitor, open Finder, click Applications, and then double-click Activity Monitor within the Utilities folder. Some users with troublesome systems keep Activity Monitor as an icon on the Dock for just such contingencies!

Tip 142

Share Your Contacts with Others

Macs use vCard files to store contact details, although end users aren't aware of this because the files are invisibly handled by the Contacts application. The vCard system records all the details about a particular contact in a single file, and it's an open file format that's understood by many operating systems, including Windows (and Microsoft Outlook).

Exporting a Single Contact

To export a contact in order to send it to somebody, open the Contacts app (open Finder, select Applications, and then double-click Contacts in the list), and locate your contact in the list. Then simply click and drag the contact from the main list into a new email window, or click and drag to the desktop if you want to turn it into a file to send manually.

Usually, all recipients need to do is double-click the vCard (.vcf) file to import the data, but they might have to use a special import function of their email or chat client. They should check their documentation for instructions.

You can Quick Look a .vcf just like any other file—select it and hit `Space` to see its contents.

Exporting Multiple Contacts

You can export many or even all of your contacts at once either by selectively clicking them (that is, holding down `Command` while selecting) or by selecting all by clicking one and hitting `Command`+`A`. Then click and drag to an email or the desktop as usual. All the details will be contained with a single .vcf file. Note that Microsoft Outlook can't deal with multiple contacts in a single file, but other Macs will be able to import the data just fine.

Tip 143

Set Your IM Status—Even If Messages Isn't Running

When Messages quits, it takes your instant messaging (IM) accounts offline. Therefore, a knee-jerk reaction is to assume you need to have Messages running at all time if you want your friends to be able to message you.

As you might expect with OS X, Apple engineers have provided an alternative solution. You can add an icon to the top right of the desktop (near the clock and Wi-Fi menulets) that will let you set your IM status and see which of your buddies are online, all without having to start the Messages app. Any new messages sent to you appear as notifications that, when clicked, start the Messages app so you can continue the conversation. You'll also see a numbered notification on the Messages Dock icon showing how many messages you have not yet read.

To add the Messages menu icon, start Messages, and then click the Preferences item under the application menu. Ensure the General tab is selected, and then check Show Status In Menu Bar. For what it's worth, you might also want to remove the check alongside When I Quit Messages, Set My Status to Offline. Then close the Preferences dialog box, and close Messages.

A menu icon—that of a small speech balloon— will be added to the menu bar. Clicking it will let you set your IM status and see which of your IM buddies are online.

Note that if you have several IM accounts configured within Messages, you might find one or more sometimes go offline, in which case they'll be listed at the top of the menu under the Offline heading. This might be the case if you use the same IM account on other devices, like an iPad. The Messages menu offers no way to take individual accounts back online without starting the Messages app, but a quick and effective solution is to take all accounts offline by clicking the Offline entry on the menu and take them all back online by clicking Online. Hey, presto—all your accounts should now be back online.

Tip 144

Change Fonts Used in Finder

Here is a personalization tip with a little productivity usefulness thrown in. Like all Mac apps, the Finder uses the Lucida Grande font. However, you can change both the title bar font and the font elsewhere in the program window, such as the font used for displaying file and folder names. Doing so can improve at-a-glance viewing of Finder windows.

Changing the Main Finder Font

To change the fonts used throughout Finder (except for Icon view), open a Terminal window (open Finder, select the Applications list, and then in the list of applications double-click Terminal within the Utilities folder), and type the following:

```
defaults write com.apple.finder NSSystemFont -string AmericanTypewriter;
    killall Finder
```

I've specified the American Typewriter font, but the key is to type the whole name of the font as it is listed in applications like TextEdit, but remove any spaces between the words in the font name. So, the American Typewriter font becomes AmericanTypewriter.

Changing the Title Bar's Font

To specifically change the font of a title bar, type the following into a Terminal window:

```
defaults write com.apple.finder NSTitleBarFont -string ArialBlack;killall
    Finder
```

Here I've specified the Arial Black font, again removing the spaces between the words in the font title.

You might also want to increase the size of the title bar font. Use the following Terminal command to increase the point size to 16:

```
defaults write com.apple.finder NSTitleBarFontSize 16;killall Finder
```

Reverting to Defaults

To remove your font choices within Finder and revert to the default Lucida Grande font, open a Terminal window, and type the following four lines:

```
defaults delete com.apple.finder NSSystemFont
defaults delete com.apple.finder NSTitleBarFont
defaults delete com.apple.finder NSTitleBarFontSize
killall Finder
```

Changing the Fonts for Other Apps

This tip can be used to change the fonts of other apps in a similar way, although not always with a high rate of success. To give it a try with an app, first quit the app in question, and then type the following into a Terminal window, typing the app's name after the -app component (type it exactly as it appears in the Applications list of Finder); the following will set the American Typewriter font to be used in the title bars of TextEdit windows:

```
defaults write -app TextEdit NSTitleBarFont -string AmericanTypewriter
```

The following line will set the title bar font for the Notes app to the Stencil font:

```
defaults write -app Notes NSTitleBarFont -string Stencil
```

To revert to the default system font, modify the following line, again typing the app's name after the -app component; the following reverts TextEdit:

```
defaults delete -app TextEdit NSTitleBarFont
```

Tip 145

Stress Test Your Mac's CPU

If your Mac has been experiencing random crashes, you might want to run a CPU stress test. This will load the processor to 100 percent, and you'll therefore be able to determine whether it's faulty or, more likely, whether the cooling system is faulty.

Testing

There are various ways of stress-testing a Mac, but the easiest way is as follows. Before starting, be sure to save any open files and close any unnecessary applications. If you're using a portable Mac, attach the power cord.

Before starting, find out how many processor cores your Mac has. Unless you're using a Mac Pro desktop system, the answer will be either two or four. To see a quick trick to view the number of cores in the system, check out Tip 135, *Watch CPU Load and Activity*, on page 154—just view the number of bars in the CPU performance graph; each represents a core of your CPU.

Open a Terminal window (open Finder, select the Applications list, and then in the list of applications double-click Terminal within the Utilities folder), and type the following at the command prompt:

```
yes > /dev/null
```

Then hit Command+T to open a new tab in the Terminal window, and type the command one more time. If you have a four-core processor, repeat the step twice again so that a total of four tabs are open and running the command. If your computer has eight cores, then, yes, you've guessed: you'll need to do this eight times in total so that Terminal is running the command within eight tabs.

The yes command merely creates a stream of characters, but it does so as quickly as it can, to the extent that it soon consumes all the available processing power. Elements after the command direct the output of the yes command to /dev/null, which is like a black hole in the system that consumes as much data as is thrown at it.

Terminating the Test

Wait for a few minutes. You'll probably hear your computer's fans start to spin. This is normal, as is the computer getting hot. You might also find the computer becomes a little sluggish when responding to your interaction.

If the computer hasn't crashed after five minutes, terminate the test by closing the Terminal window (don't worry about any warning that doing so will terminate currently running apps). If your Mac crashes or freezes up before you terminate the test, it's very likely your computer has a fault that requires repair.

Tip 146

Find Files by Tagging Them

Every single Mac file can be tagged, which will help Spotlight prioritize the files should you search for them. Tags are simply memorable words that are invisibly attached to the file (technically speaking, they're stored as *metadata*). For example, suppose some friends send you a photograph of them. You can tag the file with their names so that at a later point you can find the photo by simply typing their names as a search term within Spotlight.

Folders can be tagged too, but this isn't recursive—applying a tag to a folder won't apply it to the files it contains.

Tagging Individual Files and Folders

To tag a file or folder, first select it; then hit Command+I to open the info window. Under the Spotlight Comments field at the top, type as many tags as you need, separating each word or phrase with a comma. For example, let's say I received a photo of John Smith and Jill Jones on a water sports holiday in Aruba. I could type the following: John Smith, Jill Jones, water sports, swimming, snorkeling, scuba, holiday, Aruba.

Once you're done, simply close the info window. You can test any of the tags instantly by using it as a search term within Spotlight. Highlight any entry in the list of results, and when the Quick Look window appears, hold down Command to see the tags listed beneath the preview pop-out window (although they'll be listed alongside a Comments heading, rather than a tag heading).

You can tag any type of file in this way, including business documents. The only limitation is how much time you want to spend tagging!

Tagging Multiple Files

There's no quick and easy way to tag multiple files within OS X, although the following Automator action lets you create a small app that will do the job (see *Exploring OS X: Automator*, on page 347):

1. Start the Automator program. It's among the first programs listed in the Applications view of Finder—its icon is a robot.

2. In the Choose a File Type dialog that appears, click the Application icon (the icon is a robot here also), and then click the Choose button. If no Choose a File Type dialog box appears, click File→New.

3. The Automator program window is a little daunting, but you can ignore most of it. In the Search field above the second column on the left, type Set Spotlight. This should thin down the list of actions to one choice. Click and drag this to the right of the window in the area that reads Drag Actions or Files Here to Build Your Workflow.

4. In the New Spotlight Comments field, type a comma (,) and nothing else. However, click the Options button beneath and put a check next to Show This Action When the Workflow Runs.

5. Click File→Save to save your new Automator app. Save it to the desktop and call it something like Group Tagger.

6. Close Automator.

Now and in the future, drag and drop the files you want to be tagged on top of your new app. A dialog box will pop up, asking what tags you want to apply. Type them as prompted, after the comma that's already in the text field, and when you click OK, the files will be tagged instantly and invisibly. Note that there'll be no feedback that anything has happened.

Tip 147

Bring Back the Library

Those who've been using a Mac for some time might have noticed that, since the OS X Lion release, the Library folder within their user folder has vanished. It's still there, of course. It's just that Apple has decided you shouldn't be confronted with it every day, so it's hidden now. The Library folder is where all your personal app and OS X settings are stored. It's not intended for the files there to be manipulated by anything other than apps, but often it's useful to delve in there to remove an errant configuration file.

finger off the mouse button, move it up into the Stack listing. Note that you'll instantly select the item your mouse is hovering over when you release the mouse button.

You can also simply click to activate a stack in the usual way and then start to type the filename of any entry within the list. OS X will automatically highlight the file that matches what you type. Hit `Return` to open the file/folder that's highlighted.

Tip 149

Always See File Info

Click a blank spot on the desktop, and hit `Command+J`. This will bring up the View dialog box. Check Show Item Info. You'll then see useful details beneath each file. For example, documents will have their file size listed beneath. Images will show their physical dimensions. MP3 songs will show how long they are. Folders will show how many files they contain.

This works inside folders, too, provided icon mode is active (hit `Command+1`) —just open the folder in Finder, hit `Command+J`, and check Show Item Info. Each folder will remember the individual settings.

Tip 150

Create One-Click Shortcuts

With the title bar of any program that's able to edit files (that is, an app like TextEdit rather than one like iTunes), you'll see the name of the file currently being worked on—assuming you've saved it, of course!

To the left of this will be an icon representing the file. This is known as the *proxy icon*. Click and hold it for a few seconds without moving the mouse, and then drag the icon to the desktop or to a Finder window to instantly create an alias to that file. Aliases are essentially shortcuts pointing to a particular file that, when double-clicked, open the file. By holding down `Option` before releasing the mouse button, you'll create a copy of the file instead.

If the file has been modified and not saved, the icon might appear grayed out and will stubbornly resist being clicked and dragged. The solution is simply to save the file before clicking and dragging.

This works in most Mac applications, although in Microsoft Office apps you'll need to hold `Option`+`Command` to create an alias. Note that if you click and drag the icon from the title bar of a Finder window, then instead of creating a shortcut, the folder you're currently browsing will be copied to the desktop.

Tip 151

Quickly Move Toolbar Icons

To quickly reposition an icon on the toolbar of most programs that allow toolbar reconfiguration, such as Finder or Preview, hold down `Command` for a few seconds and then click and drag the icon.

Tip 152

Delete iCloud Files (Without Going Insane)

Each and every time you delete an iCloud document you'll see a dialog box warning you that the file will be deleted on all the devices you own that access iCloud. Needless to say, if you're in the process of cleaning up iCloud and deleting many documents, this warning can become annoying.

One solution is to create a new folder within iCloud (see Tip 13, *Create iCloud Folders*, on page 25), name it Trash, and then drag all the files you want to delete into it. Then, when you've finished, just drag this single folder to the trash—or just leave your new Trash folder there, because it'll do no harm!

The only downside with this trick is that you can't place folders within other folders in iCloud, so if you want to delete a folder, you'll have to do so manually in the usual way by either dragging it to the Dock's trash icon or right-clicking it and selecting Delete.

Tip 153

Shrink PDF Files

All applications capable of editing documents or pictures on a Mac can output files as PDFs. To do so, just click File→Print on the menu of the application, and click the PDF drop-down at the bottom left. Then select Save as PDF, and enter a filename as usual (be sure to add a .pdf file extension if you want the file to be read on computers other than Macs).

However, PDFs created by Macs tend to be large. The solution is simple: repeat the previous steps to output a PDF, but choose the Open PDF in Preview option from the PDF drop-down list. Then, when the Preview window appears, click File→Export. In the Save As dialog box, click Reduce File Size in the Quartz Filter drop-down list.

Note that shrinking PDFs in this way will also reduce the quality of the images slightly.

This technique can also be used to shrink large PDF files you might have received by email. Just open then in Preview, export them, and choose the Shrink option. However, if the PDF contains sophisticated functions such as security features, it may lose these functions in the shrinking procedure.

Tip 154

Turn On Key Repeat

With recent releases of OS X, Apple made a break from years of computing development. As just one example, Apple deactivated key repeat in favor of a method of inserting accented or non-English characters (see Tip 114, *Type Symbols and Diacritical Characters*, on page 121).

This technique of inserting foreign or accented characters works only in a handful of applications, including built-in Apple apps such as Mail, Safari, and TextEdit. In other apps, holding down a key does nothing.

If you find this feature annoying, it can be turned off so that keys will repeat in the standard way when held down. To do so, open Terminal (open Finder, select Applications, and then double-click Terminal within the Utilities folder), and type the following:

```
defaults write -g ApplePressAndHoldEnabled -bool FALSE
```

Then log out and back in again for the changes to take effect.

To revert to inserting accented or foreign letters on key hold, open a Terminal window, and type the following:

```
defaults delete -g ApplePressAndHoldEnabled
```

Tip 155

Save Text Snippets

Here's a neat trick for those who work with words on their Macs.

Creating a Clipping

If you highlight text in an application and click and drag it to a folder or to the desktop, the text is turned into a file. These are called *text clippings*, and they will take their filename from the first few words of the excerpt. If there's any formatting applied to the text, it will be saved too. This is an excellent way of filing away anything you've had to edit out of a document but want to keep for other purposes.

Viewing and Inserting Clippings into Documents

To view the contents of the clipping, just double-click it or select it and hit Space to bring up Quick Look. Note that you won't be able to edit the file. However, to reinsert the text into a document, just click and drag the clippings file on top of the program window after positioning the cursor where you'd like it to be inserted.

Once used this way, the text clippings file won't be deleted, so you can use it again in other documents.

Exploring OS X: Mac Server

Those interested in using OS X as a server can do so by purchasing the server upgrade via the Mac App Store. As well as adding server applications of various kinds, including a calendar and a wiki, the server upgrade adds several GUI user management and system monitoring tools to a standard OS X installation. It also adds support for the Xsan cluster filesystem. However, key OS X tools like Time Machine are also included, which can make the ordinarily complex procedure of server backup as easy as backing up a desktop computer.

A key feature of OS X Server compared to other server operating systems is that the purchase price of OS X Server allows an unlimited number of clients. This indicates the smaller-business orientation of OS X Server, a market that Apple claims includes "small studios, retail shops, even home-based businesses" and "people who never thought they could run a server."

Apple ceased production of dedicated Mac server hardware in 2010 and currently recommends either the Mac Pro or high-end Mac Mini desktop systems be used for those who require server hardware.

Tip 156

Hide Files

There are two ways of making files invisible on your Mac. Neither is bulletproof from a security standpoint, and anybody with know-how would be able to uncover them in seconds. But for quietly hiding a file or two for a short period, they're worth considering. If you need to protect files from prying eyes, take a look at Tip 126, *Secure All Your Files Against Hackers*, on page 137 and Tip 209, *Create Encrypted Archives for All Computers*, on page 234.

Hiding Files via Unix

Your Mac's operating system, OS X, is actually a version of Unix. In Unix, you can make a file invisible by adding a period (.) in front of its filename, and this works on Macs too. This means the file won't show up in Finder windows, in file open dialog boxes, or on the desktop. Those browsing at the command line won't be able to see it unless they specifically request to view hidden files (that is, ls -a).

For example, typing a filename of .document.docx when you're saving a file will render it invisible. You'll probably be warned that putting a period in front of a filename is reserved for system files, the type of file this technique is typically used to hide, but you can still choose to save the file.

Hiding Files So Mac Apps Can't See Them

The chflags can be used to hide files so they don't show up in graphical user interface (GUI) applications. However, they'll still be visible if anybody browses files using a Terminal window.

To hide files in this way, open a Terminal window (open Finder, select the Applications list, and then in the list of applications double-click Terminal within the Utilities folder), and use the chflags hidden command, specifying the file or folder name immediately afterward. For example, to hide secret.doc, type the following:

```
chflags hidden secret.doc
```

To unhide the file so it's visible via GUI software again, use the chflags nohidden command:

```
chflags nohidden secret.doc
```

Viewing Hidden Files

So, if a file is hidden, how can you see it in order to open it again? In expanded file open/save dialog boxes within apps (see Tip 294, *Always See Expanded Save Dialogs*, on page 313), hitting Shift+Command+. (period) will display hidden items in the file listing. Hitting the key combo again will hide them. However, be aware that you'll suddenly see lots of system files that are hidden in this way. (Steer clear of these—don't delete or open them.)

The only way to see hidden files in Finder windows is to activate a secret setting that shows them alongside other files. This will cause them to always be visible within Finder windows and on the desktop, although hidden files will have a washed-out appearance to indicate their status. Open a Terminal window, and type the following:

```
defaults write com.apple.finder AppleShowAllFiles -bool TRUE;killall Finder
```

Even after making this change, you'll still have to hit Shift+Command+. within file open/save dialog boxes to see hidden files.

To revert to hidden files being hidden within Finder, type the following:

```
defaults delete com.apple.finder AppleShowAllFiles;killall Finder
```

Tip 157

Supertip: Make Better Screenshots

Macs have powerful screenshot facilities built in, with which you can produce a snapshot of what's on your monitors at any given time (see Tip 233, *Take a Picture of the Screen*, on page 258). Here's how you can tweak a few things relating to screenshots: the file type, where files are saved, and whether they have a shadow effect applied to them.

Changing the File Format

By default screenshot files are saved in Portable Network Graphics (PNG) format (.png). This is as good as any for a file format, but you might find that people you work with demand JPEG or GIF files. To change the default file format, first look up the format you need in the left column of the following table, open a Terminal window (open Finder, select the Applications list, and then in the list of applications double-click Terminal within the Utilities folder), and add it to the end of the following command:

```
defaults write com.apple.screencapture type -string
```

Here are the format options:

Filetype	Description
BMP	Windows Bitmap; ideal for any type of image but produces large file sizes. Can't be used online.
GIF	Graphics Interchange Format; used primarily for diagrams. Can be used online.
JPEG	Joint Photographics Expert Group file format; best for photographic images. Can be used online.
PDF	Portable Document Format; can be used for any type of image file. Most modern web browsers support PDF.
PNG	Portable Network Graphics; can be used for both photographs and diagrams but perhaps better suited to the latter. Can be used online.
TIFF	Tagged Image File Format; ideal for any kind of image but produces large file sizes. Popular in the publishing industry but can't be used online.

For example, to change the default screenshot file format to GIF, you can type the following:

```
defaults write com.apple.screencapture type -string GIF
```

Then log out and back in again.

To change back to the default PNG format, open a Terminal window, and type the following:

```
defaults delete com.apple.screencapture type
```

Don't forget to log out and back in again afterward.

Changing the File Save Location

You can also alter the default save location where your Mac places screenshots it captures. By default this is the desktop, but the following command will save them to the Documents folder, for example (replace USERNAME with your username, which you'll usually find listed just before the $ prompt in the Terminal window):

```
defaults write com.apple.screencapture location /Users/USERNAME/Documents/
```

You'll need to log out and back in again for the change to take effect. To revert to the standard location (that is, the desktop), open a Terminal window, and type the following, logging out and back in again afterward:

```
defaults delete com.apple.screencapture location
```

Getting Rid of the Shadow

Screenshots of program windows taken by hitting Shift+Command+4 followed by Space always have a shadow effect applied to them. You can turn this off in two ways. The first is temporary and involves simply holding down Option while taking the screenshot. The second is permanent and involves altering a secret setting. Open a Terminal window (open Finder, select the Applications list, and then in the list of applications double-click Terminal within the Utilities folder), and type the following:

```
defaults write com.apple.screencapture disable-shadow -bool TRUE
```

Log in and out for the change to take effect.

To revert to screenshots having shadows once again, open a Terminal window again, and type the following, logging out and back in again for the changes to take effect:

```
defaults delete com.apple.screencapture disable-shadow
```

Tip 158

Set Movie Thumbnails

If you import a movie file into iTunes, it will automatically set the thumbnail preview you see when looking at a listing of movies in Grid and Cover Flow view modes. The thumbnail is usually based on the first frame of the movie file, which can be annoying if the movie starts with a fade from black or a film/TV studio logo.

You can replace the thumbnail with your own choice by watching the movie and then pausing it on something suitably illustrative. Then right-click the playback area and select Set Poster Frame from the menu that appears.

Note that you might have to quit and then restart iTunes for the thumbnail change to take effect.

Tip 159

Create a Clever Color Picker

This tip is primarily for web developers and graphic artists.

A lot of Mac apps feature the built-in OS X color picker tool. In TextEdit, for example, clicking the color chooser icon on the toolbar and then choosing Show Colors from the pop-out menu will display this tool. It's a floating window showing a color wheel, although you can also switch to predefined palettes by clicking the relevant toolbar button on the floating window.

Creating a Simple App

The color picker is not available as a stand-alone app, but it's easy to turn it into one with a little AppleScript. This way, it can be used whenever you need to choose a color and find the RGB (or CMYK) values.

Open AppleScript Editor—it's in the Utilities folder within the Applications list of Finder. Open a new file (File→New); then in the main code area, type the following:

```
choose color default color {65535, 65535, 65535}
```

Click File→Save As; give your new app a name, such as Color Picker; and choose a location (you can save it in the Applications folder if you want, alongside all your other apps). In the File Format drop-down list, near the bottom of the Save dialog box, select Application. Then click Save.

Your new app is now ready for use. When it's running, you can close it by clicking either the Cancel or OK button—it doesn't matter.

To see the RGB or CMYK values of a color, click the Color Sliders icon on the color picker window's toolbar (second icon from the left), and select RGB Sliders or CMYK Sliders from the drop-down list (see Figure 27, *Creating a homemade color picker app*, on page 183).

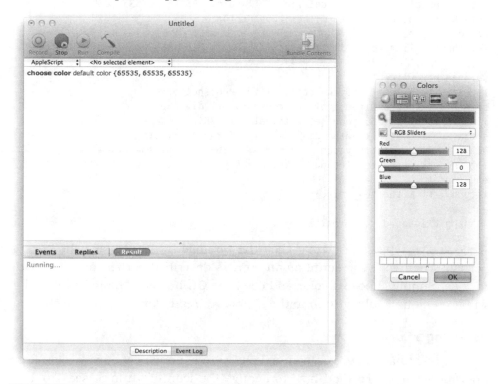

Figure 27—Creating a homemade color picker app

If you want to sample colors anywhere on the screen to get their RGB or approximate CMYK values using the color picker tool (CMYK has a smaller color gamut compared to RGB, so any values returned by the color picker will be nearest approximated values), click the magnifying glass icon next to the large color bar, and click the area of the screen you're interested in. (Note that there's already an app for sampling on-screen colors, available in the Utilities folder of Applications—DigitalColor Meter, but it doesn't show CMYK values.)

Creating a More Sophisticated App

A few extra lines of code can boost our new tool substantially and turn it into a web developer's dream. The following AppleScript, when saved as an app as described earlier, will write the color value chosen to the clipboard as a hex value (that is, something like #6BACFF). This can then be pasted into HTML code, for example.

```
set chosencolor to choose color default color {65535, 65535, 65535}
set the formattedColor to my hex(chosencolor)
on hex(chosencolor)
set the hex_list to {"0", "1", "2", "3", "4", "5", "6", "7", "8", "9", "A",
        "B", "C", "D", "E", "F"}
set the hex_value to ""
repeat with i from 1 to the count of the chosencolor
set this_value to (item i of the chosencolor) div 256
if this_value is 256 then set this_value to 255
set x to item ((this_value div 16) + 1) of the hex_list
set y to item (((this_value / 16 mod 1) * 16) + 1) of the hex_list
set the hex_value to (the hex_value & x & y) as string
end repeat
return ("#" & the hex_value)
end hex
set the clipboard to formattedColor
```

Once you've typed the listing, click the Compile button to see whether it's correct. Then save the script as an app, as described earlier, and it's ready for use. Simply choose a color and click the OK button. The RGB hex value will then be invisibly written to the clipboard, ready for pasting elsewhere.

Assigning a Custom Icon

There's one final tweak you can make to perfect your new app—assign it an appropriate icon. To read how to change the icon of an app, see Tip 116, *Personalize Every Icon*, on page 127.

Also, you'll find an ideal image at /System/Library/ColorPickers/NSColorPickerWheel.color-Picker/Resources/NSColorWheelImage.tiff. To open this file, start Preview, click File→ Open, make sure On My Mac is selected at the top left, and then hit Shift + Command + G . Then type the path shown earlier, and click Open to open the file for viewing and converting into an icon, as described by the aforementioned tip.

Tip 160

Back Up Without a Time Machine Disk

When Time Machine is used on a portable Mac, such as a MacBook Air, OS X is clever enough to realize there are times when the computer won't be attached to the Time Machine disk (or within range of the Time Capsule). Therefore, it temporarily backs up to the computer's hard disk, creating what are known as *snapshots*.

With desktop Macs like the iMac, this feature isn't activated because it's assumed the Time Machine disk will always be connected or that the computer will always be in range of the Time Capsule. But this might not always be the case. Perhaps you sometimes disconnect your Time Machine disk because you temporarily need the USB port it uses for other things, for example.

Enabling Local Snapshots

If your desktop machine is not always connected, you can enable the same local disk backup that portable Macs use. Open a Terminal window, and type the following:

```
sudo tmutil enablelocal
```

You'll need to type your password when prompted. A new snapshot will be created within the hour, but if you're impatient, you can force one to be made by typing the following at the Terminal window:

```
tmutil snapshot
```

Note that no indication is given that a snapshot is taking place. If you enter Time Machine, snapshots are identified by gray bars in the time display against the right side of the screen. Regular backups are colored purple.

Deactivating Local Snapshots

To deactivate the local backup feature, type the following:

```
sudo tmutil disablelocal
```

All the local backup data will be deleted (this might take some time but will take place in the background), so ensure you create a new external backup of the system by attaching the Time Machine disk and clicking the Back Up Now option on the Time Machine menu.

Tip 161

Make the Dock Really, Really Small

You can shrink and enlarge the Dock by clicking and dragging the "Abbey Road" bar lines that separate the application icons from the stacks on the Dock (that is, the bars that look like the road-crossing stripes on the *Abbey Road* album cover). Alternatively, you can open System Preferences, select the Dock preference pane, and click and drag the Size slider.

However, your Mac will let you shrink the Dock only to a certain size. This setting is pretty small, but it's possible to go even smaller.

Shrinking the Dock

To shrink the Dock even more than what is usually allowed, open a Terminal window (open Finder, select the Applications list, and then in the list of applications double-click Terminal within the Utilities folder), and type the following:

```
defaults write com.apple.dock tilesize -int 8;killall Dock
```

This will shrink the Dock to half of the supposedly smallest size—for an example, see Figure 28, *Shrinking the Dock to a minuscule size*, on page 186. The number at the end of the command can range from 1 (too small to be useful) up to 16, which is the smallest size achievable by clicking and dragging to resize. You can set values higher than this too, but you might as well use the built-in Mac tools, such as the System Preferences tool.

Figure 28—Shrinking the Dock to a minuscule size

However, if used with Dock magnification (which you can set using the same Dock pane of System Preferences), it is entirely possible to use a tiny Dock size, especially if screen real estate is limited.

Restoring a Normal Size

Using the Dock pane of System Preferences is the best way of returning the Dock to a normal size (just click and drag the size slider), although you can return the Dock to the default size by opening a Terminal window and typing the following:

```
defaults delete com.apple.dock tilesize;killall Dock
```

Tip 162

Get a Better Stack List

Stacks are the spring-out displays that appear when a folder in the Dock, such as Documents, is clicked. There are three view modes that you can select by right-clicking the folder: Fan, Grid, and List.

Getting a Better List

As its name suggests, List view simply presents the files and folders in a rather dull list that you can scroll by nudging the mouse at the top and bottom of the list. To change List view to a rather more aesthetically pleasing display complete with a scrollbar that you can click and drag (see Figure 29, *Hidden stack list mode (left) and the default stack list mode (right)*, on page 188), open a Terminal window (open Finder, select the Applications list, and then in the list of applications double-click Terminal within the Utilities folder), and type the following:

```
defaults write com.apple.dock use-new-list-stack -bool TRUE;killall Dock
```

The Dock will disappear for a split second, but don't worry—this is fine. You should be able to test the changes right away.

Tweaking the Size

You can increase or shrink the size of icons in the new look by activating the stack and then holding Command and tapping the minus and equals keys, which are on the top right of your keyboard, next to the main number row.

Figure 29—Hidden stack list mode (left) and the default stack list mode (right)

Reverting to Normal List Mode

To revert to the standard List view at any time, open a Terminal window, and type the following:

```
defaults delete com.apple.dock use-new-list-stack;killall Dock
```

Tip 163

Supertip: Make Finder Your Hub

Finder is much more flexible than you might realize. Its toolbar and sidebar offer significant potential for boosting productivity.

Creating a Copy of the Dock

You can drag and drop practically anything onto the Finder toolbar to create a shortcut for quick access. For example, you can drag an application icon there, and it will act like an icon in the Dock, so you can click it to launch the app and drag and drop files onto it for opening. You can even replicate your entire set of Dock icons, or at least the key applications you use daily, if there's enough space.

File, Folder, and Storage Device Shortcuts

You can also drag data files and folders to the toolbar that, when clicked, will open instantly. Removable storage devices like USB memory sticks can also be dragged there—just click and drag their entry from beneath the Devices list in Finder.

You can drag and drop folders to the Favorites section of the Finder sidebar to create shortcuts there.

Printing Easily

You can also add to the Finder toolbar a shortcut to your printer(s), which will let you drag and drop files to instantly print them or allow you to click the icon to see the print queue. Just open System Preferences (Apple menu →System Preferences), click Print & Scan, and then drag and drop any of the printer(s) from the list to the toolbar of any open Finder window.

Adding System Preferences Shortcuts

It's also possible to add entries from within System Preferences to the Finder's toolbar or sidebar. Follow the instructions in "Adding Specific System Preferences Icons to the Dock," in Tip 244, *Get Quick Access to System Preferences*, on page 270. However, rather than dragging the .pref files to the Dock, drag them to the Finder's toolbar or sidebar instead.

Removing a Toolbar Entry

To remove an icon you've added, just hold down `Command` and drag the icon up and away from the toolbar in the case of toolbar icons or to the left and away from Finder in the case of sidebar icons. The icon will disappear in a puff of smoke (literally, although don't worry—only the shortcut will be deleted).

You can also delete default toolbar entries this way, such as the Search box, which will free up a lot more space for your own icons.

To restore the default set of icons to the Finder toolbar at any point, right-click in the toolbar area, and then click Customize Toolbar in the menu that appears. Then in the drop-down dialog box, drag and drop the default icon set to the toolbar over what's already there.

Tip 164

Hide Every Single Window

To send every program window that's open to the Dock—apart from the one that you're currently working in—hit `Option`+`Command`+`H`. To restore the program windows to the screen, you'll need to click their individual Dock icons.

Hold down `Option`+`Command`, and click a blank spot on the desktop (such as the space on either side of the Dock) to instantly hide all windows except Finder windows, revealing the desktop. Click the Dock icon of each app to unhide it.

Tip 165

Work Better with Column View

Column view within Finder is probably my favorite way of browsing files. To access it, open a Finder window, and click View→As Columns, or hit `Command`+`3`.

The only issue I sometimes have is that long filenames get truncated because of the narrow column widths. To get around this, I double-click the small double-bar icon at the bottom right of the column beneath the scrollbar (for an annotated example, see Figure 30, *Resizing columns in Finder*).

Figure 30—Resizing columns in Finder

This double-bar icon can also be dragged to resize the column. Holding down `Option` while resizing columns will both resize *all* columns proportionately within the Finder window and cause Finder to remember the resizing the next time you open a Finder window, rather than resetting the column width. Double-clicking the double-bar icon will cause the column to revert to its default size once it has been manually resized by clicking and dragging.

Tip 166

Maximize iTunes Windows

If you click the green "maximize window" blob at the top left of the iTunes window, something unexpected happens. Rather than maximizing the window, which is what happens with every other app, you'll switch iTunes to its Mini Player mode, where the entire iTunes interface shrinks down to just the play/skip buttons and a volume control. Hitting the green button again causes the iTunes window to return to normal.

So, how do you actually maximize an iTunes window? Simply hold down Option before clicking the green button. It'll then work like it does in other apps.

You can permanently deactivate the Mini Player activation via the minimize blob by using a secret setting. Quit iTunes, open a Terminal window (open Finder, select the Applications list, and then in the list of applications double-click Terminal within the Utilities folder), and type the following:

```
defaults write -app iTunes zoom-to-window -bool YES
```

You can still activate the Mini Player from the Windows menu when iTunes is active.

Should you decide to reverse Mini Player deactivation, again open a Terminal window, and type the following:

```
defaults delete -app iTunes zoom-to-window
```

Tip 167

See All Your Mac Knows About Somebody

By selecting an individual's entry within the Contacts app and then clicking Edit→Spotlight, you can instantly find every email you have from them (and to them), every instant message conversation you've had with them, every document they've created, every web page you've visited that mentions them, every file you've tagged with their name, and so on (provided relevant details are contained within their card within the Contacts app—you won't be able to find their instant message conversations if their IM address isn't on the contact card, for example).

Tip 168

Print Wall Calendars

By selecting File→Print in the Calendar app, you can print monthly or weekly calendars that resemble commercially available wall calendars (select the choice from the View drop-down list). You can print a calendar showing your events for that month/week or remove the check(s) under the Calendars heading to remove them and print a completely blank calendar. By selecting a higher number in the Months counter, you can print as many months as you want from the current month onward. Each will be printed on a separate sheet. If your printer is capable of printing bigger sizes of paper, select this from the Paper drop-down list.

Tip 169

Keep a Folder Update Log

If you have a folder containing files that multiple users of your Mac access on a regular basis, you can make it so a dialog box showing a message pops up whenever the folder is accessed. Users can then add their own comments to the message (that is, something like "2/23/2013—Added some image files"), forming a log that describes who did what to the contents of the folder and why. You could even use this if you're the only person using the Mac to remind yourself of additions or edits!

You can set this up as follows:

1. Right-click the folder and select Get Info from the menu that appears. This trick uses the Spotlight Comments field of the Info dialog box to store the comments, and it's necessary to add something to start off with. Something like the date, followed by Setup folder logging, will be sufficient.

2. Close the info window, right-click the folder, and select from the menu that appears Folder Actions Setup (or possibly Services→Folder Actions Setup). See Figure 31, *Creating a folder logging system*, on page 194.

3. In the Choose a Script to Attach dialog box that appears, select open - show comments in dialog.scpt. Then close the dialog box.

Setup is now complete. When anybody opens the folder, a dialog box will appear where they can either click OK to dismiss the dialog, click the Open Comments button to add comments to the log (which will simply open the info window where they can type into the Spotlight Comments field, as earlier; to create a new line when typing, hold down Option), or click Clear Comments, which will wipe clean the Spotlight Comments field. Note that the dialog box stays on-screen for only a few seconds before it automatically dismisses itself. Note also that if you choose to clear the comments, the dialog won't appear

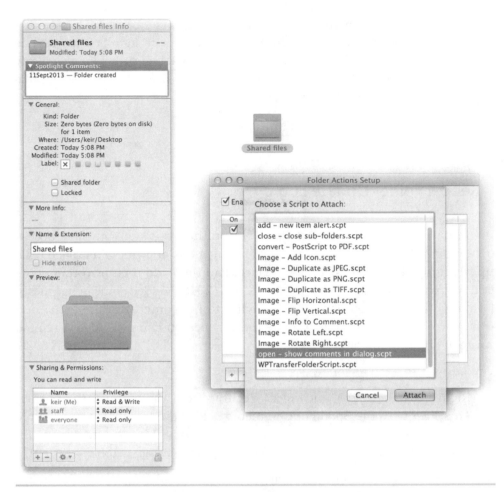

Figure 31—Creating a folder logging system

again until you repeat the previous step 1 and manually add new text to the Spotlight Comments field.

To remove the dialog box and log later, again right-click the folder, select Folder Actions Setup (or possibly Services→Folder Actions Setup), and then click Cancel within the list of scripts that appears. In the Folder Actions Setup dialog box, select the folder on the left, and then hit the minus button beneath. Note that this won't delete the folder. Instead, it will simply remove it from the list of folder actions.

Tip 170

Start Terminal in an Instant

After you click its icon, it can take more than a few seconds for Terminal to start sometimes. This is because it's reading in various log files built up since you began using OS X as part of the process initiated by the default login shell (/usr/bin/login). However, by specifying that Terminal should simply use bash, you can cause Terminal to start up almost instantaneously every time.

To do this, open Terminal, and then open its Preferences dialog box (Command + , (comma)). Then ensure the Startup icon is selected, and click the Command (Complete Path) radio button, under the Shells Open With heading. And that's all you need to do—bash will already be specified. Close the Preferences dialog box, and you should find Terminal opens much more quickly the next time you start it from cold.

Tip 171

Enable Apache and PHP

Here's a corollary for the sidebar *OS X for Admins and Software Developers*, on page 251. Although the Apache 2 web server and PHP 5 scripting language are both included with a standard desktop installation of OS X Mountain Lion, neither is configured to work out of the box. If you're a web developer, you'll most likely want to change this; the following instructions explain how.

Starting and Configuring Apache

To start Apache, open a Terminal window, and type sudo apachectl start. Type your password when prompted, and note that you'll need to do this several times when prompted during the following steps. To stop Apache, type sudo apachectl stop. You can test Apache by visiting http://localhost in your browser.

Document root is located at /Library/WebServer/Documents/. To enable user-level root (that is, something like http://localhost/~keir), you'll have to create a Sites folder in your home folder, although this might already exist if you've upgraded from a previous release of OS X. This is where you should place your site files in the future.

You'll also need to add a text .conf file within the /etc/apache2/users folder named after your short Unix username (that is, something like keirthomas.conf; to find your short Unix username, type whoami at the prompt).

To do so, type sudo nano /etc/apache2/users/USERNAME.conf, replacing USERNAME with your short Unix username. Then paste the following into the Terminal window, again replacing USERNAME with your username:

```
<Directory "/Users/USERNAME/Sites/">
Options Indexes MultiViews
AllowOverride All
Order allow,deny
Allow from all
</Directory>
```

Save the file, and quit the text editor by pressing Ctrl+O, Return, then Ctrl+X.

Finally, set the correct permissions on the file by typing sudo chmod 644 /etc/apache2/users/USERNAME.conf, again replacing USERNAME with your Unix username, and restart Apache: sudo apachectl restart. To have Apache start automatically as a background service each time the computer boots, type the following into a Terminal window:

```
sudo defaults write /System/Library/LaunchDaemons/org.apache.httpd Disabled
      -bool FALSE
```

If you ever want to disable automatic starting of Apache on boot, again open a Terminal window, and type the following:

```
sudo defaults write /System/Library/LaunchDaemons/org.apache.httpd Disabled
      -bool TRUE
```

Enabling PHP

To enable PHP, open a Terminal window, and open the httpd.conf file for editing by typing sudo nano /etc/apache2/httpd.conf. You can navigate within the text editor using the cursor keys. Look for the line that begins #LoadModule php5_module, and remove the hash at the start of the line. Then save the file and quit the editor by hitting Ctrl+O, Return, and then Ctrl+X. Restart Apache by typing sudo apachectl restart.

Note that MySQL is not installed by default but can be downloaded from the MySQL website.[13] Alongside the main MySQL package are additional components that allow the starting and stopping of the MySQL server from within System Preferences.

---

13. http://dev.mysql.com/downloads/mysql/

Tip 172

Change Preview Markup Colors

If you use the markup (highlighter) pen tool in Preview (see Tip 229, *Supertip: Take Control of PDFs*, on page 252), you can change the color of any markup you add to text by right-clicking the markup and selecting a different color from the menu that appears—no need to highlight it again!

Tip 173

Download Files Fuss-Free

Although OS X doesn't include a download manager—a program whose job it is to take care of downloads, including resuming those that stall or fail—it does include a similar style of tool at the command line. curl can download (and even upload) just about any type of file or even entire websites (a process known as *crawling*).

To use curl to download a large file, open a Terminal window (open Finder, select the Applications list, and then in the list of applications double-click Terminal within the Utilities folder); then switch to the folder into which you'd like to download the file. This can be done easily by locating the folder in Finder and then dragging and dropping it onto the Terminal window while holding down Command.

Type curl -C - -O (that's the letter O at the end, not zero), and then drag and drop from Safari the link to the file you want to download. Note that the link must directly point to the file and shouldn't be within a password-protected section of the site—such sites typically rely on cookies to authenticate you, and those cookies can't be shared with curl.

Once you hit Return, the download will commence, and you'll be shown a status display. If the download fails with an error, just repeat the entire command —this can be done by hitting the Up cursor key and then hitting Return. curl will resume the download where it left off. Similarly, if the download appears to stall, which is to say the download speed slows to zero or just a trickle, hit Ctrl+C to abort the download, and then again repeat the command as described earlier. The download will again resume from where it left off and in all likelihood with a better transfer speed.

Don't close the Terminal window while the download is in progress. The best plan is to minimize the Terminal window until the download has finished.

Hide a File from Spotlight

You might already know that by opening System Preferences (Apple→System Preferences), clicking the Spotlight tab, and selecting Privacy, you can choose to "hide" folders from Spotlight, which will stop any files within them from appearing in the list of results. Just drag and drop the folders onto the Spotlight window.

What isn't obvious is that you can drag and drop single files onto this window to hide them from Spotlight's list of results. While this isn't an infallible way of stopping others from finding private files (they can simply repeat what you've done and see the listing in System Preferences), it's enough to stop you from being pestered in Spotlight results by files that you've archived and want to forget about.

Create Groups of Contacts

The Contacts app lets you create groups, which are logical collections of people whose entries within your address book have things in common. For example, you could create a group for people employed by a particular company. You could even create a group for a certain set of your friends. Clicking the group's entry within the groups listing (click View→Groups) will then show only the people in that group.

Smart Groups take groups one step further by automatically detecting and adding people who fulfill certain criteria. To create a smart group, click File →New Smart Group. Then in the text field alongside the Card and Contains drop-down lists, enter some text that you know will be somewhere within the address book entry of each individual you'd like to be included in the list. This might be a company name, or even something like a telephone area code, if you want to create a smart group for people who live in a city or district.

By clicking the first drop-down in the smart group creation dialog box, headed Card by default, you can select specific address book fields that you want the smart group to filter by, such as Email or even Birthday. By clicking the Contains drop-down, you can select Does Not Contain to create a smart group that *doesn't* include the text you specify, which is useful if your address book contains mostly people within your company and you want to create a group showing people employed by others.

Note that, in the future, you can hold down Option while clicking or viewing an entry within the overall list of Contacts to see any groups they're in. When you click, the group(s) will briefly flash blue.

Tip 176

Calm a Bouncing Dock Icon

Some apps bounce their Dock icons when they want to tell you something, such as when a task has completed. Some apps bounce their icons for a short while, while others will keep bouncing the icon until you do something about it. This can be annoying if you're busy doing something else.

Temporarily Calming a Dock Icon

While clicking the Dock icon to activate the app is one solution, another is simply to move your mouse cursor over the icon. It will instantly stop bouncing, and you can then return to the task at hand.

Deactivating Dock Bouncing

If you finding it irritating, you can turn off the Dock icon bouncing entirely, although bear in mind this means you won't know when an app requires your attention.

The Dock bounces when one of two events occur: when an app launches and if an app requires attention. The former can be turned off by opening System Preferences (Apple→System Preferences) and then clicking the Dock icon, before removing the check from the Animate Opening Applications box.

The latter can be switched off via a hidden setting. Open a Terminal window (open Finder, select the Applications list, and then in the list of applications double-click Terminal within the Utilities folder), and type the following:

```
defaults write com.apple.dock no-bouncing -bool TRUE;killall Dock
```

The changes will take effect straightaway.

To reactivate Dock icon bouncing, repeat the previous steps with System Preferences, open a Terminal window, and type the following:

```
defaults delete com.apple.dock no-bouncing
```

Tip 177

Spawn New Finder Windows

This is an obvious and simple tip yet is one that eluded me and several people I know until recently. If you want to open a new, additional Finder window—perhaps to drag a file from one Finder window to another—you can hold down Command while double-clicking a folder on the desktop or within a Finder window.

If you don't hold down Command, the default action when double-clicking a folder is to "reuse" the same Finder window.

To close all Finder windows at the same time, just hold down Option while clicking the Close button at the top left. (This works for all apps, not just Finder.)

Tip 178

Pool Printers for Quick Printing

This is a tip for anybody who uses a Mac on a network and prints to network printers or perhaps has several printers connected to the Mac via USB.

One of the biggest issues with using a shared printer is that it might be busy or just switched off. To overcome this, Macs let you pool printers. Once a pool is created, you can select the pool when printing, and your Mac will send the job to the first printer it detects that isn't already busy or offline.

Alas, printer pools aren't perfect. You're given no indication of which printer has printed the job. If you create a pool that, for example, includes printers on different floors of the building, then you'll have to visit each until you find your output!

Creating a Pool

To create a printer pool, open the Print & Scan component of System Preferences. In the list of printers on the left, select the printers you want to include by holding down `Shift` or `Command` when selecting them (just as you do when selecting files). On the right of the panel, a new button will appear: Create Printer Pool. Clicking this will let you create the pool, and the final step is to give it a name. Once you're done, you'll see the printer pool appear in the list of printers on the left.

All you need to do in the future is select the printer pool you created from the File→Print dialog box within any application, in the same way you'd select a single stand-alone printer. Printer pools have their own print queue, the icon for which will appear in the Dock when you print.

Deleting a Printer Pool

Deleting a pool is just like deleting any other printer: open System Preferences, select Print & Scan, select the printer pool in the list on the left, and then click the minus button at the bottom of the list. Then click Delete Printer [sic] in the dialog box that appears.

Tip 179

View Photo or Movie's Hidden Info

When you open an image in Preview or a movie in QuickTime Player, hitting `Command`+`I` will bring up the information window that will show every scrap of technical and metadata information about the file, including EXIF data in the case of images (click the "i" icon, and then select the EXIF tab). Hit `Command`+`I` to hide the info window again.

Figure 32—You can Quick Look just about anywhere, including within Mail.

Delete Files While Quick Looking

If you hold down the Command key while using Quick Look to view a file and then hit Delete (the key above the Return key, sometimes called Backspace on PC keyboards), you'll instantly send the file you're currently looking at to the trash. The next file in Finder's file list will then appear in Quick Look, and you can then delete this in the same way or hit the Down cursor key to jump to the next file without deleting it. In this way, you can very quickly prune a list of files while looking at what they contain.

This same trick works when you're viewing multiple files within Preview (that is, when several files are thumbnailed in the sidebar drawer).

Zoom In While Quick Looking PDFs

If you're using Quick Look to view a PDF, you can zoom in on a page if using a trackpad by making the pinch-to-expand gesture (that is, placing your finger and thumb together on the trackpad and moving them apart; contracting them again will zoom out). If you're using a mouse, you can hold down `Option` and scroll the mouse wheel up and down to zoom in and out (for what it's worth, this also works with a trackpad—just hold `Option` and use two fingers to scroll up and down in the usual way).

However, for reasons best known to Apple engineers, this works only with PDFs and not with any other kind of file, such as images. If you use the pinch-to-expand gesture with such files, you'll switch to full-screen mode instead.

Quick Look Files at the Command Prompt

You can use Quick Look at the command line to preview any file. What you'll see is the same as what you would see if you select a file in Finder and hit `Space` or right-click it and select Quick Look.

Just use the qlmanage -p command, followed by the filename. For example, to Quick Look the file disneyland.jpg from the command line, I'd type the following:

```
qlmanage -p disneyland.jpg
```

You can Quick Look any type of file: images, documents, PDFs, and so on.

Tip 181

Print via Drag and Drop

Wouldn't it be useful to be able to print a file instantly, without first having to open it and then click File→Print? As you might expect, your Mac lets you do just that. Open System Preferences (Apple menu→System Preferences) and then click the Print & Scan entry. In the list of printers that appears on the left, simply select a printer and drag and drop it to the desktop. This will create a shortcut to the printer, which will probably be an icon-sized photograph of your actual printer.

To instantly print any file, simply drag and drop a file on top of this new shortcut.

Double-click the new icon to view the print queue.

Tip 182

Be Ultra-Accurate with Spotlight

Spotlight is precise in providing files that match your search query, but you can also force it to be even more specific, returning only certain types of files in the results, for example, or only those files with certain characteristics.

Searching for Types of Files

To force Spotlight to search only for a particular type of file that matches your search term, such as images, type kind: and then the type of file you're looking for. For example, to search only for audio files matching the word bieber, I'd type the following:

```
kind:music bieber
```

To search for documents matching the word report, type the following:

```
kind:documents report
```

You can see a full list of words that can be used in the following table. Remember that Finder includes a Spotlight search field at the top right of each file browser window, and this technique works there too.

If specified without anything following, Spotlight will return a list of every particular file type on your system.

kind:modifier	Description
kind:alias	Returns only file aliases.
kind:app	Returns only applications within Spotlight results.
kind:bookmark	Returns only Safari bookmarks (not those of other browsers you may have installed) and also entries within your browsing history.
kind:contact	Returns entries from the Contacts application.
kind:document	Returns documents, although this is a broad term applying to any file that is a container for text and not just office documents. You can use kind:word to return only Microsoft Word documents and kind:pages to return only iWork Pages documents.
kind:email	Returns only mail messages (kind:mail can also be used).

kind:modifier	Description
kind:event	Returns calendar entries from the Calendar app.
kind:exe	Returns only developer files (files generated by Xcode, for example).
kind:folder	Returns only folders.
kind:font	Returns only fonts installed on the system.
kind:movies	Returns only movie files, as .mov or .avi files, or downloaded iTunes movies; to return only QuickTime movies, use kind:quicktime.
kind:music	Returns only audio files, such as MP3s or downloaded iTunes songs (kind:audio can also be used).
kind:pdf	Returns only PDF files.
kind:pic	Returns only images, such as JPEG or TIFF files ("kind:image" can also be used)—use kind:jpeg to return only JPEG images kind:tif to return only TIFF images, and use kind:gif to return only GIF images (sadly, kind:png will not return PNG files!).
kind:preferences	Returns only System Preferences configuration tools.
kind:presentation	Returns only presentations (that is, Microsoft PowerPoint or iWork KeyNote files)—use kind:powerpoint to return only PowerPoint files and kind:keynote to return only KeyNote files.
kind:spreadsheet	Returns only spreadsheets (that is, Microsoft Excel or iWork Numbers files)—use kind:excel to return only Excel files and kind:numbers to return only iWork Numbers files.

Searching via Label

You can also use label: to search for color-labeled files (that is, files that you've applied a color to by right-clicking them and selecting a color under the Label heading—see Tip 189, *Manage Projects with Colors*, on page 213). label: needs to be followed by the name of the color. For example, to use Spotlight to search for files colored red, you'd type label:red. The choices are red, orange, yellow, green, blue, purple, and gray.

Searching by Author

Using the author: keyword, you can specify the author of the document—the person who sent the email, for example, or the person listed within a Microsoft Office document as the author. Enclose the name in quotes if you specify more than one word: author:"keir thomas" will return documents and emails created by Keir Thomas, for example.

Limiting Spotlight Results to Particular Dates

You can have Spotlight return results only for those files created or modified on a particular day. To do so, type date: followed by today or yesterday in the search field to see only those files created or modified today or yesterday. You can also specify a date: date:10/3/2011 will return files created or modified on October 3, 2011, for example. (Those outside of the United States should use native date formats instead: date:3/10/2011, for example.)

You can also specify date ranges: date:8/1/2011-8/31/2011 will return files created or modified in the month of August 2011, for example.

Specifying Words NOT to Search For

Let's say you're using the Spotlight search tool to find emails mentioning getting an iPad as a present for your friend John. You perform a search using the keywords *ipad* and *john* and find that, along with the emails you're looking for, there are also emails from Frank discussing how cool the iPad is. You don't want to see those emails.

To stop a particular word from appearing in Spotlight's results, you can add a minus before it.

Using the previous example, the following would return results that specifically don't include any mention of Frank:

```
john ipad -frank
```

Another way to refine searches is to use AND, OR, and NOT (these are known as *Boolean operators*). For example, to search for a message containing either the word *ipad* or *tablet*, you could type the following:

```
ipad AND tablet
```

It's important that AND, OR, and NOT are typed in uppercase, because otherwise Spotlight will consider them part of the search string.

Tip 183

Jump Between Views in Finder

Finder offers four separate ways of viewing your files and folders: Icon view, List view, Column view, and Cover Flow. You can switch between them using the icons on Finder's toolbar (just above the file display area), but a quicker way to do so is to hold down Command and press 1, 2, 3, or 4 for Icon, List, Column, and Cover Flow views, respectively.

Tip 184

Reset Hardware Settings

Sometimes your Mac's hardware might start doing odd things. If you're having hardware problems, you might try one of two methods to reset various hardware settings.

Resetting the System Management Controller

The System Management Controller (SMC) controls power management hardware and lights on your Mac. If your Mac has problems such as constantly blowing its fans at full speed, refusing to turn off when you close the lid (if it's a portable Mac, of course), or LED lights doing odd things (particularly those that show battery charge), then you might try resetting the SMC.

To do so on a portable Mac that has a battery that can't be removed, shut down the computer and ensure the power cable is attached. Then hold down Shift+Control+Option and press the power button. Release, and then restart your computer in the usual way.

On a Mac with a battery that can be removed, shut down the computer and remove the battery. Disconnect the power supply, and then press and hold the power button for five seconds. Then reconnect, reattach everything, and boot as usual.

If you have an iMac or Mac Pro, simply shut down the computer and remove the power cable for at least fifteen seconds. Then reattach it and boot as usual.

Resetting the Parameter RAM

The Parameter RAM (PRAM) holds hardware settings that are set by the user and that are carried across reboots, such as the speaker volume or the key repeat rate. If you have problems such as your computer displaying a question mark each time it boots, external monitors not working as they should, or the computer seems unable to remember the sound settings across each boot, then you might like to try resetting the PRAM. To do this, reboot and—before the Apple logo appears and you hear the boot-time chime—hold down `Command` and `Option`, and then hold `P` and `R`. The system will restart. Release all keys, and let the computer boot as usual.

Tip 185

Force-Open a Document

You can drag and drop files onto any Dock icon to open them, but only if that application believes it can understand that particular type of file (for example, .doc files are understood by Microsoft Word). Unfortunately, some applications don't realize they can read certain types of files when they actually can.

Forcing an App to Open a File

To force an application in the Dock to at least attempt to open a file it doesn't believe it can, hold down `Option+Command` before clicking and dragging the file to the Dock. If the application genuinely can't understand the file, either nothing will happen or you'll see an error message.

Increasing the Chance of Success

For a higher probability of success when dragging to the Dock icon as described earlier, you might also try removing the file extension from the file before opening it as described (that is, the part after the dot in a filename, such as .jpg). To do so, select the file and hit `Command+I`. In the Name & Extension field of the dialog box that appears, remove the extension.

Note that removing the extension by simply renaming the file by any other method probably won't work, depending on your system's settings—the file will retain the extension but give the appearance of not doing so.

Don't forget to restore the file extension after attempting to open it!

Exploring OS X: iCloud

iCloud seamlessly synchronizes data and documents across all your Mac computers, as well as any Apple iPad, iPhone, or iPod touch devices you might own (provided they run the latest version of the iOS operating system). iCloud invisibly and silently uploads and downloads the data to and from Apple's server computers.

iCloud will ensure the same address book details are always used across all devices, for example, and will keep calendars and Safari bookmarks in sync without the user having to do a thing.

Provided the apps concerned are compatible, you can also save office documents to iCloud rather than your hard disk. Examples of iCloud-compatible apps include the most recent updates to Apple's iWork suite, along with the built-in OS X tools TextEdit and Preview. You could, for example, use Pages to create a document on your Mac and then instantly switch to your iPad to continue working on it, without the need to manually transfer files.

iCloud also includes the Photo Stream service, which automatically shares photos from your iPhone, iPad, or iPod touch between your devices. You can access the Photo Stream photos on a Mac too, but only if you have the latest versions of iPhoto or Aperture installed, although it's also possible to create shared photo albums that anybody can access on any computer via http://icloud.com.

iCloud includes the Find my Mac service, which lets you track down the approximate physical location of a lost or stolen Mac and lock the screen or show messages to anybody using the computer. You can remote wipe the computer to stop anybody from getting their hands on your data.

Also included as part of iCloud is the Back to My Mac service, which allows you to access your Mac across the Internet as if you're on the same local area network: you can share your Mac's screen, access your Mac's files, and SSH into the computer.

Setting up iCloud is usually done while installing OS X but can also be done by selecting the iCloud entry within System Preferences (Apple menu→System Preferences). You'll need an Apple ID to so do, and new iCloud accounts come with 5GB of free storage.[a] Within System Preferences, you can also choose which items are synced to iCloud by putting checks next to each entry in the list, and you can purchase more storage in addition to the gratis 5GB.

---

a.   https://appleid.apple.com

Tip 186

See What Free Disk Space There Is

You can find out how much disk space is free by right-clicking the icon in the title bar of any Finder window (the one to the left of the name of the folder) and selecting the bottom entry in the list, which will probably be the name of your computer.

Then right-click your Mac's hard disk icon in the Finder window and select Get Info. Look at the Available heading in the dialog box that appears.

To always have this info available, open Finder, and click View→Show Status Bar. Then look at the bottom of the Finder window to see the figure. You can also hit `Command+/` to toggle the status bar on and off, if you don't want to have it stick around all the time.

Tip 187

Find Forgotten Passwords

Often your Mac will ask whether you want to let it remember your login details for websites and even applications like Yahoo Messenger.

I make such heavy use of this feature that I often forget what the password was or even the account name in some cases. However, Macs make it easy to recover such details.

All passwords are stored in a secure keychain file, and you can use the Keychain Access program to get to it. It's found in the Utilities folder of the Applications list within Finder. When the program starts, ensure All Items is selected under the Category heading on the left, and then simply type the name of the website or application into the search field at the top right of the program window. Then double-click the entry you want in the list of results.

In the dialog box that appears, put a check in the Show Password box. You'll need to type your login password to authorize this, but once you're done, it will appear in plain text (ensure nobody can see your screen at this point, of course). Your login name will be listed above in the Account text field.

Tip 188

Get the Size of Multiple Files

You probably already know about the File Info window, which you can open by selecting a file and hitting Command+I. This shows details about the file, such as its size, where it was downloaded from (if applicable), and so on.

Highlighting several files at once and hitting Command+I doesn't do what you might expect. Instead of showing a combined info window, it opens individual Info dialog boxes for every single file you've selected.

The solution is to highlight the files in question and hit Option+Command+I instead. This will open the less-well-known Multiple Item Info dialog, showing the combined size of the files (useful if you're planning to burn them to CD or DVD, for example).

The Multiple Item Info dialog is dynamic; that is, you can Command+click additional files while it's open, and it will update to reflect the new total size.

Tip 189

Manage Projects with Colors

Files and folders can have color labels applied to them, which is to say that you can color them so that their filenames and icons in listings are outlined in red, blue, green, and so on. This is done by right-clicking the file or folder and selecting the color under the Label heading in the menu that appears.

The intention is to help users organize files. You could label all files for a particular project in the same color, for example, so they're easily identified.

Label colors can also be combined with saved searches as a method of instantly viewing all of a project's files, no matter where they've been saved on your hard disk.

Setting Up

Here's how to set it up:

1. Ensure files and folders you create for the project in question always have the same color label applied. Apply the color label to any existing files. Files can be bulk labeled by selecting them all and opening the Multiple Item Info dialog (see Tip 188, *Get the Size of Multiple Files*, on page 213)—just select from the entries beside the Label heading in the dialog box. Obviously, for this trick to work, you won't be able to use the color label you choose with any nonproject files!

2. Open Spotlight search (hit `Command`+`Space`) and then type label:, followed by the color. So if the project files are colored blue, I would type label:blue.

3. Listed beneath should be all the project files. At the top of the list of results in Spotlight will be an entry: Open All in Finder. Click this.

4. In the Finder window that appears, click the Save button near the top right, and—in the dialog box that appears—give the saved search a name, perhaps relating to the project. Be sure the Add to Sidebar button is checked, and then click the Save button.

Accessing the Saved Search

From then on, you'll see the saved search on the left of the Finder window in the Favorites list. Clicking it will show all the project files, no matter where you've saved them or what type of file they are. To create an alias of the search somewhere else, such as the desktop, right-click the search and select Open Enclosing Folder. In the Finder window that appears, click and drag the saved search to wherever you want the alias to live, but before releasing the mouse button, hold down `Option`+`Command`. Later, double-clicking the alias will open the search.

Tip 190

Make Movies, Screencasts, and Podcasts

Despite its name, QuickTime Player can help if you want to record a movie of yourself using your Mac's built-in camera and if you want to create a screencast (that is, a movie of what you're doing on-screen). You can also create audio podcasts using QuickTime Player.

Creating a Recording

Just start the application (open Finder, select Applications, and then double-click QuickTime Player), and click File→New Movie Recording, New Audio Recording, or New Screen Recording, depending on what you want to do.

In the window that appears, hit the red record button to start recording; hit it again to stop. When recording screencasts, there's an option to record the entire screen or to click and drag to record just a section of the screen area. Note that when recording the screen, the playback/record controls are visible while you're recording but don't appear in the actual movie.

To save the file, click the Close button on the QuickTime Player window. Note that for reasons fathomable to Apple's engineers, there *won't* be a Save option on the File menu, and the usual keyboard combination of Command+S won't work.

Altering Input Sources

To alter which camera or sound input is used, click the small down arrow to the right of the recording/playback controls before clicking the Record button. Note that when recording screencasts, no audio is recorded unless you specifically set your Mac's built-in microphone as an input source—to do so, click the down arrow at the right of the QuickTime controls, and choose an entry under the Microphone heading. See Figure 33, *Selecting a sound source when recording a screencast*, on page 216.

Exporting Your Creation for Use Online

Once a screen or movie recording has been made, you can instantly shrink it down for use online or sending via email by clicking File→Export To→Web. QuickTime will even save an HTML file (iFrame.html), which you can open by double-clicking for specific instructions on how to use video online.

You can also select an entry on the menu that appears when you click the Share Sheet button (top right on the controller bar) to automatically process and upload the file to social networking sites such as YouTube or Facebook. You'll need to provide your login details when prompted and provide posting details afterward (that is, any description text you might want to accompany the video).

To learn how to trim your home-recorded movies using QuickTime Player, see Tip 230, *Edit Movies*, on page 255.

Figure 33—Selecting a sound source when recording a screencast

Tip 191

Print from Finder

This tip is blindly obvious but little known: selecting one or more files in Finder and then clicking File→Print on the menu will automatically open the file(s) in the default editor (that is, a photo will open in Preview and so on) and automatically print it/them.

Tip 192

Add an Eject Button

Ejecting CDs or DVDs on Macs with optical drives can be a little cumbersome, especially if you're not using an Apple keyboard and therefore lack an eject key. Clicking the Eject icon next to the CD/DVD entry in Finder is perhaps the best method, but an even quicker way is to add an Eject button to the menu bar or Finder. Here's how to set it up.

Adding an Eject Icon to the Menu Bar

Open Finder, hit `Shift`+`Command`+`G`, and then type /System/Library/CoreServices/Menu Extras. Then double-click Eject.menu. The new button will instantly appear at the top right of the menu bar near the clock and will stay across reboots. Clicking it will show a menu that allows you to eject discs from the CD/DVD drive.

Holding down `Option` while clicking the icon and then selecting the Eject option beneath will force the CD/DVD drive to eject, even if it doesn't believe it has a disk in it—useful for when discs get "stuck" (see also Tip 231, *Eject a Stuck CD/DVD Disc*, on page 257).

To get rid of the new icon at any time, hold down `Command` and click and drag it away from the menu. Upon releasing the mouse button, it will disappear instantly.

Adding an Eject Icon to Finder

Right-click the toolbar within Finder, and select the Customize Toolbar option. Then, in the dialog box that appears, click and drag the Eject icon to a blank spot within the toolbar area (the Eject icon is in the top row of the dialog box icon listing).

In the future, all you need to do is select the CD/DVD disc in the list of Devices in the sidebar of Finder and then click this icon on the toolbar. Note that this button can also be used to eject things like USB memory sticks in the same way—just select them in the Devices list, and click the button.

To remove the new icon in the future, hold down `Command` and drag it up from Finder. Release the mouse button, and it'll disappear in a puff of smoke.

Tip 193

Access Hidden Menu Options

Holding down `Shift`, `Control`, or `Option` while viewing virtually any application or system menu will display various alternatives to standard menu choices. For example, selecting a file and then holding down `Option` and clicking Finder's File menu changes the Open option to Open and Close Window, which will open the selected file and then close the Finder window immediately afterward.

Try holding down a combination of the keys—for example, holding down Shift in addition to Option will reveal further hidden options.

The number of alternative options displayed varies depending on the support within the application, with the Mac's built-in applications being particularly well supported.

On some menus you might notice that holding down Option removes the ellipsis after an entry (that is, the three dots). This means that clicking that menu option will activate it right away without any confirmation or questions. For example, clicking the Apple menu, holding down Option, and hitting Shut Down will cause the Mac to attempt to shut down instantly, without a confirmation dialog box appearing (although you'll still be prompted to save files).

Incidentally, try this trick when a dialog box appears too—often you'll see that the dialog box buttons change to alternative options!

Tip 194

Instantly Search Google

Highlight some text in any application, and then drag and drop it onto the Safari icon in the Dock. This will instantly search Google (or your preferred search engine) using the text as a search query.

Tip 195

Enhance Your Login Picture with Visual Effects

On Macs that have a built-in camera, there's an option to take a quick snapshot of yourself when you first set up a new Mac. This photo then appears in the login window next to your username. But the pic can be easily enhanced, as follows:

1. Open the Contacts app (open Finder, select the Applications list, and double-click Contacts), and select your own entry in the list of contacts. If there's more than one entry, look for the one that—when selected—has the word *me* beneath the thumbnail preview of the login pic.

2. Double-click the thumbnail preview picture, and then click the pencil icon at the bottom left of the pop-out dialog box. Then click the circular button to the right of the preview of your login image.

3. This will open an effects palette similar to the one seen in Photo Booth, and clicking any of the previews will instantly apply the effect to your picture. See Figure 34, *Apply effects to your login pic*, on page 219. Click the left/right arrows beneath the effect previews to see more effects.

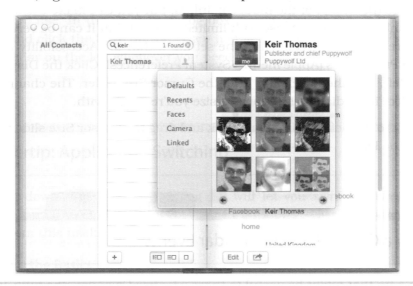

Figure 34—Apply effects to your login pic.

4. By holding down Option and clicking and dragging the image after you've applied the effect, you can also rotate it (also hold Shift to "snap" the image to points on the compass-like circle that appears). Simply clicking and dragging without Option will let you reposition the image within the frame, and clicking and dragging the zoom slider will let you zoom in and out.

5. Once you've finished, click the Done button at the bottom right of the pop-out window. Note that you can repeat these steps later and will be shown the original iSight/FaceTime HD snapshot once more without the effects you added, ready for a different set of effects to be applied.

You can also click the Camera tab on the left of the pop-out effects window to take an entirely new photo for your login pic—pose, and then click the Camera icon at the bottom left to take the snap.

Application Windows mode, which shows only the open windows for the current program. At this point, you can release the `Command` key and select a program window using the mouse.

Be aware that if a program is active (that is, there's a spotlight by its icon in the Dock) but it has no open windows, then all you'll see when you switch to Application Windows mode is a blank screen. You can resume switching through apps by once again holding down `Command` and tapping `Tab`.

Restoring Minimized Programs

It sounds complicated, but it's actually quite useful once you've mastered it.

If you switch to an app whose program windows are all minimized, it won't maximize, which is somewhat counterintuitive! However, a simple trick gets around this limitation, although it works best when there's only one app window open or when all an app's windows are minimized—if there's a mixture of minimized and maximized windows, it becomes a little unreliable.

Once the minimized application is highlighted in the switcher icon listing, press and hold `Option` and then release `Command`. The most recently minimized application window will now restore from the Dock. It's odd, but it works!

If the program isn't minimized but is simply open and not editing a document, holding down `Option` in this way will either create a new document—the equivalent of opening the app and clicking File→New—or open a File→New dialog box. Which you see depends on each app.

Quitting or Hiding Apps

To quit an application, just highlight the app in the list by tapping `Tab` and then tapping `Q`, keeping `Command` depressed. This is an excellent and quick way of pruning from memory apps that you're no longer using. Hitting `H` instead will hide the app in question in the Dock. If the app is already hidden, tapping `H` will unhide it.

Tip 199

Lock Files for Safety

You can manually lock any file on your Mac, which will prevent edits or deletion until the file is specifically unlocked. This can be useful if you have a master version of a file, for example, that you want to ensure remains sacrosanct. Folders can also be locked, which will prevent the folder or its contents from being edited or deleted.

If you try to edit a locked file, you'll be warned and will have to specifically opt to unlock the file.

Locking Files via File Info

There are several ways to lock a file or folder. The easiest is simply to select the file or folder in Finder or on the desktop and hit Command+I to open the File Info dialog box. Then put a check in the Locked box under the General heading.

To unlock a file or folder later, simply repeat the steps and remove the check.

Locking Files via Applications

Certain applications, including those built into OS X such as TextEdit, support file locking from within the application. Click the filename in the window's title bar, and select Lock from the pop-up menu that appears. For an example, see Figure 35, *Locking a file from within an application*. You can also select to unlock a locked file and browse previous versions (see *Exploring OS X: Autosave and Versions*, on page 280).

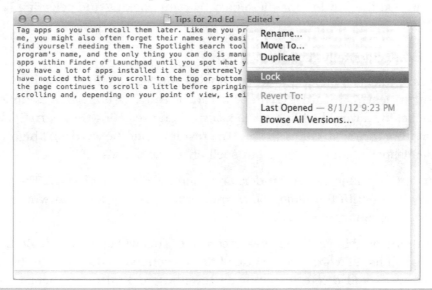

Figure 35—Locking a file from within an application

Tip 200

Correct Your Mac's Dictionary

Here's how to correct a few issues that arise with the built-in Mac spell-checking software that works in most apps.

Forcing Autocorrect to Learn Words

Some apps automatically correct what you type, replacing words with what OS X thinks are the correct ones. Needless to say, this doesn't work 100 percent all the time, and in particular autocorrect has an irritating habit of correcting slang or unusual names into other words.

The solution is dogged persistence: if you see that autocorrect has changed a word you've typed correctly, hit `Command`+`Z` to undo the correction, hit the Right cursor key, and then type the word a second time. Autocorrect will again correct the word, so again hit `Command`+`Z`. On the third time you'll find that autocorrect has now learned the word. This doesn't mean the word won't be highlighted as being incorrectly spelled—autocorrect's list of words is separate from the main dictionary used by OS X. However, as with any word, you can add the word to the dictionary by right-clicking and selecting Learn Spelling.

Deleting Accidentally "Learned" Words

Your Mac will spell-check text when you type, but you might have accidentally told it to "learn" a word that's spelled incorrectly. Usually this is done by right-clicking a word highlighted as incorrect and selecting the Learn Spelling option from the menu that appears. The result is that the word isn't highlighted as misspelled and is ignored in spell-checking passes.

To undo the damage, open Finder, and then hit `Shift`+`Command`+`G`. Then type ~/Library/Spelling into the dialog box, which will open the location where your personal dictionary is stored.

Once there, double-click the LocalDictionary file. This will open in TextEdit, and you'll see a list of words you've added to the dictionary. Just locate the misspelled word and delete it, removing the line break also (so there's still a continuous list of words without any blank lines). Then save the file. The changes should take effect immediately, but if they don't, try logging out and back in again.

Tip 201

Make the Volume Ultra-Quiet

If your Mac has built-in speakers, you'll be familiar with altering the volume using keyboard shortcuts (usually via the F11 and F12 keys). What you probably don't know is that there's a secret ultra-low volume setting.

To access it, press the volume decrease hotkey until the sound is muted (that is, the speaker icon on-screen is struck through). Now press the actual mute hotkey (usually F10). You'll see that the volume level is set at no bars. However, the sound *isn't* muted. In fact, it's a notch quieter than the lowest setting usually allowed—enough to hear things in a very quiet room.

Tip 202

View Application Icons Close-Up

This isn't the most useful tip in the world, but it's worth a try if you're a fan of your Mac's look and feel and want to explore more. Here are a variety of ways to view most Mac application icons, which are often high-quality works of art.

Using Preview

Go to the Applications folder within Finder, click the application whose icon you'd like to examine, and hit Command+C to copy it to the clipboard. Start Preview (open Finder, select the Applications list, and then double-click Preview) and hit Command+N to create a new file based on the clipboard contents. Hey, presto! You should now be able to view (and even save) the application icon in glorious high resolution. Several different sizes will be available, shown in the drawer at the side.

Looking Inside Packages

You can also look inside individual app packages to find the icon, along with any other icons the app uses. To do this, just find the app in the list within Finder, and then drag and drop it on top of the Preview icon on the Dock.

Figure 36—Viewing OS X icons at full resolution

All the icons and images contained within the application will appear in the drawer to the left. If you want to export one of the images or icons, just select it in the drawer; then hold down `Option` before clicking the File menu, and select the Save As option. Then type a filename and choose a location in the Save dialog box that appears.

Viewing the Core Set of Icons

If you'd like to take a look at the basic set of OS X icons, open a Finder window, hit `Shift`+`Command`+`G`, and type /System/Library/CoreServices/CoreTypes.bundle/Contents/Resources. Then double-click any .icns file to view (for an example, see Figure 36, *Viewing OS X icons at full resolution*, on page 226). To save any of the icons, hold down `Option` before clicking the File menu, and select the

Save As option. Then type a filename and choose a location in the Save dialog box that appears.

However, be careful not to alter anything within the folder! Doing so could damage your system.

Hack Dashboard/Mission Control Backgrounds

The wallpaper backgrounds that you see behind Dashboard and Mission Control can easily be replaced. They're actually patterned wallpaper tiles rather than large images, and they're repeated from left to right and from top to bottom along the screen. To replace them, you'll need to source a similar small pattern image that's designed to be repeated when used as desktop wallpaper, or you can choose image files that are the same size as your monitor resolution (beware: if an image is too small, OS X will repeat it, creating an ugly effect). You'll find many wallpaper pattern images by searching using Google.

Sadly, because of the way they handle wallpapers, this isn't a trick that will work with MacBook Pro computers with Retina displays.

The following steps modify system files, and this tip therefore affects all users of the computer. Ensure you have an up-to-date Time Machine backup. Like all tips that involve hacking system files, you might find your changes reverted to the default settings if you install a major operating system update. The solution is simply to repeat the steps.

Replacing the Main Wallpaper Images

Here are the steps for replacing the wallpapers:

1. Once you've found your designs, you'll have to convert them to PNG images, if they aren't already. To do so, open them in Preview by double-clicking them, and then click File→Export. Choose PNG from the Format drop-down list. Finally, click Save.

2. Rename the file you intend to use to replace the Mission Control wallpaper as defaultdesktop.png. Rename the file you intend to use for the Dashboard wallpaper as pirelli.png.

3. Open Finder and hit `Shift`+`Command`+`G`, typing the following in the dialog box that appears: /System/Library/CoreServices/.

4. Look for the `Dock` file. Right-click it and select Show Package Contents from the menu that appears.

5. In the new Finder window, browse to the `Contents` folder and then the `Resources` folder. Then locate the existing defaultdesktop.png and pirelli.png files in the folder, and drag them to a backup location on your hard disk (for example, your `Documents` folder). Keep these backups safe!

6. Now drag and drop your *new* defaultdesktop.png and pirelli.png files on top of the Finder window that is browsing the `Resources` folder.

7. Click the Authenticate button in the warning dialog box that appears, and then click the Replace button in the dialog box that warns about files already existing in the location. Type your password when prompted.

8. That's it! Log out and back in again for the changes to take effect.

Replacing the Dashboard Thumbnail Image

The only negative to this tip is that the thumbnail preview of Dashboard within Mission Control still uses the old Dashboard background. The image used for this miniature background is called mini_pirelli.png, and it's located in the same folder within the Dock package, like the images mentioned earlier.

The mini_pirelli.png thumbnail of the Dashboard is always 10 percent of your screen's resolution—on my MacBook's 1280 x 800 screen, the thumbnail is 128 x 80 pixels, for example, while on my 1920 x 1080 external monitor, the thumbnail is 192 x 108. This makes creating a replacement background for the Dashboard thumbnail easy—simply create a copy of the pirelli.png image you used earlier and reduce it to 10 percent. To do this in Preview, open the image, click Tools→Adjust Size, and change the Pixels drop-down in the dialog box to read Percent. Then enter 10 in the Width and Height fields and click OK. Then click File→Export and save the image as mini_pirelli.png. Replace the default version of the file within the Dock package, as described previously, backing up the original first.

Log out and back in again for the changes to take effect.

Restoring the Default Wallpapers

To restore the default wallpapers later, open a Finder window, hit `Shift`+`Command`+`G`, and type /System/Library/CoreServices/. Once again, right-click the Dock file, and select Show Package Contents, browsing to the Resources folder. Then locate the backups you made of the original two (or three) files and drag and drop them onto this Finder window. Again, you'll need to click the Authenticate button and the Replace button in the dialog boxes that appear. Type your password when prompted, and then log out and back in again for the changes to take effect.

Tip 204

View Tech Info When Logging In

Most Mac users are familiar with the login screen, which appears whenever you boot or reboot your Mac. Here are a handful of hacks to add info and text to it, although see also Tip 345, *Create a Login Message*, on page 354.

Add Login Screen Message

You can add a sentence or paragraph of text that will appear on the login screen. This can be useful when using MacBooks to set an "if lost" or anti-theft message, such as your phone number. Don't underestimate such low-fi technology! The majority of people who buy stolen hardware usually are aware that it's stolen.

To set a login message, open System Preferences (Apple menu→System Preferences), click the Security & Privacy tab, and then select the General tab. Unlock System Preferences if necessary by clicking the padlock icon at the bottom left, and then put a check in the box Show a Message When The Screen is Locked. Then click Set Lock Message, and type your message—something like this will do: "If you're reading this, this Mac is lost or stolen. Please phone 555-1234 to arrange return." Remember that hitting Option+Command+T will open the Character Selection window, and any of the symbols there can be used.

Once done, click OK. The message will now be set. To remove it, simply remove the check alongside Show a Message When The Screen is Locked.

View Tech Info

At the top right of the screen is a brief display showing the time, along with things like details about the Wi-Fi connection and battery power, in the case of a portable Mac. Note that those using FileVault won't see this info because a different login screen technology is used, although they will see it if they log out while using their Mac.

Altering a secret setting allows you to add a little extra functionality so that when the time display is clicked, the info display will switch to showing the computer's IP address, then the name of the computer, and then the build version number of the operating system.

To make the change, which affects all users of the system, open a Terminal window (open Finder, select the Applications list, and then in the list of applications double-click Terminal within the Utilities folder), and type the following (note there is a space between AdminHostInfo and 1). You'll be prompted to enter your login password afterward, so do so:

```
sudo defaults write /Library/Preferences/com.apple.loginwindow AdminHostInfo
      1
```

Then log out to test it. Click the time display to cycle through the information displays.

To revert to the default display showing only the time, open a Terminal window, and type the following:

```
sudo defaults delete /Library/Preferences/com.apple.loginwindow AdminHostInfo
```

Tip 205

Send Somebody a Listing of your Forthcoming Events

Ever wanted to send somebody a text listing of the things you're doing over the coming week/month so they can work out when best to schedule a meeting with you?

It's easily done. Just open Calendar, switch to week/month view (and navigate to the relevant date, of course), hit Ctrl+A to select all the events, and press Ctrl+C to copy them to the clipboard. You'll be warned in the case of recurring events that you're only copying the events that fall in that week/month, but this is fine. Then start a new email, document, or IM conversation and hit Ctrl+V to paste a listing of all the appointments that you viewed within Calendar, neatly sorted by date and time, and with complete descriptions.

You don't have to select all the events. You can also hold down `Command` and click some of the events to select them individually, which you can then copy and paste into an email/document/instant message as described earlier.

Boot via an Apple Remote

If you use your Mac's Bootcamp feature to install Windows alongside OS X, you might already be aware of the menu that lets you choose between operating systems at boot time or accessing the repair system. Holding `Option` before the Apple logo appears during booting should make the menu appear.

However, another way of seeing it is to press and hold the Menu button on an Apple remote as the computer boots up.

Organize Mail by Color Schemes

You might already know that you can "flag" email messages in the Mail app by right-clicking the mail's entry in the list and selecting one of the colored flag icons. This can help you find the email in a hurry. However, you can also make each entry in the email list a particular color, and although doing so is easy, it's far from obvious how.

Select a message in the list within Mail, and then hit `Shift`+`Command`+`C` to bring up the Colors palette. Then select a color you want. You can choose any color of the rainbow. Note that you won't see the coloring until you select a different mail within the list.

To remove the coloring, again select the mail in the list and bring up the Color palette; then select the pure white color.

Exploring OS X: FileVault

FileVault lets you protect data on the start-up disk of your Mac from snoopers in a way that'll have no impact on the way you use your computer. You won't even know the disk is protected, and the only difference will be that you'll have to provide your login password immediately after powering up or rebooting rather than at the login screen a minute or two after the computer has started.

The protection offered by FileVault in OS X is industrial strength: XTS-AES 128 encryption. Anybody who steals your Mac will be simply unable to either boot the computer without your password or access any of the contents on the hard disk by removing the disk from the computer and attaching it to a different computer (so-called *forensic analysis*). However, there's one theoretical vulnerability, which is that if you sleep your computer between uses, a hacker could forensically examine the memory contents to uncover your password. This is extremely difficult to do even with the highly specialized knowledge and equipment that would be required, but in any case the possibility can be circumvented by the truly paranoid by shutting down their computer whenever they're not using it.

FileVault can be activated by opening System Preferences, clicking Security & Privacy, and then selecting the FileVault tab. The disk will have to be initially encrypted, which will take several hours, but that happens in the background, and you can still use your computer while it happens (and even sleep the computer or shut it down). Check back on the Security & Privacy pane of System Preferences periodically to see its progress.

Tip 208

Stop Automatic File Opening

When you start a program, OS X will attempt to open any files that were open the last time you quit the app. This is either very useful or extremely annoying, depending on your personal preference, but here's how to take control of this feature.

Permanently Deactivating App Restore Systemwide

You can permanently deactivate this feature in System Preferences (Apple menu→System Preferences). Click the General icon and then check Close Windows When Quitting an Application.

Temporarily Deactivating for an Individual App

However, if you want to temporarily deactivate automatic file restore for a particular application when you're quitting it (so that it'll open "clean"), simply quit the app using the `Option`+`Command`+`Q` keystroke rather than the usual `Command`+`Q` key combination. Alternatively, hold down `Option` before clicking the Quit option on the program's menu—you'll see the menu option change to Quit and Close All Windows.

Permanent Disabling for an Individual App

It's also possible to permanently deactivate the feature on an app-by-app basis. You could turn it off for TextEdit, for example, while leaving it active for all other apps. Here are the steps required:

1. Quit the app in question if it's running, open a Terminal window (open Finder, select the Applications list, and then in the list of applications double-click Terminal within the Utilities folder), and type defaults write; then follow it with -app and then the name of the app, followed by NSQuitAlwaysKeepsWindows -bool FALSE. The line for TextEdit would read as follows, as an example:

    ```
    defaults write -app TextEdit NSQuitAlwaysKeepsWindows -bool FALSE
    ```

    The following deactivates the feature for Pages, which is part of Apple's iWork Suite:

    ```
    defaults write -app Pages NSQuitAlwaysKeepsWindows -bool FALSE
    ```

2. For non-Apple apps such as Microsoft or Adobe applications, it's instead necessary to specify the *preferences domain* within the command line. Don't worry—this simply means a command similar to the following for a Microsoft Office app, which will deactivate the feature for Microsoft Word, although you could swap out Word for Excel, PowerPoint, and so on, to deactivate the feature for those particular apps:

    ```
    defaults write com.microsoft.Word NSQuitAlwaysKeepsWindows -bool FALSE
    ```

    The following will disable the feature for Excel:

    ```
    defaults write com.microsoft.Excel NSQuitAlwaysKeepsWindows -bool FALSE
    ```

    For Adobe Create Suite apps, use the following line, which will deactivate the feature for Photoshop, although you can again swap out Photoshop for the name of any other Creative Suite app, such as Illustrator:

    ```
    defaults write com.adobe.Photoshop NSQuitAlwaysKeepsWindows -bool FALSE
    ```

3. Restart the app. The changes will take effect immediately. Note that with some apps, the first time you run the app, it might restore its old windows. However, quitting and restarting once more will put a stop to it.

Should you want to reactivate window restore for the app, quit the app and open a Terminal window. Then type the following for Apple apps, again substituting the name of the app (the following will reinstate window restore for TextEdit):

```
defaults delete -app TextEdit NSQuitAlwaysKeepsWindows
```

For Microsoft Office apps, use the following, again substituting Word if necessary for the name of the app in question:

```
defaults delete com.microsoft.Word NSQuitAlwaysKeepsWindows
```

For Adobe Creative Suite apps, you can use the following, again substituting Photoshop if necessary for the name of the app in question:

```
defaults delete com.adobe.Photoshop NSQuitAlwaysKeepsWindows
```

Quit and restart the app for the changes to take effect. Again, you might have to quit and open the app once more for the changes to actually take effect. You might also try logging out and back in again.

Tip 209

Create Encrypted Archives for All Computers

Elsewhere I explained how to create encrypted archives for use under OS X (see Tip 126, *Secure All Your Files Against Hackers*, on page 137). But if you also own a Windows or Linux computer, you might want to create cross-platform encrypted archives that you can copy to, say, a USB stick and carry around with you.

Luckily, a piece of open source (and therefore free) software called TrueCrypt provides this functionality. TrueCrypt works by creating an encrypted filestore. This single file is then mounted by the operating system and accessed as a virtual disk drive in a similar way to when you attach a USB memory stick.

When you've finished, you unmount it, thus "locking" the store so that nobody can access it without typing the password.

Setting Up and Installing

Start by downloading TrueCrypt from http://www.truecrypt.com. Select the Mac OS X ".dmg package" release. You might also choose to download the versions for any other operating systems you'd like to use your new filestore under.

Once the download has finished, install the software by browsing to the location you downloaded it to, double-clicking the .dmg file and then right-clicking the .mpkg installation file, and selecting Open. You'll be warned that the package is from an unidentified developer, but this is fine—just click the Open button in the dialog box.

Creating an Encrypted Archive

Run the program (you can find it in Applications). The following instructions explain how to create an initial encrypted filestore:

1. Encrypted filestores are known as *volumes*. So, click the Create Volume button in the middle left of the program window. A wizard will appear. Ensure that "Create an encrypted file container" is selected, and click Next. (Note that the second option, "Create a volume within a partition/drive," might seem to suit your needs better, but creating a container file allows the encrypted filestore to be transferred easily from one USB key stick to another, if need be; thus, it's the best choice here.)

2. Select the type of volume you want to create. The default choice of Standard TrueCrypt volume is fine. You might want to investigate the Hidden TrueCrypt volume option at some point, but it has a specific purpose and adds some complications. When done, click Next.

3. On the Volume Location screen, click Select File to type a filename and select a location for the new archive. By default TrueCrypt archives don't need a file extension, but it's a good idea to give it one, so add the extension .tc. This will enable you to double-click the filestore to open it in Windows. Once you're done, click the Save button in the dialog box; click the Next button in the wizard to move to the next step.

4. You'll be invited to choose the encryption algorithm you want to use. You can select each in the list to read a description underneath the list showing the pros and cons of each choice. AES is a good choice for most uses. You can also change the hash algorithm if you want, but there shouldn't be any need to do this. Once you are done, click Next.

5. Now you'll be prompted to enter the size of the filestore. If you've chosen to create the filestore on a USB stick, you'll be told how much free space is available. You can't enter fractions of a gigabyte or megabyte, so to enter 1.9GB, for example, you would need to select MB from the drop-down list and type 1946 into the Volume Size textbox (bearing in mind that there are 1024MB in 1GB, so 1.9 x 1024 = 1945.6). Once you're done, click Next.

6. Now you'll be invited to choose a password for the archive. As always, a good password involves both lowercase and uppercase characters and should be as long as you can make it while still being possible to remember. Avoid clichés or anything else that might be easily guessed. Click Next when done.

7. You'll now be asked to choose the filesystem for the filestore. FAT is the best choice because it's understood by Windows, Mac OS X, and Linux. Click Next when you've made your choice.

8. Next you'll go to the volume format screen. However, first you must create some random data for the encryption process. As strange as it might seem, this is done by waving the mouse pointer around within the True-Crypt program window. So, wave the pointer around for a few seconds, and then click the Format button. After this, the filestore will be created. This might take some time for larger archives. Once it's done, click Exit.

Accessing the Filestore

After creating the filestore, you must mount it so it's accessible. Follow these steps to do so—the instructions are essentially the same for versions of TrueCrypt running on all operating systems:

1. Start TrueCrypt if it isn't already running, as described earlier, and in the main TrueCrypt dialog box, select 1 under the Slot heading.

2. Click the Select File button. Navigate to your new filestore using the file-browsing dialog box, and click the Open button. Back in the TrueCrypt window, click the Mount button. You'll immediately be prompted for the archive's password, so type it. After this, a new drive icon should appear in the Devices list in the Finder sidebar offering access to the encrypted filestore, as if a new drive had been connected to the system. It'll probably be called NO NAME. You can drag and drop files to it, just like any removable storage device.

3. Note that you'll need to keep the TrueCrypt program running while using the archive file. However, you can close the program window, which will leave TrueCrypt running in the Dock. It's also possible to configure TrueCrypt to quit without unmounting the archive: on the menu, click TrueCrypt→Preferences, ensure the Security tab is selected, and remove the check from the TrueCrypt Quits box.

4. Once you've finished using the filestore, you can simply unmount it in the usual way: open Finder, and click the Eject icon next to the filestore's entry in the devices list. Alternatively, start TrueCrypt again, select the archive's entry in the list, and click the Dismount button.

When the filestore is mounted, a useful tip is to click Favorites→Add Selected Volume to Favorites. From then on, you can quickly mount the filestore by selecting its entry on the Favorites menu when you start TrueCrypt. You should also be able to right-click the TrueCrypt icon in the Dock when the program is running and click the entry there to automatically mount it.

Tip 210

Look Up Words Instantly

One of my favorite features of my Mac is the Dictionary application, which, just like its dusty, shelf-bound companions, allows you to look up the definitions of words.

However, there's no need to go to the trouble of actually starting the app to look up definitions. It can be called from within other applications in various ways.

Using Spotlight

Typing a word or short phrase into Spotlight will return a definition, for example, although it will appear beneath all the files and folders that match the search term, alongside a Look Up heading.

If you then hover the mouse cursor over this entry, a pop-out window will appear showing the definition. Double-click the pop-out window to open the Dictionary app showing the word.

Right-Clicking for Definitions

In some apps, you can right-click a word and select the Look Up option from the menu that appears. Alternatively, you can highlight a word and click the application menu and then click Services→Look Up in Dictionary.

Using Keyboard Shortcuts

In some apps, you can hover the mouse cursor over a word and then hit Control+Command+D to see a pop-out window showing the definition of the word (see Figure 37, *Looking up a word instantly*, on page 239). This works largely in built-in OS X apps like Safari.

Gesturing for Word Lookup

If you use a multitouch trackpad, you can also hover the mouse cursor over a word and tap with three fingers bunched together (tap, not click!). This will cause a pop-out window to appear, showing the definition along with a Thesaurus lookup (if one exists) and a Wikipedia entry (again, if there is one for that word). To get rid of the pop-up window, just click anywhere outside of the pop-out. Looking up words this way takes some practice to do right, and it can take a few seconds for the pop-up to appear.

By clicking any of the headings in the pop-out window, such as Dictionary, Thesaurus, or Wikipedia, you'll instantly be switched to the Dictionary app showing the relevant entry for that word, with the window scrolled to the Dictionary, Thesaurus, or Wikipedia section, depending on which heading you clicked.

Tip 211

Turn Off Download "Quarantining"

Whenever you download a file using a web browser, your Mac might warn you when you first open it that it could be dangerous because it's from an unidentified source. It'll tell you when you downloaded it and from where. This is known as *quarantining* and can get annoying after a while, especially if you download files only from sources you know are safe.

Quarantining is separate from the Gatekeeper feature of OS X (see Tip 50, *Install Any App Without Being Blocked*, on page 55), which means that even

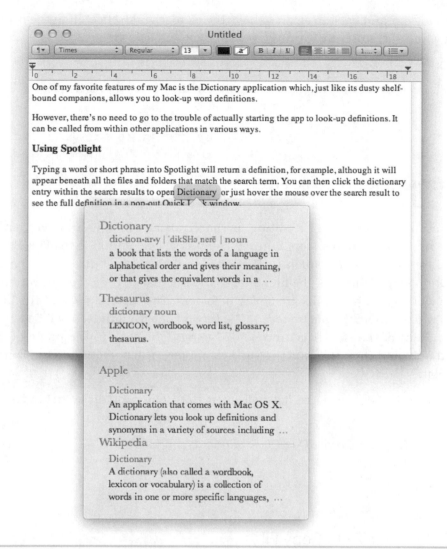

One of my favorite features of my Mac is the Dictionary application which, just like its dusty shelf-bound companions, allows you to look-up word definitions.

However, there's no need to go to the trouble of actually starting the app to look-up definitions. It can be called from within other applications in various ways.

Using Spotlight

Typing a word or short phrase into Spotlight will return a definition, for example, although it will appear beneath all the files and folders that match the search term. You can then click the dictionary entry within the search results to open Dictionary, or just hover the mouse over the search result to see the full definition in a pop-out Quick Look window.

Figure 37—Looking up a word instantly

if you bypass Gatekeeper's warnings, you'll be warned a second time because of the quarantining feature!

To permanently turn off quarantining, open a Terminal window (open Finder, select the Applications list, and then in the list of applications double-click Terminal within the Utilities folder), and type the following:

```
defaults write com.apple.LaunchServices LSQuarantine -bool FALSE
```

Then log out and back in again to have the changes take effect. If in the future you want to restore the warning system, type the following:

```
defaults delete com.apple.LaunchServices LSQuarantine
```

You'll need to log out and back in again for the changes to take effect.

Where Does This File Live?

Sometimes I open a file for editing, perhaps one attached to an email, and I have no idea where it's stored on my computer. One option is to click File→ Save to see this information in the Save As dialog box, but a much easier solution is to right-click the filename in the title bar of the program window. This will show a hierarchical display of folders. The top one nearest the file's icon will be where the file is stored. The second one from the top will be where the parent of that folder is, and so on, going right back to the name of the hard disk and then the name of your computer, which should be the last in the list.

Selecting any entry in the list will open that folder (or disk) in Finder for browsing.

See also Tip 150, *Create One-Click Shortcuts*, on page 174.

Cut Rather Than Copy Files

This is a subtle but useful tip. If you use keyboard shortcuts to copy and paste files from one place to another, you'll know that it's not possible to move files. Hitting Command+X—the keyboard shortcut for Cut—simply doesn't work, and the Cut option on the Edit menu when Finder is selected is grayed out.

You can in fact move a file using keyboard shortcuts but in a slightly obscure way. Hit Command+C to copy the file, but hit Command+Option+V when it comes to pasting it into a new folder, rather than Command+V. This will move the file from the old destination to the new one.

If you like to use the Edit menu to move files around, hold down the `Option` key while accessing it (after first copying the file in the usual way), and you'll see a Move Item Here option appear, which has the same effect as using `Command`+`Option`+`V`.

Tip 214

Avoid the Spring-Load Wait

If you drag and hover a file over the icon for a folder for long enough (in both Finder windows and on the desktop), a new Finder window will pop out, wherein you can see the contents and deposit the file. This feature is known as *spring-loaded folders*, and you can alter the delay before the new Finder window appears by changing the setting in Finder's Preferences dialog box (application menu→Preferences, and ensure the General pane is selected).

However, if you're in a rush, simply drag and hover the file as described, and then hit `Space` to cause the new Finder window to spring out immediately.

Dock icons are spring-loaded too—if an app is running, you can drag a file onto its icon, and after a few seconds, the app will switch to Application Windows mode of Mission Control, and you can drop the file into whichever of the app's window you want. However, if you hit `Space` as soon as you drag the file to the Dock icon, it'll instantly switch to Application Windows mode with no delay. You can then hover the dragged file over a window and hit `Space` again to make that app window instantly come to the foreground, ready for you to drop the file onto.

(For what it's worth and although it's hard to see a situation where this could prove useful, if an app *isn't* running, hitting `Space` while you're dragging a file on top of it will cause the app to launch instantly.)

Drag a file onto a Dock stack, and within a few seconds, a Finder window will temporarily open showing that folder for as long as you're dragging the file (that is, dragging a file onto the Downloads stack, and a Finder window appears showing the contents of your Downloads folder). Hit `Space`, however, and the Finder window will pop up instantly.

Tip 215

Print Envelopes

If your printer is compatible with envelopes, you can use the Contacts app to print addresses on them. Just select a contact, and then click File→Print. Selecting multiple contacts will let you print more than one envelope at a time. This tip works well if you create groups; see Tip 175, *Create Groups of Contacts*, on page 198.

Tip 216

Turn Off Drag and Drop

If you find you often accidentally drag and drop text within applications (which is to say, you accidentally select some text and then accidentally drag and drop it to a new location—something especially easy to do with a trackpad), you can turn it off with a secret setting.

To turn it off for all apps, type the following into a Terminal window (open Finder, select the Applications list, and then in the list of applications double-click Terminal within the Utilities folder):

```
defaults write -g NSDragAndDropTextDelay -int -1
```

Then log out and back in again.

To reactivate for all apps, type the following into a Terminal window:

```
defaults delete -g NSDragAndDropTextDelay
```

To deactivate it for a particular app, first quit the app in question. Then type what appears next, replacing the text after -app with the app's name; the following deactivates text drag and drop for TextEdit:

```
defaults write -app TextEdit NSDragAndDropTextDelay -int -1
```

The following deactivates it for Safari:

```
defaults write -app Safari NSDragAndDropTextDelay -int -1
```

To reactivate text drag and drop for that app, type the following into a Terminal window, again replacing the app name; the following reenables text drag and drop in Safari:

```
defaults delete -app Safari NSDragAndDropTextDelay
```

Tip 217

Quickly Upload Files Using Safari

If you're uploading a file to a website in Safari, you might see a button that —when clicked—opens a file-browsing dialog box in which you can choose the file. To save a little time, you can usually just drag and drop the file from the desktop or a Finder window onto the button, saving the need to use the file browser. Click it to begin the upload procedure.

Tip 218

Map an Address You've Been Sent

If you come across a contact address in a document in any of your Mac's built-in applications or come across one in a web page, simply highlight the whole thing and right-click the selection. Then click Show Address in Google Maps. As you might guess, this will perform an instant lookup of the address using Google Maps.[14]

If you see an address in a mail message, hovering the mouse over it should reveal an arrow icon that, when clicked, will show a menu offering a Show Address in Google Maps option.

In both cases, the addresses will have to be full and not abbreviated or shortened—something like "1 Infinite Loop, Cupertino, CA 95014" will work fine, but OS X will fail to recognize something like "1 Infinite Loop, 95014" as an address.

---

14. http://maps.google.com

Tip 219

Install Apps on All Your Macs

Did you know that if you have several Mac computers within your home, you can legally install any apps you buy through the Mac App Store on all the Macs without having to pay anything extra? This requires you to sign into the Mac App Store with the same Apple ID on each of the computers. Then click the Purchases tab, and you'll see listed all the apps you've ever bought. Just click the Install button alongside any of them to install them.

You can also configure the Mac App Store to automatically install on that particular Mac any apps you purchase on another Mac—keeping all your Macs up-to-date with your purchases. Open System Preferences (Apple menu →System Preferences), and then click the Software Update icon. Then check Automatically Download Apps Purchased on Other Macs.

Note that none of this applies to business or educational users, for whom a volume licensing system is available.[15]

Tip 220

Move the Cursor When Using Page Up/Page Down

Here's an annoying "gotcha" that you might find catches you out when editing text.

If you have a desktop Mac (or use a full-sized keyboard with your portable Mac), you might use the `Page Up`/`Page Down` keys to quickly navigate in documents. However, you might also be aware of an issue: although the text moves up and down, the cursor stays where it was last used. When you start typing, the document immediately scrolls back to its previous position. Grrr!

Luckily, there's a way around it. Hold `Option` while hitting the `Page Up`/`Page Down` keys. This will cause the text to scroll up or down a page and cause the cursor to jump to the middle of each page. You can then move it to where you'd like to start editing.

---

15. See http://www.apple.com/mac/volume-licensing/.

Incidentally, Mac notebook users (and those using Apple wireless keyboards) can hold down the `Fn` key while hitting the Up/Down cursor keys to emulate `Page Up` / `Page Down`.

Tip 221

Jump Around Open/Save Dialog Boxes

When saving new files, you are usually taken to iCloud, if you have it enabled, or to the last location where you saved a file on the disk (or the app's default Save location if you're using it for the first time). If you want to save the file elsewhere, it can be cumbersome navigating there.

However, if you already have a Finder window open browsing where you want to save, just click and drag the *proxy icon* from the Finder window to the Where drop-down list within the app's Save As dialog box. You'll instantly be switched to that location.

The proxy icon is the little icon in the title bar of the Finder window, to the left of the name of the folder you're currently browsing. You'll need to click and hold for a second before it detaches, and you can drag it away.

If you instead drop the proxy icon in the filename field, you'll see a Go To dialog box asking you to confirm you want to switch directories. Just click the Go button.

This trick works in File Open dialog boxes, too.

Tip 222

Regain Control of a Crashed Mac

Very occasionally an application might crash so badly that it appears to lock up your Mac. You might see the "beach ball of death," that spinning color wheel that indicates your Mac is too busy to respond to you.

There are various ways of attempting to regain control, as follows.

Forcing a Quit

If the app has crashed, right-clicking its Dock icon will probably show a Force Quit menu entry. Click this to force the app to quit. If there's no Force Quit entry, hold down `Option`, and it will appear.

You can also hold down `Option`+`Command` and tap `Esc` to bring up the Force Quit dialog box. From there you can select the app and click the Force Quit button.

Using a Keyboard Shortcut

The following might work if the app simply won't quit, but beware that it terminates the app without offering the chance to save data: click the Dock icon for the app, and then hold down `Shift`+`Option`+`Command`+`Esc` for three seconds. You'll know instantly whether it has worked because the app will vanish.

Forcibly Rebooting the Computer

If that doesn't work and the computer is simply unresponsive, the only solution might be to restart the computer. Holding down `Control` and `Command` and hitting the power button will forcibly shut down your computer (on a MacBook Air or MacBook Pro with Retina screen, you must hit `Control`+`Option`+`Command` and the power button). Be aware that you won't get a chance to save files, although OS X will otherwise shut down correctly, avoiding the possibility of system files becoming corrupted. Press the power button once after shutdown to restart.

If that doesn't work, hold down the power button for five seconds. This simply powers down the computer instantly, so, again, you won't get a chance to save any open files. Because of the slight risk of system files getting damaged, this method should be considered a last resort if nothing else works.

Tip 223

Turn a Clipboard Image into a File

If you've copied an image within a web page or a document and want to turn it into a file, just open Preview (open Finder, select the Applications list, and then double-click Preview), and then hit File→New from Clipboard. This will create a new file containing the image. Click File→Save to save the file in whatever format you want: select the format from the Format drop-down list in the Save As dialog box. Hold down `Option` before clicking the Format drop-down list for a wider option of filetypes.

Tip 224

Leap Around the Desktop via the Keyboard

Moving your hand to grab the mouse while you're working can be a concentration killer. Luckily, it's mostly possible to move around your Mac's desktop using the keyboard.

Activating the Main Menu

To activate the menu, hit `Control`+F2 (on portable Macs, or Macs with an aluminum keyboard, you'll have to hit `Fn`+`Control`+F2). You can then navigate from menu to menu using the Left/Right cursor keys, and you can open a menu using the Down cursor key. Press Up/Down to select menu options; hitting `Return` will select an option. Hit `Esc` to deactivate the selection highlight.

Activating the Dock

Hitting `Control`+F3 (or `Fn`+`Control`+F3) will do the same for the Dock. Use the Left/Right cursor keys to move the selection highlight, press `Return` to start or switch to an app, and hit the Up cursor key to activate the application menu (the same one you see if you right-click the Dock icon). Hit `Esc` to deactivate the selection highlight.

Tip 225

Make Email Desktop Shortcuts

Here's a nice trick for anybody who emails the same person frequently and would like to create a desktop shortcut that, when double-clicked, will instantly create a new message addressed to that individual.

The shortcut doesn't have to live on the desktop. You could create a folder full of these email shortcuts and access them via Finder, or you could click and drag them to the top of a Finder window to create a one-click shortcut.

Locking via a Menu Icon

A little-known way to lock the screen is to use a feature of your Mac's Keychain Access application, which ordinarily handles password and certificate security for your Mac. Start the application (open Finder, select the Applications list, and then double-click Keychain Access within the Utilities folder), and select Preferences from the application menu. After ensuring the General tab is selected in the dialog box that appears, put a check next to Show Keychain Status in Menu Bar.

You'll now see a padlock icon appear at the top right of the screen near the time display (you can now quit Keychain Access because we're finished with it). Clicking the padlock will show a menu with a Lock Screen menu option.

To remove the padlock icon later, hold down `Command` and simply drag the icon onto the desktop. Upon releasing the mouse button, it will disappear.

Locking via Touching a Screen Corner

You can also set up your Mac so that pushing the mouse cursor into a particular corner of the screen activates sleep mode. To set this up, start System Preferences (Apple menu→System Preferences), click the Mission Control button, and then click the Hot Corners button. Click the drop-down list next to whichever corner(s) you'd like to use and select either Put Display to Sleep or Start Screen Saver, if you don't want to leave the screen black. Then click the OK button.

Tip 228

Switch Which App Edits a File You're Working On

Let's say you're tweaking a photo in Preview and decide you need the full power of Adobe Photoshop.

Look at Preview's title bar. You'll see the name of the file currently being worked upon. To the left of this will be a small icon representing the file. This is known as the *proxy icon*. Click and hold it for a few seconds, and then drag and drop the icon to the Photoshop icon on your Dock or to the Photoshop icon in Applications. The most recent version of the file will open in Photoshop (to learn about *versions*, see *Exploring OS X: Autosave and Versions*, on page 280).

OS X for Admins and Software Developers

Mac OS X is a version of Unix and a POSIX-compliant operating system. The heart of Mac OS X, including the kernel, is called Darwin, which evolved from the Berkeley Software Distribution (BSD).

Within the Utilities folder in Applications, you'll find a Terminal program that will provide a Bash command prompt, although various other shells are available, such as csh, ksh, zsh, and so on. Each can be called in the usual way by typing its name at a Terminal prompt. Users can change their default shell by opening System Preferences, clicking Users & Groups, unlocking System Preferences, right-clicking their username in the list on the left, and then selecting Advanced Options. A choice can then be made from the Login Shell drop-down list.

Many contemporary Linux/Unix open source technologies and scripting languages are included in a standard Mac OS X installation. For example, the Python, Ruby, and Perl programming languages are present, as is the Apache web server software.

A standard Mac OS X desktop installation can be expanded into a fuller Unix implementation using Homebrew, MacPorts, or Fink.[a] The chflags command can be used to reveal within Finder the usually hidden Unix filesystem hierarchy: open a Terminal window, and type sudo chflags -h nohidden /*.

The Xcode package is available from the Mac App Store for free and provides a sophisticated IDE, interface builder, and other developer tools geared toward creating apps for OS X and also iOS. Note that command-line developer tools like the GNU Compiler Collection (gcc) must be installed manually from within the Preferences dialog box of Xcode.

When creating OS X apps, developers are encouraged to work within the Cocoa application programming interface, which can be accessed via a variety of contemporary languages, although Apple encourages programmers to develop in Objective-C, which adds a subset of object-oriented extensions to ANSI C.

---

a.   See http://mxcl.github.com/homebrew/, http://www.macports.org, and http://www.finkproject.org, respectively.

It's a good idea to close Preview following this. Otherwise, attempting to save the file in Photoshop will show an error message saying the file is in use.

Instead of dropping the proxy icon onto the Dock icon, while still in the process of dragging the icon you can tap Command+Tab to bring up the application switcher and drop the proxy icon on top of the program's icon in the switcher display.

Note that this same technique of dragging and dropping the proxy icon also works if you want to insert an image you're working on into a word processing document (although this example could be any file type and any kind of document). In the image editor, save the file if you haven't already, and then drag the proxy icon on top of the word processor or layout program's window where you'd like to insert it. It will be inserted instantly.

Tip 229

Supertip: Take Control of PDFs

Preview is the Mac's highly capable image viewer, and it also displays PDFs. You'll find it within the Applications list of Finder. But that's just the start of its abilities when it comes to these document files. Several tips are listed here, but see also the longer Tip 356, *Add Your Signature to Docs*, on page 370.

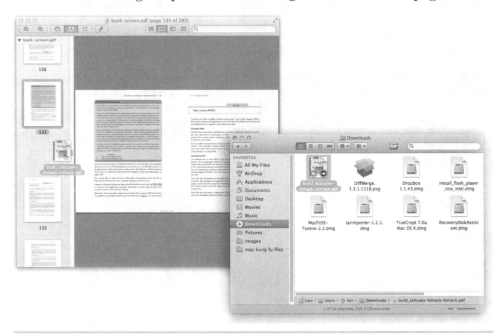

Figure 38—Merging one PDF with another

Annotating PDFs

Preview has reasonably sophisticated annotation facilities built in that you can use to add notes or markings to a PDF. Look under the Tools→Annotate menu. Once you've made a selection, click and drag anywhere on the page to add the annotation.

You can add the annotations toolbar by clicking the pen icon on the standard toolbar (left of the search field at the top right of the program window). The annotations toolbar provides quicker access to annotations functions.

Combining PDFs

To combine two or more PDFs, open the first of them in Preview and then ensure the thumbnails sidebar is visible (View→Thumbnails). Locate in Finder the second PDF you want to combine with the first, and drag it on top of the thumbnail sidebar of the first PDF in Preview's sidebar. For an example, see Figure 38, *Merging one PDF with another*, on page 252. You can insert the new document anywhere within the page order of the original file—the existing pages will slide out of the way to make a gap for you to drop in the new file.

To insert pages, you can also simply select a page within the thumbnail list on the left, after which the pages will be inserted, and then click Edit→Insert →Page from File (although the title of this menu entry is a misnomer—you can actually insert multipage PDFs). Note the other entries on the Insert menu too—you can insert a blank page and also scan in a page for insertion if you have a scanner attached to your Mac.

Once the two documents are merged, you can reorder any of the pages—old or new—by clicking and dragging them in the sidebar. If you have a multitouch trackpad, pages can be rotated using the standard picture rotate gesture—be sure to first place the mouse cursor over the body of the page in question or over the thumbnail for the page.

Note that you can keep adding more PDFs by dragging and dropping them onto the thumbnail preview drawer—you aren't limited to merging two files.

When done, click File→Export and give the merged document a new name. Beware that simply saving the file will overwrite the original PDF you selected for merging!

Adding Images to PDFs

You can also add images to a document; again just drag and drop them onto the thumbnail preview drawer (View→Thumbnails) in the same way as described earlier. Each image is given a new page. It's not possible to insert images onto an existing page using Preview, although the signatures feature can be unofficially utilized to insert hand-drawn sketches—see Tip 298, *Add Sketches to PDFs*, on page 318.

To learn how to create a new PDF from images, see Tip 315, *Convert Images into a PDF*, on page 329.

Password Protecting a PDF

You can encrypt a PDF file so that a password is required to open it. To do so, open the PDF in Preview, and then click File→Export. In the Format drop-down list of the dialog box that appears, make sure PDF is selected. Then put a check in the Encrypt box and type a password beneath this (type it again in the Verify field to confirm).

Note that the protection is primitive compared to what you might be used to with programs such as Adobe Acrobat[17]—there's no way to protect PDFs so that copying text or images is prohibited, for example. The password protection merely protects the document from being opened. Once opened, the user is free to do whatever they like in the file, including saving an unencrypted copy.

Create a New PDF from a Page of Another

Ever wanted to create a new PDF from a page within a larger PDF? Just make sure the page is displayed within the Preview window, and select `Command`+`C` (or click Edit→Copy). Then click File→New From Clipboard. This will create a new PDF containing just that page.

This trick is useful if you also want to print a single page—do the previous steps to isolate a single page, print it, and then close the new file without saving it.

Quickly Email a PDF Extract

The previous tip can be adapted to allow the emailing of PDF pages, which can be useful if you want to send the page to friends or colleagues. Just ensure the page is visible in Preview, and then hit `Command`+`C` (or click Edit→Copy) to copy the page to the clipboard. Then start a new Mail message and, in the body of the email, just hit `Command`+`V` (or click Edit→Paste). This will paste the page as a completely new PDF attachment, ready for sending.

Pasting PDF pages also works in TextEdit, although with a serious caveat—the document into which you paste will be converted into Rich Text Document with Attachments format (.rtfd), even if it's already in an alternative format

---

17. http://www.adobe.com/products/acrobat.html

such as Microsoft Word. Rich Text Document with Attachments is a format that currently only Macs understand—both Windows and Linux are unable to access them.

Tip 230

Edit Movies

QuickTime Player is the Mac's built-in movie player—you can find it on the Applications menu within Finder.

Trimming Movies

QuickTime Player is actually a trimmed-down version of the (not free) QuickTime Pro, but it's pretty powerful in its own right. For example, you can edit movies within QuickTime Player, at least in a primitive way, as follows:

1. Open the movie in QuickTime Player, and click Edit→Trim. The timeline will now change to a frame display of the movie, surrounded by a yellow boundary box—see Figure 39, *Trimming a movie file*, on page 256.

2. Click and drag the boundary box on the left and right sides to cut out any material at the beginning and end you want to lose (unfortunately, it's not possible to cut sections out of the middle of the file—for that you'll need a more sophisticated editor like iMovie,[18] although movie clips can be merged together—see the following section).

3. If you want to view the audio track of the file, click View→Show Audio Track. This switches the frame display to one showing the audio waveform, so you can edit perhaps based on quiet or loud episodes.

4. Once you're done, click the Trim button.

Merging Two or More Movies

You can combine two or more movies into one file. To do so, open the first of the movies in QuickTime Player, and then locate the next in Finder and drag and drop it onto the QuickTime Player window. It will appear in the timeline view at the bottom as a separate clip, and you can drag and drop it to the beginning or end of the existing movie file. You can add more clips in the

---

18. http://www.apple.com/ilife/imovie/

Figure 39—Trimming a movie file

same way and reposition them in the timeline view within QuickTime Player by clicking and dragging. When you've finished, click the Done button, and then close the file to bring up a Save dialog box.

Note that, prior to merging movie files, you should ensure they're the same resolution (that is, both are 720p, for example). If you merge two or more movie files of differing resolutions, the smaller file(s) will be proportionally upscaled to fit the resolution and frame size of the larger movie.

Saving an Edited Movie

When you've finished trimming or merging movie files, click File→Close. This will bring up a prompt asking whether you want to save the file. Unfortunately, it's not usually possible to simply save the file in its original format. Instead, it must be exported in an Apple-compatible format. The safest bet to retain as much of the movie's quality as possible is to select the highest-resolution output choice you're offered in the Format drop-down list: 1080p, 720p, or 480p, unless you know the movie has a smaller frame size.

Note that depending on the speed of your Mac, the export process might take several minutes and possibly even hours. A window will appear showing the export progress and will give a rough time estimate too.

Tip 231

Eject a Stuck CD/DVD Disc

Most Macs don't have a physical Eject button for the DVD drive (if indeed it has one). Instead, users must hit the Eject button on the keyboard, usually located in the top right.

For various reasons, Macs sometimes forget they have a disc in the drive, in which case the Eject button won't work. One solution is to reboot the Mac and, before the Apple logo appears or the chime sounds, press and hold the mouse or trackpad button. Within seconds the disc will be spewed out, and you can release the mouse button. Booting will then continue normally.

You can also try to force an ejection when OS X is running, using the Eject menu item—see Tip 192, *Add an Eject Button*, on page 216.

Tip 232

Cue Through Movies Using Your Fingertips

Does your Mac have a multitouch trackpad? Want to cue backward or forward in movies? Just "scroll" left or right with the cursor placed over the movie window to cue back and forth (that is, bunch two fingers together and slide them left or right on the trackpad). Do this while the movie is paused, and you'll simply move rapidly back and forth in the movie file, as if clicking and dragging the blob on the timeline within the controller bar. Do it when the movie is playing, and you'll see an icon appear at the top left of the QuickTime Player window showing the playback speed. The controller bar will also indicate the playback speed.

To return to normal playback in either case, just lift your fingers from the trackpad.

Tip 233

Take a Picture of the Screen

Your Mac has a powerful screen-grabbing facility built in, with a variety of ways of accessing it.

Using Keystrokes

The simplest way to take a shot of the screen is to tap `Shift`+`Command`+`3`. This will output an image to the desktop, although beware if you're playing a DVD movie—the DVD movie window will be blank because movies are copyrighted.

If you want to grab a specific area of the screen, hit `Shift`+`Command`+`4` instead. The cursor will change to a crosshair, and you can click and drag to define an area that will be turned into a screenshot and output to the desktop. Hold `Space` while dragging, without releasing the mouse button, and you can reposition the screenshot frame. Hit `Esc` to cancel.

To capture one program window in particular, tap `Space` once after this series of keystrokes, as in `Shift`+`Command`+`4`, and then tap `Space`. Then click the window you want to capture. It doesn't matter if it's behind another window—it'll still be captured in its unobscured entirety.

See also Tip 157, *Supertip: Make Better Screenshots*, on page 180.

Screengrab to the Clipboard Rather Than to a File

To capture a screen to the clipboard instead of creating a file so you can then paste the snapshot into your own document or image, hold down `Control` in addition to the standard capture shortcuts. For example, `Shift`+`Control`+`Command`+`3` will capture the entire screen to the clipboard. `Shift`+`Control`+`Command`+`4` will let you click and drag to capture a portion of the screen to the clipboard.

Using the Grab App

If key combinations are a little confusing, you can use the Mac's Grab utility, which is found in the Utilities folder of Applications within Finder. Once the program starts, select the entry you want from the Capture menu. Grab also gives you the opportunity to take a screen grab after only ten seconds have passed—just select the Timed Screen option on the Capture menu.

Additionally, if you click the program menu and then Preferences, you can select to include various cursor images within the screenshot (usually cursor images are hidden when using Grab and also when using OS X's built-in tools, as mentioned previously). Just select a cursor type you're interested in, close the Preferences dialog box, and then capture a screen using one of the menu options as described previously. During the capture process, the cursor will change to the one you selected.

Grab can capture images only in the TIFF format.

Using Preview

The Mac's general-purpose image viewer, Preview, also has screen capture abilities built in. The advantage of using Preview is that you can crop, edit, or annotate the image once captured. You can also save images in a variety of image formats.

Just start Preview (open Finder, select the Applications list, and then double-click Preview), click File→Take Screen Shot, and choose from the options. The captured image will appear within Preview as if it's an image file you've just double-clicked. You can annotate it by clicking Tools→Annotate. To save it, click File→Save. Select the image format you want to use from the Format drop-down list in the dialog box that appears (hold Option before selecting the drop-down list to see more file choices).

Tip 234

Ignore a Software Update

In my experience, there's a new update for my Mac every few months or so. Often this is an iTunes update, and on one of my computers, I simply never use this software. Therefore, wasting time downloading an update is pointless.

To avoid being nagged about the update, I simply right-click its entry within the Updates section of the Mac App Store and select Hide Update. This will remove it from the list.

Should you change your mind at some point, simply click Store→Show All Software Updates. You might have to quit and restart the Mac App Store for the update(s) to become visible again.

Note that you should never hide security or major operating system updates. These should always been installed, no matter how long it takes. To learn how to capture update files for manual installation on more than one computer, which can save time if you have more than one Mac, see Tip 263, *Manually Manage Software Updates*, on page 287.

Tip 235

Generate Font Samples

If you have a lot of fonts installed on the system, you may find it helpful to create a sample document displaying them all. Lots of professional designers rely on binders full of such printed examples.

There are two simple ways of doing this, depending on whether you want a simple or bespoke sample document.

Creating a Simple Font Sample Document

You can create a simple sample of one or more fonts, showing little more than the upper/lowercase letters and numbers from 0 to 9, by following these steps:

1. Open the Font Book app, which is the Mac font manager (open Finder, select the Applications list, and then double-click Font Book), and then select one or more fonts (multiple fonts can be selected by holding down `Command`).

2. Click File→Print. The print dialog will open, and you'll see previewed a simple letters and numbers sample that you can print immediately if you want by clicking the Print button. However, by expanding the print dialog box by clicking Show Details, you'll see more options.

3. Ensure Default Settings is selected in the Presets drop-down list within the print dialog box, and ensure Font Book is selected from the drop-down list beneath the paper orientation buttons. Then select from the three different options in the Report Type drop-down list: Catalog, Repertoire, and Waterfall. You'll see the preview at the top left change with each choice you make, showing the differences between the options.

4. When you're happy with your choice, click the Print button. Alternatively, to save a PDF for printing later, click the PDF button at the bottom left, and then select Save As PDF.

Creating a Bespoke Font Sample Document

You can modify a ready-made AppleScript to generate a bespoke sample using your own choice of text, as follows:

1. Start by opening the Font Book application (open Finder, select the Applications list, and then double-click Font Book), and highlight any or all the fonts you want to include in the sample document. Multiple fonts can be selected by holding down `Command`.

2. Leaving Font Book open, switch to a Finder window, hit `Shift`+`Command`+`G`, and type /Library/Scripts/Font Book. Then double-click Create Font Sample.scpt.

3. This will open the script in AppleScript Editor, where we have to insert a line and change another line. Start by switching to AppleScript Editor and then hitting `Command`+`F`; in the Find dialog box, type set numFaces and click Next.

4. This will highlight part of a line. Leave the line as it is, but in the blank space beneath (above the line that reads tell application "TextEdit"), type the following, ensuring after typing that you've typed it correctly:

```
set TextString to the text returned of (display dialog "Type a sentence or
    paragraph that you'd like to use for the font sample document:" default
    answer "")
```

Note that you might see a warning about the need to duplicate the locked file. This is fine, so agree.

5. Next, hit `Command`+`F` again, and this time type set characters to tab. This will highlight a line later in the AppleScript. Remove psName in this line and replace it with TextString so that the complete line now reads as follows:

```
set characters to tab & TextString & return & return
```

6. Those are all the edits you need to make. Click the Compile button on the toolbar to ensure you haven't mistyped—if you have, then the error will be highlighted. If there's no error, then you can now save the Apple-Script for further use (File→Save, and save it to your Documents folder, where you can run it in the future by double-clicking it), or you can just run the script immediately by clicking the Run button on the toolbar.

7. Once run, a dialog box will appear prompting you to enter the sentence or paragraph you want to use to generate the font samples. Once you've entered this and clicked OK within the dialog box, a TextEdit document will open, and, slowly but surely, it will be filled with samples of each font you selected earlier. Once it's finished, quit AppleScript Editor and then save and/or print the new TextEdit document as required.

Tip 236

Send iMessages from Within Contacts

If you're looking up a contact with the Contacts app and their phone number or email address is registered with the iMessages service (that is, you've sent them an iMessage previously), you can click the heading alongside their number or email address and select Send Message from the menu that appears. A pop-out window will appear letting you send an iMessage, without the need to start the Messages application.

Tip 237

Instantly View a Command's Man Page

Man pages are instruction manuals for command-line tools. To view the man page for any command when working at the command-line prompt, right-click it and select Open Man Page on the menu that appears.

Tip 238

Autocomplete Words

Ever had one of those days where you can't quite spell? Well, all you need to do is start typing the first few letters of the word and then hit Esc. A pop-out menu will appear showing lots of suggestions—see Figure 40, *Using OS X's word autocomplete feature*, on page 263. Then use the cursor keys to select the correct word and hit `Return` to insert it. Hit `Esc` again to close the list if you don't want to choose one of the options.

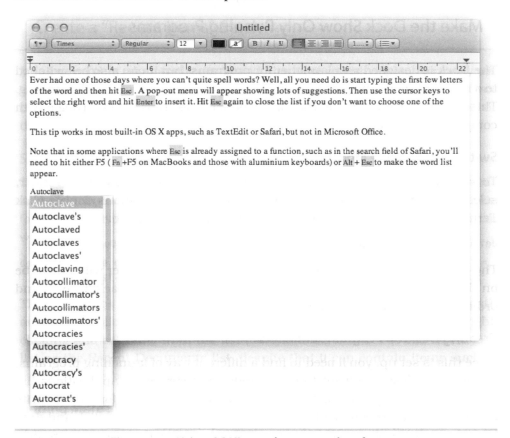

Figure 40—Using OS X's word autocomplete feature

This tip works in most built-in OS X apps, such as TextEdit or Safari, but not in Microsoft Office.

Note that in some applications where `Esc` is already assigned to a function, such as in the address and search field of Safari, you'll need to hit either F5 (`Fn`+F5 on MacBooks and those with aluminum keyboards) or `Option`+`Esc` to make the word list appear.

In the dialog box that appears, select the Verify radio button, enter your login password in the relevant field, and click Start. The scan should take a few seconds to complete. If it reports an error, which will be highlighted in red, click the Repair radio button. and again click Start. Once complete, close the Keychain Access program, log out and then back in again, and visit the errant websites to see whether the issue has been fixed.

Deleting the Entry

If the problem persists, try once again to open Keychain Access, and this time delete the entry for the website or application from the list within the Keychain Access program (right-click the entry and select Delete from the menu that appears). These will be listed to the right of the program window, although you can type the app or website name in the search field at the top right of the window.

Deleting the entry will then prompt you to enter the details anew the next time you access the website or application, where they'll also be recorded fresh for future reference.

Deleting a Website Password Within Safari

Although you can use the Keychain Access program to delete and access Safari website passwords, Safari itself offers access to this list—open Safari's Preferences dialog box (select Preferences on the application menu), and then click the Passwords tab. Select the entry in the list and click the Remove button.

Tip 243

Turn Off the Desktop

If you're using your Mac to give a presentation, you might not want everybody to see your messy desktop! If so, you can run a quick command that will hide your desktop icons.

Hiding the Desktop

To temporarily turn off the desktop, open a Terminal window (open Finder, select the Applications list, and then in the list of applications double-click Terminal within the Utilities folder), and type the following line:

```
defaults write com.apple.finder CreateDesktop -bool FALSE;killall Finder
```

Note that this will mean you can no longer right-click the desktop or drag files there. The files there will still be accessible by using Finder to browse to your Desktop folder.

To restore things to normal after your presentation, again open a Terminal window, but this time type the following:

```
defaults delete com.apple.finder CreateDesktop;killall Finder
```

Hey, presto! Everything should be back to normal. If not, log out and back in again.

Creating a Desktop Hiding App

With the use of a quick AppleScript, this Terminal command can even be turned into a stand-alone application that you can run before each presentation, saving the hassle of the command line.

Open AppleScript editor (open Finder, select the Applications list, and then double-click AppleScript Editor within the Utilities folder), and type (or cut and paste if you're reading the eBook version of this book, being careful to remove the line breaks) the following code:

```
display dialog "Desktop icons visible or hidden?" buttons {"Visible",
        "Hidden"} with icon 2 with title "Switch to presentation mode"
        default button 1
set switch to button returned of result
if switch is "Hidden" then
tell application "Terminal"
do shell script "defaults write com.apple.finder CreateDesktop -bool FALSE;
        killall Finder"
end tell
else
tell application "Terminal"
do shell script "defaults delete com.apple.finder CreateDesktop;killall
        Finder"
end tell
end if
```

Click the Run button on the toolbar to test your script. You should see a dialog box appear with two buttons: Visible and Hidden. To make sure the app works OK, click Hidden to hide the icons; then run the app again, and click Visible to reveal them.

To save the AppleScript as an application, click File→Save. Type a filename, and then in the File Format drop-down list, select Application. Save the file anywhere you'd like on your hard disk, although *not* on your desktop—when the icons get hidden, you won't be able to access the app again to unhide them unless you use Finder.

Tip 244

Get Quick Access to System Preferences

Here's a way to get quick access to system configuration tools.

Right-Clicking the Dock Icon

If you keep the System Preferences icon in the Dock, simply right-click it and select the preference you want from the list that appears. This will start System Preferences with that particular option open.

If the System Preferences window is open, you can also click and hold the Show All button at the top left to see this list and select an entry from it.

Using Spotlight

If you can remember the name of the various System Preference panes (Desktop & Screen Saver, Energy Saver, Network, and so on), then you can access them ultra-quickly using Spotlight. Just hit `Command+Space` to open Spotlight's text field, and then type the name of what you want. Before you've finished typing, you should see it appear near the top of the list of results, if not at the top. Simply select it to start System Preferences with that particular pane viewable.

Using Hotkeys

If your Mac's keyboard has hotkeys at the top for changing the volume or brightness or for activating Mission Control, you can quickly access the associated pane of System Preferences by holding `Option` before hitting the shortcut key.

For example, holding down `Option` and hitting the volume increase button will open the Sound pane of System Preferences. Holding down `Option` and hitting the Mission Control hotkey will open the Mission Control pane of System Preferences. Hitting `Option` and the keyboard brightness hotkeys opens the Keyboard pane of System Preferences.

Adding Specific System Preferences Icons to the Dock

If you find yourself using a particular System Preference option a lot, you can add it to the side of the Dock that contains the trash; you're not allowed to add them to the other side of the Dock, where app icons live.

To do this, open Finder, hit `Shift`+`Command`+`G`, and type /System/Library/Preferen-cePanes. Then click Go. In the file listing that appears, click and drag the .prefPane file you're interested in straight to the right side of the Dock.

Clicking it within the Dock will now activate System Preferences, which will then jump straight to that pane when it starts.

To remove the Dock icon, just click and drag it off the Dock, where it will vanish.

Tip 245

Temporarily Toggle Dock Magnification

If you have Dock magnification switched on (that is, the Dock icons expand when your mouse passes over them), holding down `Shift`+`Control` will cause them to remain small. On the other hand, if you *don't* have Dock magnification turned on, the same key combination will cause them to be magnified—which is useful if you want to see the unread count alongside the Mail icon, for example.

Tip 246

Remove System Preferences Icons

Here's how to tidy up and trim the list of options within System Preferences.

Removing Third-Party Icons

Some applications like to add their own icons to the bottom of the System Preferences window under the Other heading.

The trouble is that the same programs leave behind these icons when they're uninstalled. To manually remove any icon, right-click it and select Remove Preference Pane.

Note that if the app is still installed, simply removing the icon probably won't uninstall the rest of the app. To do that, you'll need to click and drag the program's icon from within Applications to the trash. If the program doesn't add an entry to the Applications list within Finder, you'll need to consult the website of the software developer to learn how to manually remove the program.

Pruning Standard System Icons from the List

To remove any of the standard system icons from System Preferences, click and hold the Show All button (top left of the program window) until the list of apps appears; then—keeping your finger on the mouse button—scroll to the bottom and select Customize. Then remove the checks next to any icons you want to remove (see Figure 41, *Removing built-in System Preferences icons*, on page 273). Click the Done button at the top left when you've finished.

Note that although the icon might have been removed, you can still access the function by clicking and holding the Show All button and selecting the entry in the list.

To restore icons, repeat the previous steps, and add a check next to the icon(s) you removed.

> ### Tip 247
> ## Speed Up Slow PDFs

Sometimes you might find that someone sends you a PDF that is very slow when you view it in Preview—scrolling takes a long time, for example, and pages draw slowly too. It's not always clear why this happens, but it might have to do with the number of layers in the document.

A quick and easy solution is to use Preview to save a copy of the file (select File→Export, and then assign a different filename). Open the copy, and you should find it's now much quicker to browse.

Figure 41—Removing built-in System Preferences icons

Tip 248

Turn Off Mail Sounds

Mail is a surprisingly noisy program—you'll hear a noise when mail is sent (a swoosh) and also a noise when new mail arrives.

Turning off sound effects is very easy. Open Mail's Preferences dialog box (application menu→Preferences), and then ensure the General tab is selected. In the New Messages Sound drop-down list, select None. Then remove the check alongside Play Sounds For Other Mail Actions. Finally, close the Mail Preferences dialog box.

To restore Mail sound effects, repeat the previous steps but in reverse—choose the New Message Sound entry from the New Messages Sound drop-down list, and then put a check in the Play Sounds For Other Mail Actions checkbox.

Tip 249

Supertip: Take Control of Zip Files

Macs can read and write .zip compressed archives, the most popular type of compressed file format used under Windows. As you'd expect, everything is automated, but here are some tricks you can employ.

Unpacking and Creating Archives

To unpack an archive, simply double-click it. The contents will automatically be extracted to the same folder as the archive file. To create an archive, right-click a file or folder, and select the Compress option.

Setting Archive Preferences

You can change the location where all zip files are extracted to and also make your Mac delete the original zip files after extraction by setting the preferences of the program called Archive Utility, which your Mac uses in the background to perform zipping actions. You'll find it in /System/Library/CoreServices: open a Finder window, press Shift+Command+G, and type the path before hitting Go. Double-click the program, although note that it doesn't have a program window. Instead, on its application menu, click the Preferences entry. Then make your choices from the drop-down menus of the dialog box that appears.

You can also choose what happens when creating an archive (that is, when you right-click a file or folder and select the Compress option)—just make your selection from the Save Archive, Use Archive Format, and After Archiving drop-down menus. Close the application when you've finished with it.

If you'd like these options at hand so they can be changed easily, right-click the Archive Utility icon in /System/Library/CoreServices, as mentioned previously, and select Show Package Contents. Then navigate to Contents/Resources/, and double-click the Archives.prefPane file. Then click the Install button. This will permanently add an option to set the file archive preferences to System Preferences.

Extracting to Destinations You Choose

You can add an entry to the right-click menu that will cause the unzipped output to be placed on the desktop, regardless of preference changes you made earlier. Another entry you can add will cause a file-browsing window to appear, prompting for a destination where you'd like to unarchive the files.

To make either a reality, open System Preferences (Apple menu→System Preferences), and then click the Keyboard icon. Click the Keyboard Shortcuts tab, select Services in the list on the left, and scroll to the very bottom of the list on the right, where you'll find two options that read Unarchive to Desktop and Unarchive To. Put check marks in the boxes alongside both.

The change will take effect immediately. Whenever you right-click an archive file, no matter where it is, clicking the Unarchive to Desktop option will unzip the contents to your desktop. Clicking Unarchive To will open a file-browsing dialog box, in which you can select a destination.

To remove the menu options later, repeat the previous steps, and simply uncheck the entries in the list within System Preferences.

Create Password-Protected Zip Archives

Although OS X can unzip password-protected archives, it offers no way via Finder to create them. However, you can create a simple Automator service that does the trick. It makes use of the command-line zip tool, although you won't be aware of this—after you type a password when prompted to, the creation of the zip file will be automated. The action will appear as an option in the menu that appears when you right-click a file or folder.

1. Open Automator, which you'll find near the top of the Applications list within Finder. In the Choose a File Type For Your Document dialog box, select Service (the cog icon). If the Choose a File Type dialog box doesn't appear, hit Command+N.

2. On the right of the program window, change the Service Receives Selected drop-down list to Files or Folders, and change the second drop-down list almost immediately alongside to Finder.

3. In the search field in the middle top of the Automator program window, type Run AppleScript. This will filter the list beneath to just one entry. Drag and drop it on the right of the program window, over the text Drag Actions or Files Here to Build Your Workflow.

4. In the main text area beneath the Run AppleScript heading, delete the purple text that's already there, and type the following (or copy and paste if you're reading the ebook):

```
on run {fileList}
repeat with singleFile in fileList
set filePath to quoted form of (POSIX path of singleFile)
tell application "Finder"
set fileName to name of singleFile
set parentFolder to POSIX path of (container of singleFile as alias)
end tell
set zipName to quoted form of (parentFolder & fileName & ".zip")
tell application "System Events"
activate
display dialog "Enter Password" default answer "" with hidden answer
set the passwd to text returned of the result
end tell
set cmd to "zip -P " & passwd & " -r " & zipName & " " & filePath & " -x
        *.DS_Store"
do shell script cmd
end repeat
end run
```

5. Click the icon representing a hammer above the textbox. This will check the code to make sure it's correct. If it isn't, the error will be highlighted. If it's fine, the code will be reformatted neatly, but you can ignore this—it has no bearing on whether the script works.

6. Click File→Save to save your new service. There's no need to choose a destination, but for the filename type Compress with Password.

7. Once done, close the Automator window.

You can test your new service immediately by right-clicking any file or folder in a Finder window or on the desktop and selecting Compress with Password at the bottom of the menu that appears (you might have to click Services→ Compress with Password). A dialog box will appear where you can type the password you'd like to use to protect the zip file you're about to create.

Note that when you unzip your password-protected file, it will always be in a Users folder and then a folder named after your username. This is because of a limitation of the zip command.

To remove your service in the future, open a Finder window, and hit Shift+Command+G. Then type ~/Library/Services, and click Go. Then drag the Compress with Password file to the trash and log out and back in again.

Tip 250

Take Better Snapshots

Here are a few quick tips to better control Photo Booth, the Mac application that uses the iSight or FaceTime HD camera to take pictures of users.

Stopping the Flash

When using Photo Booth, the Mac's screen flashes white to illuminate the subject an instant before the picture is taken.

Sometimes, however, you might simply want to make use of ambient light. To avoid the firing the flash, just hold down `Shift` when clicking the camera button. There's no need to keep holding it down while the photo is taken.

Turning Off the Countdown

To avoid a countdown before the photo is taken (that is, to take a snapshot as soon as you click), hold down `Option` before clicking the snapshot button. You can combine this with `Shift` to prevent the flash from firing.

Using a Photo for Twitter

If you take a particularly good snapshot, you can click the Share Sheet button at the bottom right of the window to automatically replace your Twitter profile photo with it. You can also select to use the photo as your Buddy image within Messages and also to replace your login photo on OS X.

Tip 251

Select Text like a Pro

In some built-in Mac apps like TextEdit, as well as in Microsoft Office and Mozilla Firefox, it's possible to select text in a variety of useful ways above and beyond simply clicking and dragging.

Selecting Noncontiguous Regions

Holding down `Command` while clicking and dragging lets you select disparate sections of text. You could highlight one sentence at the beginning of a paragraph, for example, and while holding down `Command`, select another sentence at the end of a paragraph. Hitting `Command`+`C` will copy both to the clipboard. If you hit `Command`+`V` to paste, the two sentence components will be pasted on two separate lines.

Selecting Square or Rectangular Blocks of Text

Holding down `Option` will let you select rectangular blocks of text within a paragraph. This is hard to describe, so give it a try by holding down `Option` and clicking and dragging within a paragraph of text (hold `Option`+`Command` in Microsoft Word). Again, hitting `Command`+`C` will copy it, and hitting `Command`+`V` will paste it. It's hard to imagine how this would ever be useful, but you might find a use for it!

Selecting Without Dragging

By clicking at the beginning of the region you want to select and then holding `Shift` and clicking at the end of the region, you'll select everything in between.

If you've already made a text selection, you can hold down `Shift` and click either side of it to add text to the selection. Clicking within the selection while holding down `Shift` will let you subtract letters and words from the selection.

`Shift` can be combined with `Option` to define square or rectangular blocks of text that you can define without the need to click and drag. It's a little hard to describe, so give it a try!

Tip 252

Create Cool Dock Stacks

Almost everything that appears under the Favorites and Devices heading in the side pane of Finder can be turned into a Dock stack for quick access. Simply drag and drop its icon from the Finder window to the stacks area of the Dock (that is, the side containing the trash). You can drag and drop Applications, Desktop, Pictures, and so on, including removable storage devices such as USB memory sticks. Turning Applications into a stack offers a quick way to start apps akin to Launchpad—see Figure 42, *Turning the Applications list into a stack*, on page 279.

Figure 42—Turning the Applications list into a stack

Any item under the Favorites heading within Finder can also be added to the Dock by right-clicking it and selecting Add to Dock from the menu that appears.

Two items can't be converted into a stack: AirDrop and All My Files. The latter can be added to the Dock, but clicking it simply opens a Finder window with All My Files selected.

Note that in the case of removable storage devices added as a stack, when the device isn't attached to the computer, the Dock icon will turn into a question mark on top of a hard disk. This is only temporary, and the stack will function correctly once the memory stick is reattached.

Exploring OS X: Autosave and Versions

Since the computer was invented, users have been familiar with saving files. OS X Lion and subsequently Mountain Lion made a brave step away from this strict requirement. In apps that are compatible with the new autosave and versioning features, files are automatically recorded to disk as soon as you start editing—even if you haven't chosen to save them or given them a name. Create a file in TextEdit, for example, and you can quit the app right away. When you next open TextEdit, the unsaved file will be there waiting for you.

In those same apps (that is, they were either designed or specifically updated for Lion/Mountain Lion's new features), OS X also periodically saves versions of files so you can step back in the file's history to restore an older rendition. Every time you close a file, a new version is recorded, and a new version is also recorded after every hour that passes while the document is open. You can also hit Command+S to save a version whenever you want, such as before making a big edit, although this will also update the saved file in the standard way.

To restore a previous version, just click File→Revert to→Browse All Versions on the menu (or click the filename in the title bar and select the same option). This will open a timeline view of the document rather like that offered by the Time Machine backup function, but, crucially, Versions can work independently of Time Machine. In fact, there's no requirement for Time Machine to be set up.

All you need to do is select the version of the file you want from the vertical timeline display at the right of the screen. The current version of the file will be shown on the left, with the archived version on the right. When you find the one you want to restore, just hit the button beneath.

Even if you restore to an older version of the file, the version of the file you're abandoning will also be added to the version list, making the purpose of autosave and versions very clear: except for a catastrophic hard disk failure, it is impossible to lose any data, and you therefore don't have to worry about saving files.

Tip 253

Clean Caches for Smooth Running

To speed things up, most OS X applications and system tools cache data on the hard disk that they access frequently. While this works fine most of the time, sometimes the caches can become corrupted, and this can slow down either the application or the entire system. Therefore, if you run into a mysterious problem of an app working slowly or perhaps not working at all, deleting the caches might be worth trying. Don't worry—the caches will be re-created as soon as the app next opens.

Clearing Local Caches

Start by quitting any apps that are open. Then open a Finder window, hit Shift+Command+G, and type the following: ~/Library/Caches. Then drag all the files and folders you see to the trash. Enter your login password if prompted.

Clearing Application Caches

As described earlier, ensure all applications are closed, and then open a Finder window. Hit Shift+Command+G, and type the following: /Library/Caches. Then drag all the folders and files you see in the Finder window to the trash, typing your password when prompted, and reboot for the changes to take effect.

Note that the first time you reboot, the system might seem slower. This is because the caches are being rebuilt.

Tip 254

Turn the Numeric Keypad into a Launcher

If you never use the numeric keypad of your full-sized keyboard for its proper purpose (that is, quickly typing numbers), you can turn it into a range of hotkeys that activate various OS X functions.

This is possible because OS X sees the numeric keypad as a separate range of keys. As far as it is concerned, hitting 3 on the numeric keypad is not the same as hitting 3 on the main keyboard. The same is true for the other numbers and also for the symbols on the numeric keypad.

Creating a Hotkey Shortcut

You can define new keyboard shortcuts and redefine existing ones by starting System Preferences (Apple menu→System Preferences), selecting the Keyboard icon, and then ensuring the Keyboard Shortcuts tab is selected.

Just select an entry in the list on the right, and then double-click the right side of the entry. Then press the keyboard shortcut or combination you'd like to use. Switch between categories using the list on the left.

To use one of the numeric keypad keys as a hotkey, double-click the entry for the function you want to define or redefine, as mentioned earlier, and press the numeric keypad key. For example, because my keyboard lacks a hotkey to make Launchpad appear, I selected the Launchpad & Dock entry on the left, and then I double-clicked the Show Launchpad entry in the list within System Preferences and hit the `0` (zero) key on the numeric keypad.

Removing Shortcuts

As strange as it might seem, there's no way to remove individual keyboard shortcut combinations once you've created them. All you can do is restore the default keyboard shortcuts for *all* entries within that particular keyboard shortcut listing. For example, to remove the shortcut I created earlier—Show Launchpad—I would again select its entry on the Keyboard Shortcuts tab within System Preferences and click the Restore Defaults button. Unfortunately, this restores the default keyboard combinations for all other entries in the Launchpad and Dock list, but there's no way to avoid this. This is one area of OS X where there are strictly limited options, although a semiofficial add-on is available for download from one of the Mac OS X developers employed by Apple. Services Manager[19] allows full control over the right-click menus and keyboard shortcuts.

Tip 255

Open a Terminal Window Where You're Browsing

Command-line junkies will like this one: you can make it possible to open a new Terminal window automatically switched to the location you're viewing in a Finder window. Open System Preferences (Apple menu→System Preferences), and click the Keyboard icon. Then click the Keyboard Shortcuts tab, and in the list on the left, select Services. In the list on the right, scroll down until you find New Terminal at Folder under the Files and Folders heading. Then put a check mark next to the entry in the list—this will cause the entry to appear on the menu that opens whenever you right-click a folder (although on some systems you might first have to click the Services submenu to see the option). Close System Preferences, and give your new tweak a try in a Finder window or on the desktop.

---

19. See http://macosxautomation.com/services/servicesmanager.

Note that although it's theoretically possible to also assign a keyboard shortcut to open a Finder window with System Preferences, this does not work in practice because of limitations placed on how Finder works with keyboard combinations.

Tip 256

See Mini-Calendars in the Calendar App

Click the Calendars button in Calendar app, and a sidebar will appear, where you'll see a list of the calendars you're currently subscribed to, as well as a mini-calendar showing the current month at the bottom. However, if you click and drag up the bar above the small calendar, you can see up to five additional "mini-calendars" for forthcoming months, which is useful for finding out forthcoming dates "at a glance." The only limitation on how many mini-calendars you can see is the size of the Calendar program window and therefore, ultimately, the size of your screen!

Tip 257

Install Only Printer Drivers and Not Their Add-Ins

If you download and install printer drivers from a manufacturer's site, you might find that they come with bundled software that you don't need, such as programs that warn you about low ink levels. There's no need for this on a Mac because the feature is already built in—just open System Preferences, then click Print & Scan, and finally click the Options & Supplies button for the printer you're interested in. Click the Supply Levels tab in the dialog box that opens.

Sometimes it's possible to delve into the installation package you download to install only the actual printer drivers, which may well be in a package of their own. It's something of a black art because different manufacturers name files differently, but it's worth a try. The actual printer driver packages are often identified by the name of the technology they use—Common Unix Printing System (CUPS)—so look for this in the filename.

Assuming that what you download from the manufacturer's website arrives as a disk image, double-click it in the usual way so the disk image mounts it in Finder. Then right-click the .mpkg or .pkg file representing the installation package, and select Show Package Contents. In the Finder window that opens, browse to the Packages folder. If there isn't a Packages folder, then look in the other folders in the package, but the chances are you're out of luck and will just have to install the entire thing in the usual way.

If there is a Packages folder, look for anything that looks like it might just contain the actual drivers. In the package for my Brother multifunction printer, for example, I found two packages named with variations of Brother_Inkjet. To install both, I right-clicked the first package, selecting Open from the menu in order to bypass Gatekeeper; then after installing it, I repeated the process on the second. This gave me the printer drivers I needed but not the irritating software that starts at boot-up and is intended to help with scanning.

Tip 258

Reveal the Desktop

Although it's a very useful feature, the Show Desktop feature isn't given its own hotkey on Mac keyboards—unlike Mission Control and Dashboard. While you can hit F11 to activate it (Fn+F11 on portable Macs, or perhaps Ctrl+Down depending on your system configuration), you might like to know that the Mission Control hotkey (usually F3) doubles up as a Show Desktop hotkey. Just hold Command before you tap it.

Tip 259

Avoid Trackpad Confusion When a Mouse Is Used

In my experience, Apple designs its portable Macs well and positions the trackpad to avoid accidental touching while typing. But if you're using an external mouse, you might still find that you occasionally brush against it, causing the mouse pointer to skitter.

Fixing this is easy, but Apple has buried the setting you must alter. Open System Preferences (Apple menu→System Preferences), and click the Accessibility icon. Click the Mouse & Trackpad icon on the left, and then check Ignore Built-in Trackpad When Mouse or Wireless Trackpad Is Present.

Tip 260

Send Somebody an App Link

Did you spot something in the App Store that you think would be perfect for a friend? Just right-click the product image above the price/install button, and select Copy Link from the menu that appears. Then switch to Mail or iChat, and paste the link into a message to your friend. When clicked, it will open the product page at Apple's website. Your friend can then click the View in Mac App Store button to actually install the app via App Store.

Tip 261

Copy Calculator Results

Any result displayed on the Calculator app's LCD screen can be instantly copied into the clipboard for pasting into any other application.

Copying and Pasting

After hitting the equal key, hit the usual copy keyboard short-cut—Command+C—to copy the result in the clipboard. Then paste it into other applications in the usual way—either by clicking Edit→Paste or by hitting Command+V.

It works the other way around too—if you have a figure from another app that you want to use in Calculator, just copy it to the clipboard and then, making sure the Calculator window is on top, hit Command+V to paste it into Calculator's LCD display (note that any existing numbers within the LCD display will be cleared).

Using the Paper Tape

If you're doing a series of complex calculations that you'd like to copy and paste into other apps, open the Paper Tape window, which can be found on the Window menu. All calculations and results are recorded on it, even if you clear the calculator, and you can click and drag to select anything "printed" on it and then copy and paste as usual.

Tip 262

Bookmark Images and PDFs

Preview lets you bookmark files in various ways, as follows.

Bookmarking Files

If there are images or PDFs that you view frequently, you can bookmark them within Preview. This works just like bookmarking websites within a web browser like Safari and uses the same keyboard shortcut—just load the image or PDF and hit Command+D. From then on, click the image or PDF's entry on Preview's Bookmarks menu to open it instantly.

If you bookmark a multipage PDF file, you'll also bookmark the page you were reading at the time so that clicking the bookmark in the future will return you to that page.

Rather cleverly, even if you move the original file from one folder to another, Preview's bookmark will still link to the file—even if the file has moved into the trash!

Bookmarks can be renamed or deleted by selecting Bookmarks→Edit Bookmarks. To delete a bookmark, select an entry on the list, and click the Remove button. To rename a bookmark, just double-click its name within the list.

Bookmarking Sentences or Paragraphs

You can also use the Preview's markup tool to create makeshift bookmarks within documents that, when clicked, will take you straight to that sentence, paragraph, or page, as follows:

1. Open the PDF that you want to create bookmarks in, and activate Preview's markup (highlighter) pen tool. This can be done by clicking the button

on the toolbar (on a default icon set within Preview, which is the fifth icon from the left). It doesn't matter which color you choose for the highlighting. If you want, you can choose the underline or strikethrough options too.

2. Click View→Highlights and Notes. This will expand a drawer on the left side of the program window.

3. Highlight some text that you'd like to serve as a bookmark within a page. You'll see that this instantly adds an entry to the drawer on the left, named after the text you've highlighted.

4. Highlight more text that you want to bookmark elsewhere in the PDF. Again, you'll see that it's added to the drawer on the left. Clicking any entry in the drawer will take you straight to that highlight. Effectively, you've created a series of bookmarks.

5. When you've finished highlighting, don't forget to save the file (File→Save) complete with your highlights. In the future, to see the annotated bookmarks when you open the file, again select the View→Highlights and Notes option.

Tip 263

Manually Manage Software Updates

Approximately every few months, Apple updates OS X with a point release. This is usually several hundred megabytes in size, and if you have more than one Mac in the house, downloading the updates for each computer can put significant strain on your Internet connection.

The command-line softwareupdate tool can help. This gives much more control over the updating procedure compared to using the Mac App Store for updates, and it allows you to download the update packages before manually installing them. This way, you can download the updates and transfer them to other computers using a USB memory stick.

Viewing and Installing Updates

Open a Terminal window and begin by listing what downloads are available, as follows (typing your login password when prompted):

```
sudo softwareupdate -l
```

It'll take a few minutes for the list of results to appear.

At this stage, installing any entry mentioned in the results list is simply a matter of specifying its name after the softwareupdate -i command (specify the name alongside the asterisk in the list—with some updates, this might simply be a series of numbers, such as 041-0846-2.7). For example, if the list includes an entry by the name of MacOSXUpd10.8.1-10.8.1, the following will both download and install it:

```
sudo softwareupdate -i MacOSXUpd10.8.1-10.8.1
```

Downloading Updates

To simply download the update without installing it, use softwareupdate -d. Using the same example, this will download but not install the MacOSXUpd10.8.1-10.8.1 update package:

```
sudo softwareupdate -d MacOSXUpd10.8.1-10.8.1
```

To download but not install all available updates, type the following:

```
sudo softwareupdate -d -a
```

You'll see a progress display as each file downloads, indicating the quantity of the file downloaded so far and the estimated time until the download completes.

In each case, the downloaded update packages are stored in the /Library/Updates folder, and each will probably be in a numbered folder (from your Terminal window, you can type open /Library/Updates to browse this location more easily in a Finder window). Each update package can be installed simply by double-clicking it; or, if you want to remain at the command line, you can type open and specify the package name (that is, something like open MacOSXUpd10.1Patch.pkg).

Tip 264

Add Blank Spaces to the Dock

All the Dock icons sit next to each other and are equally spaced, but it's possible to add spacers to the Dock so you can separate some of the icons. You may find this helps you to avoid misclicking, for example.

Adding a Spacer Between App Icons

To add any number of spacers to the side of the Dock containing the application icons, open a Terminal window (open Finder, select the Applications list, and then in the list of applications double-click Terminal within the Utilities folder), and type the following two lines:

```
defaults write com.apple.dock persistent-apps -array-add '{tile-data={};
        tile-type="spacer-tile";}';killall Dock
```

The new spacer will appear alongside the app icons. Repeat for more spacers. You can click and drag each spacer to where you want it to go. To get rid of it, just click and drag it off the Dock to the top half of the screen (bear in mind that because the spacer is invisible, it will look like you're not dragging anything!). It will disappear upon releasing the mouse button.

Adding a Spacer Near the Stacks/Trash

To add a similar spacer to the side of the Dock containing the trash and stacks (or any number of spacers), open a Terminal window, and type the following two lines:

```
defaults write com.apple.dock persistent-others -array-add '{tile-data={};
        tile-type="spacer-tile";}';killall Dock
```

The new spacer will appear beside the trash, and again you can click and drag it to where you'd like it to go. Click and drag it off the Dock to the top half the screen to dispose of it (again bear in mind that because the spacer is invisible, it will look like you're not dragging anything!).

Tip 265

Work with Background Windows

Often you might find yourself transferring information from one program window to another—from a browser window to a text editor, for example. Here are some tips to make that easier.

Repositioning Windows

Repositioning program windows in such a situation can be annoying, because each must be selected and then repositioned before you return to the window you're working in—that's a lot of clicking around!

However, holding down `Command` and clicking any nonactive window's title bar lets you move that window without losing focus in the window you're working in, although you should be careful not to click the filename within the title bar—doing so will bring up the standard file manipulation menu that appears whenever you click the filename in any title bar.

Copying Text and Images from a Background Window

Holding down `Command` before clicking and dragging in the editing area of a background window will let you select text. You can then right-click the selected area to copy to the clipboard for inserting into another app (select the Copy entry from the menu that appears; unfortunately, the `Command`+`C` keyboard shortcut won't work).

Just right-click the image in a background window and select Copy from the menu that appears to copy it to the clipboard for insertion in another app—there's no need to hold down `Command`.

Scrolling

Position the mouse over the background window, and you'll be able to scroll it in the usual way—by using a multitouch trackpad gesture or by rolling the mouse ball.

Clicking Links in a Background Window

Holding down `Command` and clicking a link in a background window will open the link in the default web browser.

Tip 266

Find Files Created Today or Yesterday (and More)

Wouldn't it be useful to click a link in Finder that showed only files accessed or created today, yesterday, or within the last week? That would make it significantly easier to find files you've saved but forgotten the location of.

To make this a reality, open a Finder window and hit `Shift`+`Command`+`G`; then in the dialog box that appears, type /System/Library/CoreServices/Finder.app/Contents/Resources/CannedSearches. Then hold down `Command`, and click and drag the Today, Yesterday, and/or Past Week files to the sidebar within Finder (hover and nudge the mouse cursor over the sidebar until a blue bar appears between the existing entries). Clicking any of these sidebar entries in the future will show just the files, as discussed previously.

Log out and back in again, and File Open/Save As dialog boxes will also show the shortcuts in their sidebars within expanded dialog boxes (see Tip 294, *Always See Expanded Save Dialogs*, on page 313).

Tip 267

Download Any File via Safari

Downloading any file for which you have the full URL (that is, something like http://example.com/filename.txt) is easy using Safari. Highlight the link text and copy it to the clipboard (Command+C).

Then expand the pop-out Downloads window in Safari by clicking the button to the right of the Google search box (or hitting Option+Command+L). This will open the download progress window, and you can just hit Command+V to invisibly paste in the download address. The file will start downloading right away.

If you can't see the download pop-out icon, hold Option, and click any web link on the site you're browsing. This will download the HTML file for the page, which you can instantly delete, but the download window will now be activated and ready for use as described earlier.

This URL pasting technique works on pictures you might want to download from a website—just right-click them, select Copy Image Address, and then select the Downloads window and hit Command+V.

Tip 268

View Two Weeks of Appointments

The Calendar app has four view modes by which you can view forthcoming appointments: Day, Week, Month, and Year. You can switch between them by clicking the tabs in the middle of the Calendar program window.

Here's a quick hack to switch the Week view to showing two weeks (or more), which is useful if your working life is arranged around two-week periods or if you'd just like to see a little further into the future.

1. Quit Calendar if it's open, open a Terminal window (open Finder, select the Applications list, and then in the list of applications double-click Terminal within the Utilities folder), and type the following:

    ```
    defaults write com.apple.iCal CalUIDebugDefaultDaysInWeekView -int 14
    ```

2. Restart Calendar, and you should find that Week view now shows two weeks of appointments. In fact, you can alter the command to make Calendar show any number of days in Week view—just change 14 at the end of the line to, say, 21 for a three-week view (although bear in mind that this will require quite a wide screen in order to fit in the entire Calendar window!).

To revert to showing only one week in Week view, again close Calendar; then open a Terminal window, and type the following:

```
defaults delete com.apple.iCal CalUIDebugDefaultDaysInWeekView
```

Restart Calendar, switch to anything other than Week view (i.e., Day or Month view), and then switch back to Week view. You should now find that the display shows only seven days per week, as before.

Tip 269

Scrap the Mac Start-up Chime

Macs are distinctive among the computing fraternity in the melodious chime they make while booting. While PCs that do nothing more than beep might look on enviously, the fact is that the chime isn't always welcome—boot your MacBook Pro in a library, for example, and several annoyed faces will willingly hand out censure.

Creating a Silent Boot

Here's how to deactivate the chime. Because there's no official way of doing this (via a hardware switch, for example), the following solution is a hack that works by muting your computer's volume when you shut down and then unmuting it when you log in again upon rebooting. Unfortunately, this works only if you don't have FileVault turned on, because that uses a different login procedure.

1. Open Terminal (open Finder, select the Applications list, and then in the list of applications double-click Terminal within the Utilities folder), and type nano to open the nano command-line text editor. Then type the following within nano:

```
#!/bin/bash
osascript -e 'set volume with output muted'
```

2. When you've finished typing, hit Control+O, and then type the following for the filename: ~/Documents/mute.sh. Hit Return to save the file.

3. Don't close the Terminal window, but alter the second line within nano to read as follows (that is, change with to read without):

```
#!/bin/bash
osascript -e 'set volume without output muted'
```

4. When you've finished typing, hit Control+X, hit Y, and then type the following for the filename: ~/Documents/unmute.sh. Hit Return to save the file, and then hit Y to confirm you want to save the file with a different name. nano will quit after this.

5. In the Terminal window, type the following series of commands, typing your login password when prompted:

```
sudo chmod u+x ~/Documents/mute.sh
sudo chmod u+x ~/Documents/unmute.sh
sudo mv ~/Documents/mute.sh /Library/Scripts/
sudo mv ~/Documents/unmute.sh /Library/Scripts/
sudo defaults write com.apple.loginwindow LogoutHook /Library/Scripts/
      mute.sh
sudo defaults write com.apple.loginwindow LoginHook /Library/Scripts/
      unmute.sh
```

If you reboot, you should find the chime volume is now muted.

Reactivating the Chime

To restore the chime at a future date, open a Terminal window, and type the following series of commands, again typing your login password when prompted:

```
sudo defaults delete com.apple.loginwindow LogoutHook
sudo defaults delete com.apple.loginwindow LoginHook
```

Tip 270

Supertip: Be a Mission Control Power User

Mission Control is the Mac feature that, among other things, shows small previews of all open program windows (see *Exploring OS X: Mission Control*, on page 127). Although seemingly simple, there's a handful of useful tricks that can make it the center of your Mac universe, as follows.

Using Quick Look Windows

Quick Look also works in Mission Control. In this case, Quick Look expands windows so it's possible to fully see their contents. Simply hover the mouse cursor over the window preview you're interested in, and hit Space. Hitting Space again will cause the Quick Look preview to shrink.

Moving All Windows at Once

Windows can be moved from one desktop space to another space by dragging them onto the desktop thumbnails showing each space that is along the top of the screen. You can move all the windows of a particular app to a new space by clicking and dragging the program's icon to the alternative space. The icon appears beneath the window previews.

Navigating Easily Using the Keyboard

I prefer to activate Mission Control by holding Control and tapping the Up cursor key. Keeping Control pressed, I can then use the Left/Right cursor keys to switch between desktop spaces within Mission Control (for what it's worth, holding Control and tapping left and right when Mission Control isn't active will also switch desktop spaces).

Switching Desktop Spaces

After you've switched to Mission Control, holding Option when clicking a different desktop space thumbnail with the mouse will switch to that space so you can see its apps, but the space won't be activated.

Turn Off App Grouping

By default windows of each app are grouped together within Mission Control. You can turn this off so that all windows for any app are semi-randomly arranged as previews within Mission Control, regardless of which app they are. If you used OS X prior to the Lion release (10.7), you might recall that this was how Exposé worked (the predecessor of Mission Control).

To do so, open System Preferences, click the Mission Control tab, and remove the check mark from the Group Windows by Application box.

Unclustering Apps at 100 Percent Preview Size

By hovering the mouse cursor over a cluster of program windows and scrolling up on a multitouch trackpad or Magic Mouse (or scrolling up the mouse wheel with other mice), you can cause the cluster to expand, showing more detail in those behind the main window. Scrolling down again will contract the windows back to their preview sizes.

This trick can be enhanced with a small tweak to a hidden system setting. To make clustered windows expand to full size (as if you were viewing them on the desktop) rather than merely a little larger than they normally are, open a Terminal window (open Finder, select the Applications list, and then in the list of applications double-click Terminal within the Utilities folder), and type the following:

```
defaults write com.apple.dock expose-cluster-scale -float 1;killall Dock
```

The changes take effect immediately. A variation of this tweak is to substitute a value of 0.6 rather than 1 in the line above (after the -float component of the line). This will cause the windows to expand to a larger size than the default but not to 100 percent of their normal dimensions.

To undo this tweak later, open a Terminal window, and type the following:

```
defaults delete com.apple.dock expose-cluster-scale;killall Dock
```

Press and Hold for Mission Control

Here's a cool trick that works for not only Mission Control but also the Dashboard or Launchpad.

You might be used to tapping a hotkey once to activate that function and then tapping it again to deactivate. However, if you press and hold a hotkey, that particular function will remain active only for as long as you hold down the key. For example, press and hold the Mission Control/Exposé hotkey, and it will disappear as soon as you take your finger off the key. Give it a try!

Tip 271

Switch Between App Windows

The `Command`+`Tab` key combination lets you switch between open applications, but what if you want to switch between open documents or files within the same application?

Simply hit `Command`+`` ` ``. That last one is the backtick key, which is located to the left of the number row on most English keyboards, but you might find it to the left of the `Z` key on some keyboards.

You won't see a fancy list showing which windows are open, like with the main task switcher. Instead, you'll simply cycle through the open windows of the app on each tap of the key, bringing each window to the fore.

You'll cycle through *all* program windows using this trick. For example, if you have a Find dialog box open in a text editor, you can switch between that and the main editing window using `Command`+`` ` ``.

Tip 272

Zoom Into the Desktop

Ever wanted to examine something on a web page in more detail? OS X includes a screen zoom tool that's deactivated by default but can be extremely useful.

Setting Up

To activate the screen zoom tool, start System Preferences (Apple menu→ System Preferences), and click the Accessibility icon. Make sure the Zoom icon is selected, and then check Use Scroll Wheel with Modifier Keys to Zoom. Then close System Preferences.

Zooming In

From then on, if you hold down `Control` and vertically scroll the mouse wheel/ ball (or drag two fingers Up/Down a multitouch trackpad), you can zoom into the screen at the cursor position. This feature is designed for people who have impaired vision, but it's also a quick, albeit low-fi way of zooming into pictures or videos if you don't want to use the application's own zoom tools. Note that you won't actually increase the amount of detail in the picture using this method. Instead, you simply make the pixels larger.

Using a More Accurate Zoom

By default the zoomed image is antialiased; that is, the rough edges of pixels are smoothed over, giving a slightly blurry effect. To quickly switch off antialiasing while zooming, which can give you a less blurred zoomed image, hit `Option`+`Command`+`\`. Hit the same key combination again to reactivate antialiasing.

Tip 273

Quickly Rename a File

There's a couple of cool ways to quickly rename files, as follows:

- To quickly rename a file or folder, select it in Finder or on the desktop, and then hit `Return`. Unlike with Windows computers, this won't open the file but will highlight the filename so you can type over it with something else. If you change your mind and want to leave the name as it is, just hit `Esc`. If you want to rename the entire file including its file extension, simply hit `Command`+`A` to select the entire filename after hitting `Return`.

- You can rename a file as you're editing it, although only in compatible apps (which include most of OS X's built-in apps). To do so, click the filename in the title bar, and then select Rename from the menu that appears. Then type the new filename in the highlighted text field.

Tip 274

Sleep Hard Disks Sooner

Portable Macs include a feature in the Energy Saver pane of System Preferences that will put the hard disk to sleep when it isn't being used (for example, if you're simply browsing the Internet while out and about and not editing files). This can save battery life, especially if your Mac uses traditional mechanical hard disks rather than solid-state disks, but it kicks in only after ten minutes of inactivity—that is, ten minutes after the disk has not been written to or read from.

Going to Sleep Faster

You can reduce this time delay at the command line, causing the hard disk to go to sleep faster. You might find this helps save battery life, although there might be a very brief system freeze each time as the hard disk spins up again.

The following command will make the delay five minutes, but only when the battery is in use and not when the power cable is connected:

```
systemsetup -setharddisksleep 5
```

Restoring Default Sleep Times

To restore things to the default, repeat the command, replacing the 5 with a 10 so that the default delay of ten minutes is reinstated:

```
systemsetup -setharddisksleep 10
```

Tip 275

Force a File to be Found via Spotlight

Sometimes you might find a particular file simply won't appear in Spotlight's search results, even though you know it should. For example, you're searching for files containing the text quarterly report, but you later find that the file Quarterly report 2012.xls in your Documents folder simply didn't show up.

Forcing Files to Be Indexed

The solution is as follows. Open a Terminal window (open Finder, select the Applications list, and then in the list of applications double-click Terminal within the Utilities folder), and type mdimport; then specify the filename and location (or just drag and drop the file onto the Terminal window to autocomplete these details).

For example, to import the file mentioned earlier, contained in my Documents folder, I'd type the following:

```
mdimport ~/Documents/"Quarterly report 2012.xls"
```

Note that I've enclosed the entire filename in quotation marks in the previous example because it contains a space.

Forcing Folders to Be Indexed

Folders can also be specified, in which case all files within will be indexed. The following will index all of a folder called accounts in your Documents folder. Here's an example:

```
mdimport ~/Documents/accounts
```

Tip 276

Turn Off New Time Machine Disk Requests

If you don't use Time Machine, you might notice that every time you attach an external hard disk to the computer, you get asked whether you want to use it for backups.

While it's possible to stop the request happening for each individual disk by clicking the option within the dialog box, you disable this request dialog box from ever appearing again for any disk by opening a Terminal window (open Finder, select the Applications list, and then in the list of applications double-click Terminal within the Utilities folder) and typing the following:

```
defaults write com.apple.TimeMachine DoNotOfferNewDisksForBackup -bool TRUE
```

Then log out and back in again for the changes to take effect.

If you'd like to restore the request dialog later, type the following (log out and back in again after for the changes to take effect):

```
defaults delete com.apple.TimeMachine DoNotOfferNewDisksForBackup
```

Tip 277

Add Your Own System Sounds

With a little hacking you can use your own sound files for system alerts. You can find a variety of sound effect files online—just try Google. However, the files must be in AIFF format. Most sound files you might download from

Exploring OS X: Time Machine

Time Machine will invisibly back up the entire system plus your personal data to one or more external hard drives that are physically attached to your computer. It can also back up or across a Wi-Fi network to a Time Capsule device.[a]

Time Machine makes *incremental* backups, which means you can restore not only the last version of a file but versions going back to when the file was first created. Time Machine stores hourly backups for the past twenty-four hours and then switches to saving a single backup representing every day for the past month. Eventually, it switches to saving one backup representing each week.

Reverting to an earlier version of a file is simply a matter of clicking the Time Machine icon at the top right of the screen and then selecting Enter Time Machine. You'll then see a display of Finder windows stretching back in time. Against the right edge of the screen will be a vertical listing of the times and dates when backups were taken. Clicking any backup will magically return the Finder to that time and show how the files and folders appeared back then—any deleted files will reappear.

It's possible to restore an entire system via Time Machine should a disaster occur—see Tip 322, *Make Use of Boot-Time Options*, on page 335.

---

a.   http://www.apple.com/timecapsule/

websites are in other formats (usually .wav). However, you can convert them to AIFF format using iTunes, as described next.

Remember that alert noises need to be no more than a second or two in length. There's no point in using a three-minute pop song as an alert because it'll continue playing long after you've forgotten what the alert was for.

When you find a sound effect you like on a website, right-click the link to it, and select Downloaded Linked File. Simply clicking the link will play the sound within the browser window.

Converting Sounds to AIFF Format

Assuming you downloaded a .wav file (which is likely), you'll need to convert it to an .aif file. Here's how that can be done:

1. Open iTunes in the usual way—click Finder, select the Applications list, and then double-click iTunes. Then click the application menu, and click Preferences.

2. In the dialog box that appears, make sure the General icon is selected, and then click the Import Settings button.

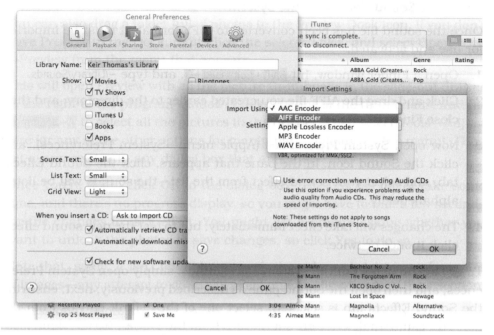

Figure 43—Adjusting iTunes settings to output AIFF files

3. In the new dialog box that appears, click the Import Using drop-down list, and select AIFF Encoder (see Figure 43, *Adjusting iTunes settings to output AIFF files*, on page 301). Then close all the dialog boxes and return to the main iTunes interface.

4. Click and drag your sound file to the iTunes window so that it's imported into your playlist. Locate it in the list (hint: type its name into the Search box at the top right of iTunes), and then right-click it and select Create AIFF Version.

5. Conversion is instant, and you'll find you have two versions of the file. Select the second of the two, and click and drag it to the desktop. You should now have an AIFF file (the file will have an .aif file extension).

6. Now you need to return iTunes to its original settings, so click the application menu again and select Preferences. Click the Import Settings button, and this time select AAC Encoder from the Import Settings drop-down list. You can now close all dialog boxes and quit iTunes.

Tip 280

Quickly Email Text or Pics

Click and drag a text selection, picture, or file to the Mail icon in the Dock to instantly compose a new email with the text or picture in the body or the file attached to the new mail.

Tip 281

Quickly Create a New Sticky Note

The Stickies application is one of the hidden gems of your Mac's built-in software list. You can find it in the Applications list within Finder. The app borrows from the real-life sticky notes, and you can stick virtual notes anywhere on the desktop. Whatever you type on them is automatically saved across reboots.

Sometimes I want to make a note of text on a web page, but this can be a cumbersome experience—I have to highlight the text, copy it, switch to Stickies, and create a new note before I can paste in the text.

Here are two potential solutions to this issue.

Creating New Notes Using Keyboard Shortcuts

The first solution is to highlight the text in the usual way and hit Shift + Command + Y. This will automatically create a new sticky note containing the text.

If photos are included within the block of selected text, they'll be included in the note, but any layout is usually lost (that is, the pictures might not appear where they did on the web page, for example).

Dragging and Dropping

An alternative is to create a Dock icon for Stickies (just drag the Stickies program icon from Applications to the Dock) and then simply drag and drop selected text onto it to create a new note containing the text. So, in Safari, I would highlight text and then click and drag it down to the Stickies icon before releasing the mouse button to create a new note.

If images and links are included in the block of selected text, they too will become part of the note, although—as earlier—the formatting of the web page will probably be lost, and everything will look a little skewed.

Additionally, dragging and dropping image files from Finder or the desktop straight onto an existing note will insert them at the cursor position. You can also drag text clippings into the Dock icon to create a note from the clippings content (see Tip 155, *Save Text Snippets*, on page 177).

Tip 282

Open Finder When Saving or Opening Files

Hitting Command+R while using the File→Open or File→Save As dialog boxes will open a Finder window displaying the contents of the folder you're currently in (provided you're browsing the files on your hard disk and not iCloud). You may find this useful when trying to locate files.

Tip 283

Rename Sidebar Folders

As mentioned in Tip 163, *Supertip: Make Finder Your Hub*, on page 189, you can drag and drop folders onto the Favorites section of the Finder sidebar to create one-click shortcuts to that location on your hard disk. What isn't obvious is that you can rename any folder listed under the Favorites menu by right-clicking the shortcut under the Favorites heading and selecting Rename from the menu that appears. Note that this renames the shortcut and also the original folder.

Tip 284

Choose Music—Via a Screensaver

The iTunes Artwork screensaver is built into OS X and can be chosen using the Desktop & Screen Saver pane within System Preferences (Apple menu→ System Preferences). However, it has a feature that elevates it above a mere display of album cover art—hovering your mouse over an individual cover image will reveal a play button, allowing you to start playing that album (or start the track if the image represents a single song). It doesn't matter if iTunes is not already running—clicking the Play button will start iTunes in the background. If iTunes is already playing music, your selected track will override it.

To quit the screensaver, click the Exit button at the bottom right or hit any key.

Note that if you performed a clean install of OS X Mountain Lion, rather than an upgrade from Lion, the iTunes Artwork screensaver will not be installed on your system.

Tip 285

Know Whether a PDF Is Multipage at a Glance

The file icon for a PDF containing more than one page has a black binder at the left (just as a real multiple-page document would be bound). Single-page PDFs are shown as just one page, sans binding.

Tip 286

Grab Photos and Movies from Your iPhone/iPad

When you attach your iPhone or iPad to your Mac via USB, open Preview and click the File menu. At the bottom of the list you'll see an option to import from the device. Selecting this will show a new window full of pictures and movies on the phone. You can click and drag individual files (or groups of files selected by holding down `Command` or `Shift`) to a Finder window or the desktop, or you can click the Import buttons at the bottom of the screen, in which case a File Save dialog box will open letting you choose a destination. In both cases, a new Preview window will appear showing the pictures as they're imported.

Tip 287

Copy Web Pages to Disk

There are a variety of ways to save web pages to disk within Safari so you can view them later.

Using the Reading List

Perhaps the quickest is to use the Reading List, which is built into Safari and is designed to let you read pages even if your computer is offline. Browse to the page in question and hit `Shift`+`Command`+`D`, or select the Add to Reading List entry on the Bookmarks menu. You can access your stored Reading List pages by clicking the eyeglasses icon at the left of the shortcuts toolbar. You can access your Reading List pages even if you have no Internet connection, making this a useful way to collate pages to read while on a flight, for example.

Reading List only saves the web page text and images. If there are any movies or music in the page, then they won't be saved.

Saving Web Archives

The biggest issue with the Reading List is that only you can read any pages it stores—there's no way to export a Reading List page. To save a web page to disk so it can be opened on any other Mac or on a Windows PC that has Safari installed, click File→Save As; then in the Format drop-down list of the dialog box that appears, select the Web Archive option. This will create a single file that you can email to others or pass to them via a USB memory stick.

Saving as a PDF

To save the web page so it can be viewed on any computer, save it as a PDF file. Click File→Print; then, in the dialog box that appears, click the PDF button at the bottom left. Select Save As PDF in the pop-up menu that appears.

Beware that saving the page as a PDF will strip out most of its formatting, although it should leave the content readable (that is, text and images should be in roughly the correct order).

You might be able to avoid a messy layout by first switching to Reader view of the web page. Reader view is designed to present the body of the page in easy-to-read format without any advertising or other page furniture. Reader will likely work only if the page is article-based (that is, something like a story at a news website). To create a PDF of the page in Reader format, click the Reader button at the right of the address bar before clicking the File→Print button, as described earlier. If the Reader button isn't visible, then Safari doesn't think it's able to reformat the page correctly, and nothing can be done about this.

Tip 288

Recycle Your Apple Hardware (and Get Paid!)

If you have an old Mac or other Apple hardware such as an iPhone, you can recycle it via Apple's official partner, PowerON. If the item has any worth, you'll be given an Apple gift card.

Deciding whether an item has any worth depends on whether the item is functional and also on its age. However, PowerON will also accept broken or very old devices and will even pay for shipping, although it's unlikely you will receive any money for it.

For more information, visit http://store.apple.com/us/browse/reuse_and_recycle. Note that this scheme runs only in the United States, although Apple's website offers advice on recycling elsewhere in the world; some Apple Stores worldwide offer recycling and discount schemes whereby you can bring in old Apple items and receive a modest discount on new hardware.[20]

---

20. http://www.apple.com/recycling/nationalservices/europe.html

Tip 289

Make Calendar Appointment Times Shorter

The Calendar app has a clever feature whereby you can create new calendar events by typing a sentence describing them. Just click the plus icon at the top left of the window and start typing. For example, typing Lunch with parents at 12pm weds will create an appointment on Wednesday starting at 12 p.m. called "Lunch with parents."

However, unless you add how long the event will last, Calendar will always create hourlong appointments. If you're using Calendar to schedule appointments for a business, it might be more convenient if Calendar defaulted to thirty- or even fifteen-minute appointments.

Shortening Default Appointment Times

A secret setting can be tweaked to make this happen. Quit Calendar, open a Terminal window (open Finder, select the Applications list, and then in the list of applications double-click Terminal within the Utilities folder), and type the following, which will shorten the default time to thirty minutes:

```
defaults write com.apple.iCal "Default duration in minutes for new event"
        -int 30
```

Change the number at the end to the number of minutes you want events to last for. For example, the following will shorten the time to fifteen minutes:

```
defaults write com.apple.iCal "Default duration in minutes for new event"
        -int 15
```

Reverting to Default Appointment Times

To revert to an hour, open a Terminal window, and type the following:

```
defaults delete com.apple.iCal "Default duration in minutes for new event"
```

Tip 290

Make Your Mac Speak

Your Mac includes a high-quality speech synthesizer that sounds almost like a natural voice.

Speaking Within Applications

In some applications, especially the built-in apps like Safari or TextEdit, you can make your Mac read by selecting text, right-clicking the selection, and selecting Speech→Start Speaking from the menu that appears. Some people find this useful for proofreading, because hearing the words allows them to pick up on errors their eyes might glide over.

Recording Speech Synthesis

You can also record your Mac's speech synthesis and turn it into an iTunes track for downloading to an iPod/iPhone. In this way, you can turn long articles into home-made podcasts that you can listen to while out and about.

Just select the text, right-click the selection, and click Add to iTunes as a Spoken Track from the pop-up menu. A pop-up window will appear, asking you to define a filename for the new file. Once you're done, click the Continue button. iTunes will automatically start, and clicking the Spoken Text heading on the left of the program window will reveal your new creation.

Changing the Voice

You can change the synthesis voice by selecting the Text to Speech tab in the Speech pane within System Preferences (Apple menu→System Preferences). Click the System Voice drop-down list. The built-in voices aren't very good, but by clicking Customize in the System Voice drop-down list, you can download several high-quality voices. Be aware that these come as very large (multigigabyte) files, however, so they are perhaps best downloaded at home rather than across public Wi-Fi in a coffee shop.

Speaking at the Terminal

Using the Terminal (open Finder, select the Applications list, and then in the list of applications double-click Terminal within the Utilities folder), you can make your Mac read entire text (.txt) files. Just type the following, replacing FILENAME.txt with the name of your file:

```
say -f FILENAME.txt
```

You can also use the say command to make your Mac say anything. For example, you could type the following:

```
say The Mac is the best computer the world has ever known
```

Finally, you can convert any text you type (or a text file) into an AIFF audio file for playing within iTunes or QuickTime Player. The following adapts the previous command to create an audio file called filename.aiff:

```
say -o filename The Mac is the best computer the world has ever known
```

...while the following will convert textfile.txt into a spoken audio file called spokenword.aiff:

```
say -o spokenword -f textfile.txt
```

Tip 291

Get the Most from the Mac Dictionary App

Your Mac includes a fantastic Dictionary application that you can find in the Applications folder of Finder.

Reading the Front and Back Matter

The Dictionary app relies on the prestigious Oxford Dictionary for its word definitions, but the app also contains *all* of the dictionary's pages, including introductory chapters and reading guides. To access these, open the application, and click Front/Back Matter at the bottom of the Go menu. Then click the hyperlinks to individual sections within the Dictionary program window.

Adding New Languages and Variations

You can also search a British version of the English dictionary and thesaurus, plus Spanish, German, and Simplified Chinese dictionaries, as well as Japanese and a Japanese/English dictionary. To activate these, click Preferences on the Application menu and select them in the list within the dialog box that appears. You can click and drag entries in the list to define which results are shown first when you search for words.

Tip 292

Scroll Finder Windows Better

If you drag a file to the top or bottom of a Finder window while in Column or List view and hold it there, the window will eventually begin to scroll up or down. This can be useful, but it's a rather difficult trick to master—often the window will scroll jerkily or scroll a little and then stop.

Activating Better Scrolling

A secret setting can help enhance this feature and make it a useful part of your workflow. To activate it, open a Terminal window (open Finder, select the Applications list, and then in the list of applications double-click Terminal within the Utilities folder), and type the following:

```
defaults write com.apple.finder NSDraggingAutoscrollDelay -int 0;killall Finder
```

The changes take effect immediately, so give it a try by dragging a folder to the top or bottom of a Folder window full of files. You'll see how the Finder window becomes far more responsive to scrolling suggestions.

Reverting to Default Settings

If you decide the change isn't for you, open a Terminal window, and type the following:

```
defaults delete com.apple.finder NSDraggingAutoscrollDelay;killall Finder
```

Tip 293

See Numbers in Huge Type for Easy Jotting

Have you ever wanted to jot down a phone number from the screen but found it difficult because you had to keep looking back and forth from screen to page, constantly losing your place on the screen?

In TextEdit you can simply highlight the telephone number, right-click it, and select Large Type. This works in Mail messages too, although you might also be able to hover the mouse over the phone number until an arrow icon appears and click it, selecting Large Type from the menu that appears. Note that this works only for messages you've received in Mail and not for ones you're composing.

This also works when using Calculator, letting you view the result of calculations—right-click the numbers on the LCD screen and then select Large Type.

In each case, the text will then be displayed in large floating text that fills the width of the screen. To get rid of it, just click anywhere.

Tip 294

Always See Expanded Save Dialogs

This is a tip for those either who don't have iCloud enabled (or don't have the Documents & Data component of iCloud enabled) or who use a lot of apps that are not iCloud compatible.

In Save As dialog boxes, your Mac offers two modes when it comes to saving files onto your hard disk: compact and expanded (see Figure 44, *Dialog boxes can be set to expanded (above) or compact (below) views*, on page 314). Compact size keeps things simple, deliberately offering few choices other than typing the filename, while the expanded size usually displays a file listing and various other options. You can switch between the two using the small down arrow next to the filename (or by hitting Command+=), but small size is the default unless the user changes it.

Your Mac will remember your choice for any particular application once the change is made, but it's possible to force all Save As dialog boxes in all applications to always appear in expanded format, even for applications you haven't used before.

Activating Large Dialog Boxes

To force save dialog boxes to always use large format, open a Terminal window (open Finder, select the Applications list, and then in the list of applications double-click Terminal within the Utilities folder), and type the following:

```
defaults write -g NSNavPanelExpandedStateForSaveMode -bool TRUE
```

Log out and then back in for the changes to take effect.

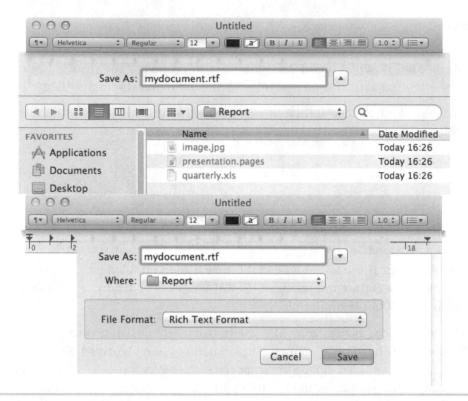

Figure 44—Dialog boxes can be set to expanded (above) or compact (below) views.

Reverting to Default

To revert to compact dialog boxes by default later, open a Terminal window, and type the following:

```
defaults delete -g NSNavPanelExpandedStateForSaveMode
```

Again, log out and back in again for the changes to take effect.

Tip 295

Check Your Grammar as You Type

Your Mac will check your spelling as you type in many applications, underlining mistakes in red, but did you know that it can also check your grammar?

Activating Grammar Checking

To activate the feature in any application where you want to use it (such as Safari, TextEdit, or Mail), open the application and click within a document or new mail window. Then click Edit→Spelling and Grammar→Check Grammar with Spelling. It will remain active for that app when you quit and restart the application until you deactivate it in the same way. You will have to repeat this step for every app in which you want to enable grammar checking.

Correcting Bad Grammar

What OS X considers bad grammar will be underlined in green, but beware that grammar checking is nowhere near as accurate as spell-checking, and—quite simply—OS X will probably get it wrong quite a bit (see Figure 45, *OS X can check your grammar but doesn't always get it right*).

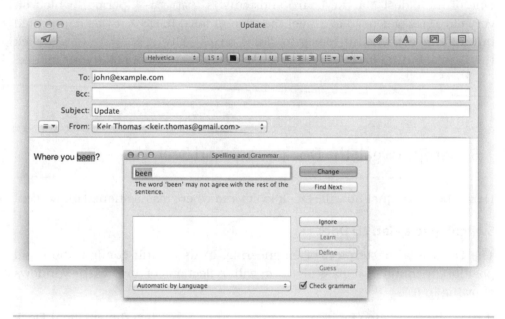

Figure 45—OS X can check your grammar but doesn't always get it right.

Right-clicking any words or phrases highlighted as bad grammar probably won't provide a suggested correction of the suspected error, as with spelling mistakes, or even a description (although suggested corrections might appear for simple mistakes, such as mistaking "it's" for "its").

However, to see the nature of the error, you can hover the mouse cursor over the underlined phrase until a tooltip appears, which will explain the problem, or you can perform a complete spell and grammar check using the Spelling and Grammar dialog box. To begin a full check, click Edit→Spelling and Grammar→Show Spelling and Grammar. Clicking the Find Next button will cycle through any highlighted errors (both spelling and grammar), with a description of what your Mac thinks the error is for grammar mistakes.

Tip 296

Cancel Dialog Boxes Instantly

One of the oldest Mac keyboard shortcuts is `Command+.` (period), which on very old Macs was used to cancel the current task. In OS X it was deprecated but still lingers when it comes to dialog boxes—hitting `Command+.` will click the Cancel button for you, saving you the bother of reaching for your mouse.

Tip 297

Supertip: Tweak the Dock's Look and Feel

Here's how to adjust how the Dock looks and where it's positioned on-screen.

Switching to a Flat, 2D Dock

The Dock is a masterpiece of engineering. In its default configuration and position, it emulates a glass platform with reflections of any nearby windows showing in it.

If that all sounds too fancy, you can switch to a flat, two-dimensional Dock quite easily. Open a Terminal window (open Finder, select the Applications list, and then in the list of applications double-click Terminal within the Utilities folder), and type the following:

```
defaults write com.apple.dock no-glass -bool TRUE;killall Dock
```

The changes will take effect immediately—for an example, see Figure 46, *Switching the Dock to a flat, 2D representation*, on page 317. The flat Dock will work in the same way as before.

To revert to a 3D Dock again, open a Terminal window, and type the following:

```
defaults delete com.apple.dock no-glass;killall Dock
```

Figure 46—Switching the Dock to a flat, 2D representation

Shifting the Dock to a Side of the Screen

You can move the Dock from its original position at the bottom of the screen to the left or right via the Dock pane within System Preferences (Apple menu →System Preferences). However, a quicker way is to hold down Shift and click and drag the bar that separates the application icons from the stacks and the trash.

Just click and drag to the left or right of the screen and then release when the Dock takes its new position. To return the Dock to the bottom of the screen, just click and drag it there in the same way. When the Dock is positioned at the left or right of the screen, it switches automatically to the 2D appearance.

It's possible to shift the Dock to the corner of the screen rather than having it centered. To do this, open a Terminal window, and type the following to shift it to the left if it's at the bottom or to a top corner if it's positioned on the left or right of the screen:

```
defaults write com.apple.dock pinning -string start;killall Dock
```

Or you can type the following to shift it to the right if the Dock is at the bottom of the screen or to a bottom corner if the Dock is positioned on the side of the screen:

```
defaults write com.apple.dock pinning -string end;killall Dock
```

To return it to the middle of the screen, open a Terminal window, and type the following:

```
defaults delete com.apple.dock pinning;killall Dock
```

Make the Dock See-Through

The 3D Dock in OS X Mountain Lion is essentially opaque, like frosted glass. A secret setting can make it translucent to match the menu bar, if you have the translucent setting activated within the General section of System Preferences. To turn on Dock translucency, open a Terminal window, and type the following:

```
defaults write com.apple.dock hide-mirror -bool TRUE;killall Dock
```

To return the Dock to its default opaqueness, type the following into a Terminal window:

```
defaults delete com.apple.dock hide-mirror;killall Dock
```

Tip 298

Add Sketches to PDFs

We discuss in another tip how to insert your signature into PDFs (Tip 356, *Add Your Signature to Docs*, on page 370). However, the system can also be used to insert hand-drawn sketches like maps or diagrams into documents. Just hold the drawing up to the camera instead of your signature, and then resize it appropriately once it's inserted into the document—the drawing will be captured in surprisingly high resolution that makes it suitable for inclusion, even in documents intended for printing.

It's not possible to append such sketches to existing image files, although you can add textboxes and various other annotations to images—just click Tools→Annotate and select an option.

Tip 299

Prune the Right-Click Menu

Is your right-click menu getting a little full, making it hard to see the options you're interested in at a glance? This can be a real issue in Finder because many apps like to add their own entries to the right-click menu that appears for files, but other right-click menus can get filled up too, such as the one that appears when you right-click text.

To control what entries appear in right-click menus, open System Preferences (Apple menu→System Preferences), and click the Keyboard icon. Then click the Keyboard Shortcuts tab, and select Services on the left. Then, to prune the file-browsing right-click menu, look under the Files and Folders heading in the list on the right of the window. Clearing the checkbox next to any entry will immediately remove it from the menu.

To prune the menu that appears when you right-click text, look for entries in the rest of the list under the various other headings in the list on the right of the System Preferences window, with particular reference to the entries under the Text heading.

Tip 300

Quit Finder

You can quit all applications except one: Finder. Finder is designed to always be running, and with good reason—it's responsible for displaying files on the desktop. Quit Finder, and all the desktop icons will disappear. However, there are certain instances when it's useful to quit Finder. Some of the tips in this book require you to restart Finder, for example, although we use the killall Finder command, which is a quick and dirty way of doing so within a Terminal window.

Adding a Quit Option

To add a Quit option to the File menu of Finder's application menu, all you need to do is enter the following line within a Terminal window (open Finder, select the Applications list, and then double-click Terminal in the Utilities folder):

```
defaults write com.apple.finder QuitMenuItem -bool TRUE;killall Finder
```

Starting Finder again once you've quit is easy—just click its icon in the Dock.

Removing the Quit Option

To remove the Quit menu option, open a Terminal window, and type the following:

```
defaults delete com.apple.finder QuitMenuItem;killall Finder
```

Tip 301

Undo File Operations

Just copied or moved a file and changed your mind? The standard undo keyboard shortcut—`Command`+`Z`—also works on the desktop and within Finder windows to undo the most recent actions.

Tip 302

Make a New Folder from Some Files

Want to ultra-quickly create a new folder that contains a handful of files? Just select the files in the usual way by clicking and dragging a rubber band around them (or by selecting them individually by holding down the `Command` key), and then right-click any one of them. The topmost entry in the menu will be New Folder with Selection. Clicking it will do exactly as the description says—you'll find yourself with a new folder containing the files! Rename it in the usual way (see Tip 273, *Quickly Rename a File*, on page 297).

Tip 303

Align Desktop Icons When Dragging

Holding down `Command` while dragging a desktop icon will cause it to align to an invisible grid when you release the mouse button (the equivalent of clicking the Clean Up option on the right-click menu). This also works with multiple files—click and drag to highlight them, and then hold down `Command` while moving them to align them all to a grid when you release the mouse button. This is a quick way of tidying up either the desktop or files in a Finder window if you're using Icon view—select all files (`Command`+`A`), hold down `Command`, and then drag them all a little to the left or right. When you release the mouse button, all the icons will magically slide into place according to the invisible grid.

Tip 304

See OS X Animations in Slow Motion

Holding down `Shift` while clicking just about anything in OS X that uses an animated transition will reveal the animation in slow motion. For example, holding down `Shift` while minimizing a window to the Dock will slow the minimizing process in pleasing slow motion. Holding down `Shift` while activating Mission Control using the keyboard hotkey will do the same.

This feature was added to OS X to allow former Apple CEO Steve Jobs to demonstrate the beauty of window animations while giving the first keynote speech introducing Mac OS X. It has hung around in the decade since!

Tip 305

Know Which Apps Are Hidden in the Dock

There are two ways to send app windows to the Dock on your Mac: minimizing and hiding.

The biggest difference between the two is that minimized app program windows are visibly shrunk to an icon on the right side of the Dock, while hidden program windows simply disappear from the screen and can be brought back to view by clicking their Dock icon (that is to say, they don't shrink to an icon on the right side of the Dock).

Additionally, individual app windows can be minimized, but when hiding an app, *all* its windows are hidden. You can't hide a single app window.

To minimize a program window, click the button on the program's title bar, or hit `Command+M`. To hide an app's windows, click the Hide option on the program's application menu, or hit `Command+H`.

Revealing Hidden Apps

If you choose to hide an app, there'll be no obvious sign that the program is hidden, but you can fix this with a quick Terminal command that will cause the hidden app's Dock icon to be dimmed out (that is, it'll become translucent).

Open a Terminal window (open Finder, select the Applications list, and then in the list of applications double-click Terminal within the Utilities folder), and type the following:

```
defaults write com.apple.Dock showhidden -bool TRUE;killall Dock
```

The changes will take effect immediately, so select an app and hide its program windows by hitting Command+H. The app's Dock icon will take on a ghostly see-through look. To restore the app's windows, just click the Dock icon.

Reverting to Default

To revert to the default mode of hiding apps, open a Terminal window, and type the following:

```
defaults delete com.apple.Dock showhidden;killall Dock
```

Tip 306

Cancel Drag and Drop Mid-Move

Ever found yourself changing your mind about dragging and dropping a file? The problem is that if you let go of the file, it'll be moved or copied to wherever your mouse is hovering over.

To cancel drag and drop, either hit Esc or drag the file to the menu bar at the top of the screen and release.

Tip 307

Make Time Machine Forget a File

Time Machine periodically backs up every single file on your computer, including personal data. That might include data you want to permanently eradicate from your computer so it simply no longer exists—not as a file and not within a backup. You can eradicate a file using Tip 6, *Get Rid of Files—Securely*, on page 16, but how do you remove it from all the Time Machine backups that occurred since the file was created or copied to your computer?

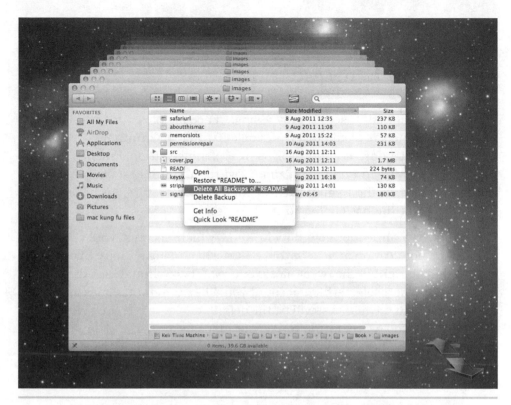

Figure 47—Making Time Machine delete a file from its backup

This is surprisingly easy to do. Start by browsing in Finder to the former location of the file you want to eradicate from backups. Then click the Time Machine icon at the top right of the screen, and if a backup is currently taking place, click Stop Backing Up. Then click Enter Time Machine. Step back to the most recent Time Machine backup in the timeline list on the right of screen, locate the file you want to eradicate, and right-click. Select Delete All Backups Of from the menu. You'll be warned this is a drastic action and asked to enter your login password. See Figure 47, *Making Time Machine delete a file from its backup*, on page 323.

Click Cancel at the bottom left of the Time Machine window when you've finished.

Tip 308

Use Multiple Twitter Accounts

While you're allowed to set up only a single Facebook account within OS X, you're not limited to configuring a single Twitter account. With the Mail, Contacts & Calendars section of System Preferences (Apple menu→System Preferences), you can add two or more Twitter accounts by simply clicking the Twitter logo on the right of the program window (you might have to click the plus icon at the bottom left to see this list).

But this raises an issue: how do you know which account you're tweeting from in the notification area or within Safari when using a Share Sheet? Just look at the top right of the tweet message area. There should be a drop-down list where you can select which account you'd like to send the message from. The account you created first will be the default choice in the drop-down each time. Should you want to make your second account the default choice, simply delete the first account within Mail, Contacts & Calendars (select it, and then click the minus button at the bottom left), and then re-create it, as mentioned earlier.

Tip 309

Connect to Stubborn Shared Folders or Servers

Your Mac can speak the same networking language as Windows computers, meaning you can share files and printers.

Using Finder's Side Pane

Connecting to a shared folder or other resource should be as easy as looking under the Shared heading in the side pane of Finder, clicking the entry for the computer in question, and then clicking the Connect As button and typing the other computer's login credentials when prompted.

Unfortunately, things sometimes don't run as smoothly as this, and it can be hard to diagnose why. The computer simply might not appear in the list.

Specifying a Network Address

Luckily, there's an alternative method of attempting to make a connection, but to use it, you'll need to know the IP address (that is, the numeric network address) of the computer in question. You can ask your local administrator for this information or, on the Windows computer in question, click Start, and in the search field, type cmd. In the command prompt window that appears, type ipconfig and look for the details that appear alongside the IPv4 Address heading.

Back on your Mac, open a Finder window, and click Go→Connect to Server. In the Server Address field, type smb:// and then the IP address. For example, a Windows PC on my network has the address 192.168.1.102, so I would type smb://192.168.1.102. Once you are done, hit the Connect button. Ideally you should now connect and be prompted for your login details.

Connecting to a WebDav Server

To connect to a WebDav server, open a Finder window, and click Go→Connect to Server. In the Server Address field, type the server's address, complete with the http:// or https:// prefix. Then hit Connect. Type the login username and password when prompted. Note that the WebDav share won't appear under the Shared heading in the Finder sidebar but will instead appear under the Devices heading. You can disconnect by clicking the Eject button alongside the entry in the list.

Tip 310

View Another Country's App Store

Are you on vacation but still want to purchase items from the App Store? You might find that the App Store you see is the one for the country you're in rather than for your home country. The solution is to click the small circular flag icon at the bottom right of the App Store home page. On the following screen, you can select which country's store you'd like to visit.

Beware: you can purchase apps only for the country where your Apple ID is registered. Therefore, it's not possible for European Mac users to beat the exchange rate and purchase apps for less in the U.S. store (or vice versa, depending on currency fluctuations!). However, this technique means it's possible for European Mac users to take a look at the U.S. App Store to get information about certain apps that are released in the United States first, before being made available elsewhere.

Tip 311

Record Your Terminal Work

Ever wanted to save your work at the command line, perhaps for showing others? Just hit `Command`+`S` (or Shell→Export Text As) to save all the commands plus output as a text file (that is, everything you see by scrolling up and down to the top and bottom of the window, including any work from the previous session that usually appears grayed out).

Tip 312

Avoid Cluttering Network Shares with .DS_store Files

If you access a network share with Windows computers, you might have heard your fellow users complain about small .DS_store files that appear like breadcrumbs wherever you browse. These are Mac system files that contain data about the directory and are hidden when a Mac browses the folder. However, they're not essential.

Deactivating the Writing of .DS_store Files on Networks

To configure your Mac so these files are not written to network shared folders, open a Terminal window (open Finder, select the Applications list, and then in the list of applications double-click Terminal within the Utilities folder), and type the following:

```
defaults write com.apple.desktopservices DSDontWriteNetworkStores -bool TRUE
```

Once you're done, log out and back in again for the changes to take effect.

Reverting to Default

If you should ever want to reverse the fix in the future (perhaps if you work in an office full of Macs, where it won't be an issue), open a Terminal window, and type the following:

```
defaults delete com.apple.desktopservices DSDontWriteNetworkStores
```

Then log out and back in again.

Tip 313

Access a Secret Dock Visual Effect

You probably know that you can change the visual effect you see when you minimize a window by opening System Preferences (Apple menu→System Preferences), clicking the Dock icon, and selecting from the Minimize Windows Using drop-down list. Two are available: Genie and Scale. Genie is the default effect, while Scale simply reduces the scaling of the window as it moves down to be stored in the Dock.

Activating the Suck

However, there's a third effect not on the list: Suck. As its name suggests, this is rather like the window is being sucked into the Dock by a powerful vacuum cleaner!

To activate the effect, open a Terminal window (open Finder, select the Applications list, and then in the list of applications double-click Terminal within the Utilities folder), and type the following:

```
defaults write com.apple.dock mineffect -string suck;killall Dock
```

The changes will take effect immediately, so give it a try by minimizing a window.

Reverting to Default Visual Effects

To restore things to normal, choose one of the two default minimize effects within System Preferences or open a Terminal window, and type the following:

```
defaults delete com.apple.dock mineffect;killall Dock
```

Note that if you switch apps using the task switcher (Command+Tab), you can still have more than one program window visible on the screen. However, as soon as you next click a Dock icon, all the other windows will again disappear.

Restoring Default Settings

To deactivate the effect later, open a Terminal window, and type the following:

```
defaults delete com.apple.dock single-app;killall Dock
```

You'll need to click the Dock icons of your apps to unhide them one by one.

Tip 317

Add the Trash to Finder

Here's how to create a shortcut to the trash in Finder's sidebar, where you'll be able to drag and drop files for deletion without having to drag them all the way to the bottom-right corner of the screen.

1. Open Finder switch to Icon view (hit Command+1); then hit Shift+Command+G, and in the dialog box that appears, type ~/Trash. Then click the Go button.

2. Switch to Column view in Finder (hit Command+3), and you'll see the trash folder is highlighted in one of the columns. It will have a slightly gray ghostly appearance to indicate that it's a hidden folder, but don't worry about this. Just click and drag it to a position under the Favorites heading on the sidebar. Placing it at the bottom of the list makes sense because then you'll always know where it is.

The shortcut you added to the sidebar is now ready for use, and you can drag files to it to put them in the trash.

Unfortunately, your homemade Trash shortcut isn't a clone of the trash icon in the Dock. As you might have noticed, the icon is incorrect. Finder doesn't allow users to change sidebar icons. Additionally, if you right-click it, you won't be offered the option to empty the trash. Emptying must be done via the trash Dock icon. But other than these quibbles, the new icon should work in the way you'd expect.

To delete the icon at a future date, hold down Command and drag it away from the Finder.

Tip 318

Save a Movie's Audio

Want to separate the audio from a movie clip so you can listen to it on your iPod or iPhone? Just open the clip in QuickTime Player, which is in the Applications list in Finder, and then click File→Export and select Audio Only from the Format drop-down list (see Figure 48, *Extracting the audio from a movie file*, on page 331). This will create an .m4a file compatible with all Apple devices and computers. Just import it into iTunes in the usual way, by double-clicking the new file.

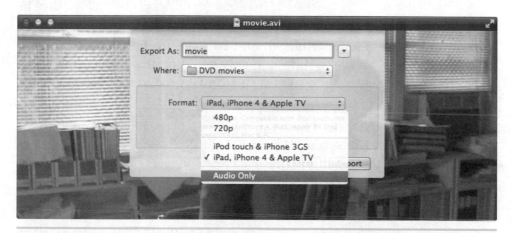

Figure 48—Extracting the audio from a movie file

Tip 319

Save PDFs Automatically to a Folder

Macs are extremely PDF friendly, to the extent that you can output just about any document as a PDF: click File→Print in any application that outputs images or documents, and select the PDF drop-down button at the bottom left of the dialog box.

If you regularly output PDFs to a particular folder, you might be annoyed that you have to navigate to the folder each time you want to save a PDF there.

Luckily, there's a simple solution that will add the folder as an option in the PDF drop-down list within Print dialog boxes. Selecting it will automatically create the PDF there.

Alternatively, or additionally, you can create a magical folder that will convert any file placed into it into a PDF.

Adding a PDF Store Folder

The steps to add a folder as an option to the PDF drop-down list are as follows:

1. Open a Finder window, hit `Shift`+`Command`+`G`, and type /Library/PDF Services.

2. Open another new Finder window (right-click the Finder icon in the Dock and select New Finder Window), and navigate to the folder where you normally save PDFs. You'll need to drag and drop this folder, so if it's in your Documents folder, for example, then you'll need to browse your home folder.

3. Click and drag the folder where you save PDFs to the Finder window that's browsing /Library/PDF Services. However, hold down `Option`+`Command` before releasing the mouse button. This will create an alias rather than copying the folder. You'll be prompted to type your password.

4. You can now close both windows.

From now on, you'll find the folder as an option in the PDF drop-down list in Print dialog boxes, listed beneath the Add PDF to iTunes entry in the list. Just select it to automatically save a PDF file to the folder.

These steps can be repeated to add as many folder destinations as you'd like to the PDF drop-down menu.

To remove the folder later, just repeat the previous steps to browse to /Library/PDF Services, and drag the alias of the folder to the trash. Again, you'll need to type your password when prompted.

Tip 320

Copy and Paste Without the Formatting

Like most modern operating systems, Mac OS X will retain text formatting when you copy and paste text from one place to another. For example, copying a paragraph of text from a website and then pasting it into a TextEdit document will mean it keeps the same font and point size.

There are several ways to avoid this, as follows:

- In some apps, you can click the Paste→Paste and Match Style entry on the Edit menu.

- In some apps, holding down Shift+Option+Command+V will paste without formatting—I usually hold down Option+Command with my thumb and hold down Shift with my pinkie before reaching across with my index finger to hit V.

- In Microsoft Office applications, you can click Edit→Paste Special and select Unformatted Text in the dialog box that appears. (In Word 2011, click Edit→Paste and Match Formatting.)

- If nothing else works, try this: hit Command+Space to open Spotlight, and then hit Command+V to paste the text. Quickly after this, hit Command+A to select all the text you've just pasted, and hit Command+X to copy it again. Then hit Command+Space to close the Spotlight window (or hit Esc twice). Finally, paste the text into your document, where you should find it has been stripped of formatting.

Tip 321

Create Secure Notes

Your Mac provides no fewer than three independent and distinct methods of creating notes.

- Using the Stickies app, found within the Applications view of Finder. This lets you "stick" notes to the desktop and is perhaps the quickest method

Tip 323

Make a "Quit All" App

Ever wanted to quit every single open application? Perhaps you want to free up memory for the launch of another app.

You can create an app using AppleScript Editor that you can place in the Dock and that will quit all open apps when clicked. Here are the steps:

1. Start AppleScript Editor by double-clicking its entry in the Utilities folder of Applications in Finder. If no new file (Untitled) window is visible, click File→New.

2. In the main code area, type the following:

```
tell application "System Events" to set quitapps to name of every
        application process whose visible is true and name is not "Finder"
repeat with closeall in quitapps
quit application closeall
end repeat
```

3. Click the Compile button on the toolbar to check the code to ensure it's correct. If it's OK, the code will be colored and indented properly. If it's incorrect, you'll see an error message, so try typing the code again.

4. Click File→Save, and choose to save the new app in your Applications folder. Call it something memorable—I chose "Quit Everything!" In the File Format drop-down list, choose Application. Then click the Save button.

5. Close AppleScript Editor, and navigate to your Applications list within Finder. Then drag and drop your new app onto the Dock, ready for use.

When using it, remember that you'll still have to deal with any dialog boxes that appear within apps asking you to confirm the saving of changes to files. Additionally, some apps such as Microsoft Word can take up to a minute to quit.

To add an appropriate icon to your app, search Google Images with a search term like *quit icon*, and then download something that looks appropriate. Then see Tip 116, *Personalize Every Icon*, on page 127 to learn how to give your app a new icon.

Tip 324

Upgrade RAM

Most Macs are designed so their memory can be easily upgraded by users, and OS X includes a utility that tells you what's currently filling the RAM slots, as well as if any are free. It also provides a link to the manual on the Apple website that gives step-by-step instructions on how to upgrade.

To access this utility, click the Apple menu, and click About This Mac. Then click the More Info button in the dialog box that appears, and in the new program window you see, click the Memory menu button within the program window. Then click the Memory Upgrade Instructions link at the bottom right. For an example, see Figure 49, *Viewing free memory slots*, on page 337.

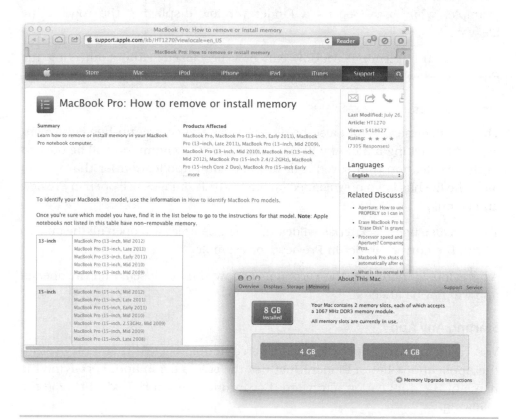

Figure 49—Viewing free memory slots

Tip 325

Start GUI Apps from the Command Line

Sometimes it's necessary to start GUI apps from within a Terminal window. Here's how that can be done.

Opening Finder

To start a Finder window displaying the location you're currently browsing at the command prompt, just type the following:

```
open .
```

That's open followed by a period. Any path will work here, along with relative paths: open ../ opens the parent of the folder currently being browsed, for example, while open / opens a Finder window displaying the root of the filesystem.

Note that the Terminal window can now be closed without affecting the Finder window.

Opening Files

The open command could also be described as the command-line equivalent of double-clicking a file. Any file specified after the command will be opened in the application that saved it or in the default application for that type of file if the file has been downloaded (in other words, images will open in Preview and so on).

You can also use the asterisk wildcard. Typing open *.jpg will open all the images within the current folder in Preview, for example.

As previously, note that the Terminal window can be closed, and the opened app will not be affected.

Starting Any App

You can also start applications as if you'd double-clicked their entry within the Applications list of Finder. Just use the open -a command, specifying the name of the application afterward. For example, to start TextEdit, type the following:

```
open -a TextEdit
```

Applications that involve two words (like Google Chrome) need to be enclosed in quotation marks:

```
open -a "Google Chrome"
```

Alternatively, you can escape the spaces in the usual way with backslashes (that is, open -a Google\ Chrome).

You need to enter the name of the application as it appears in the Applications view of Finder.

To open a file with a specific application, just list it afterward. For example, to open textfile.txt in TextEdit, type the following:

```
open -a TextEdit testfile.txt
```

Opening a Web Address in a Browser Window

To open a web address, specify it after open, but make sure you include the http:// prefix, or you'll see an error message:

```
open http://www.apple.com
```

Other URLs will work fine too: open ssh://192.168.1.1 will open an secure shell connection with the computer at 192.168.1.1, for example. See also Tip 131, *Add Magical Links for Email, Messages, Web, and More*, on page 148.

Creating a New Mail

Just type open -a Mail, and then type the filename for any attachment. For example, to create a new mail with the file Disneyland.jpg attached, I would type the following:

```
open -a Mail Disneyland.jpg
```

Tip 326

Quickly Turn Emails into Docs

If you use Mail, you can simply click to highlight any message within the Inbox, hit Command+C, and then hit Command+V to paste the message contents into an editor such as TextEdit (pasting into Microsoft Word doesn't work). There's no need to manually select all the text in the message.

By selecting multiple emails in the Inbox and then hitting `Command`+`C`, you can paste all of them into a new single document within TextEdit, and they will appear one after the other.

Tip 327

Search Spotlight from Terminal

This is a tip for those who like to use the command-line prompt. To perform a Spotlight search at the command line, use the `mdfind` command. For example, to search for any documents that contain the term `macintosh`, you could type the following:

```
mdfind macintosh
```

The `-onlyin` command option will limit the search to a certain folder, which is useful if you want to find files that are within your `Documents` folder, for example. The following would search for files containing the term `macintosh` within your `Downloads` folder:

```
mdfind -onlyin ~/Downloads macintosh
```

An interesting additional command option is `-count`, which will display how many files there are that contain your search term, for example:

```
mdfind -count -onlyin ~/Downloads macintosh
```

Tip 328

Enable the Root User

Those who have used Unix or Linux in the past might be used to the idea of a root user. This is a user with special powers who can do just about anything to the system without being challenged. It's disabled on OS X for reasons of security, and ordinary users can borrow its powers using the `sudo` command. However, if you just can't do without a proper root account on your system, you can enable it as follows.

Activating the Root Account

Open Finder, hit Shift+Command+G, and enter the following: /System/Library/Core-Services. In the file listing that appears, open the Directory Utility program. Click the lock icon at the bottom left to enable changes, if it isn't already unlocked, and enter your password when prompted.

Following this, click Edit→Enable Root User (see Figure 50, *Enabling the root user login*). You'll immediately be asked to enter a *new* password for the root user, which you'll need to type again in the Verify field to confirm.

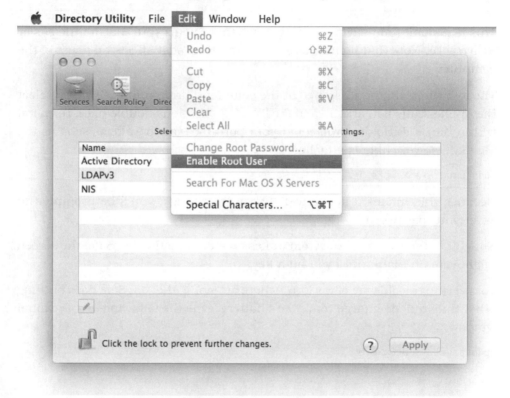

Figure 50—Enabling the root user login

The new account is created instantly.

Following this, you'll be able to switch to the root user in the usual way at the command prompt by typing su -. It appeared to be impossible to log into a GUI desktop as root in my tests, which is just as well, bearing in mind that it would be extremely dangerous to do so.

Deactivating the Root Account

To deactivate the root user account at a future date, start Directory Utility again, and click Edit→Disable Root User.

Wake Your MacBook If the Power Is Attached

This is a small time-saving tip of the type that makes your Mac a little easier to live with. Note that it changes a system setting, so it affects all users of the computer.

The following command, issued at the command prompt (open Finder, select the Applications list, and then in the list of applications double-click Terminal within the Utilities folder), will cause your portable Mac to wake as soon as the MagSafe power cable is attached:

```
sudo pmset -a acwake 1
```

Because this makes a systemwide hardware change, you'll be prompted to enter your password.

Note that even though the system wakes on attaching the MagSafe, the screen might remain blank until you hit a key.

To revert to the old way of working, where attaching the MagSafe does nothing other than quietly charge your Mac's battery, type the following in a Terminal window:

```
sudo pmset -a acwake 0
```

Tip 330

Pass Command-Line Output to GUI Apps

This is a tip for hardcore command-line fans who like a little graphical user-interface goodness in their lives.

Piping Output into Default GUI Apps

As mentioned elsewhere, you can use the open command at the command line to open files in GUI applications (Tip 325, *Start GUI Apps from the Command Line*, on page 338). The command open filename.txt will open filename.txt in TextEdit, for example.

However, the -f command-line switch will cause open to accept output piped from a command. For example, the following will pipe a detailed directory listing in a new document within TextEdit:

```
ls -la | open -f
```

Piping Output into a Specific App

To choose an application other than the default, specify it using the -a switch. I have an alternative text editor called TextMate installed on my system,[22] for example, and the following pipes the directory listing to it:

```
ls -la | open -f -a TextMate
```

Piping Output into the Clipboard

Instead of specifying the open command, you can pass the output of a command to the clipboard, ready for pasting into another app. Simply use the pbcopy command.

```
ls -la | pbcopy
```

Typing Directly into the Clipboard

Should you want to, you can type text directly into the clipboard by specifying the pbcopy command on its own and hitting Return. Type what you want to enter into the clipboard (you can include carriage returns), and hit Control+D when you've finished.

Typing Directly into the "Find" Clipboard

OS X uses a separate clipboard for what appears in find and replace boxes. So, if you want to type something directly at the command line that you'd like to then search for within an app like TextEdit, you can use the following command—just replace "search phrase" with what you'd like to put in the clipboard:

```
echo search phrase | pbcopy -pboard find
```

---

22. http://macromates.com

Then switch to an app like TextEdit and hit `Command+F`, and you'll find the text you typed waiting for you in the Find field.

This command could be used very effectively with the yank feature of Bash.

Inserting Clipboard Contents at the Command Line

It's also possible to reverse the process described previously and paste the contents of the clipboard onto the command line or into a file using the pbpaste command. For example, the following will redirect the clipboard contents—which can come from anywhere, such as Microsoft Word—into a new file:

```
pbpaste > textfile.txt
```

Obviously, any formatting applied to the text is stripped out.

Again, you can add -pboard to output the "find" clipboard contents instead:

```
pbpaste -pboard find > textfile.txt
```

Tip 331

Supertip: Turn Off OS X Features

Across various releases of the Mac OS X operating system, the people behind it have added many new features. You might not use all of them. Some of them can be annoying, especially if you're prone to accidentally hitting the wrong key (for example, activating Mission Control when you didn't mean to do so).

Here's a guide to switching off various features of OS X, along with instructions on how to turn them back on again should you change your mind later.

Note that in terms of memory or computer performance, there's nothing to be gained from turning off operating system features on modern Macs. You should turn off a feature only to remove something that you don't need and that obstructs your day-to-day use of the computer.

Turning Off Notification Center

Notification Center pop ups dialog boxes when something interesting happens, such as receiving an email or an instant message, and lists these notifications in a slide-in list. It's also how you're told about important events such as when system updates are available, so disabling it isn't advised. Remember that if it's merely a particular application that you find irritating because it seems to make too much use of Notification Center, you can stop the app from using notifications within the Notifications pane of System Preferences.

However, if you really can't stand Notification Center, the following command typed into a Terminal window will get rid of it and also remove the icon from the top right of the screen:

```
launchctl unload -w
        /System/Library/LaunchAgents/com.apple.notificationcenterui.plist
```

Log out and back in again.

To restore Notification Center, the following command typed into a Terminal window will do the trick (again, log out and back in again afterward):

```
launchctl load -w
        /System/Library/LaunchAgents/com.apple.notificationcenterui.plist
```

Disabling iCloud

Disabling iCloud is as simple as opening System Preferences, clicking the iCloud icon, and then clicking the Sign Out button. Alternatively, you disable a particular aspect of iCloud on the right side of the System Preferences program window.

To disable iCloud documents storage, which means you won't be prompted to save files to iCloud within applications, remove the check alongside Documents & Data, although be aware this will delete all your iCloud documents from the Mac you're using (you can make copies of the documents by following Tip 25, *Access (and Back Up) All iCloud Documents*, on page 36). Note that if you're doing this merely because you're irritated at always being prompted to save to iCloud rather than your hard disk, you might want to read Tip 93, *Stop iCloud from Being the Default*, on page 97.

Turning Off Mission Control

It's possible to deactivate Mission Control, but this will also make it difficult to switch desktop spaces because that's one of the things Mission Control manages. Once Mission Control is deactivated, the only way to switch desktop spaces will be by holding down `Command` and the Left/Right cursor keys.

Additionally, be aware that turning off Mission Control also deactivates the Show Desktop feature.

To turn off Mission Control, open a Terminal window (open Finder, select the Applications list, and then in the list of applications double-click Terminal within the Utilities folder), and type the following:

```
defaults write com.apple.dock mcx-expose-disabled -bool TRUE;killall Dock
```

Note that this technique disables only the main "all windows" mode of Mission Control. Application Windows mode will still work, which arranges the open windows of the active program—to use it, switch to an app, and hit Command+Down.

To enable Mission Control again later, type the following:

```
defaults delete com.apple.dock mcx-expose-disabled;killall Dock
```

Turning Off Dashboard

The Dashboard is the desktop space that features gadgets. My experience is that either people love this feature and use it all the time or they entirely ignore it.

To kill the Dashboard, open a Terminal window, and type the following:

```
defaults write com.apple.dashboard mcx-disabled -bool TRUE;killall Dock
```

The changes will take place immediately.

To enable the Dashboard again later, open a Terminal window, and type the following:

```
defaults delete com.apple.dashboard mcx-disabled;killall Dock
```

Disabling Spotlight

You can turn off Spotlight's indexing, which can avoid disk churning and occasional system slowdowns, but it's not possible to get rid of its desktop icon—this can be done only through very risky editing of system files, which I can't condone.

Be aware that Mac App Store relies on Spotlight to discover what apps you have installed. Therefore, the auto-update functionality of Mac App Store will no longer work if you disable Spotlight.

However, if in spite of this, you'd still like to turn off Spotlight indexing, open a Terminal window, and type the following, entering your password when prompted:

```
sudo mdutil -a -i off
```

To enable it again at a future date, open Terminal, and type the following, entering your password when prompted:

```
sudo mdutil -a -i on
```

Clicking the icon when Spotlight is deactivated will still perform dictionary lookups and start applications, as described in Tip 210, *Look Up Words Instantly*, on page 237, and Tip 98, *Start Apps Without the Mouse*, on page 104.

Exploring OS X: Automator

Automator allows you to automate tasks that you do frequently or that involve repetitive actions. For example, you could create a workflow to automatically email a frequently updated file to a particular group of people or to rename hundreds of images you've just downloaded from your digital camera.

Automator offers two ways of working, and both are based on *workflows*: chains of small, individual operations that pass information and/or files down the chain from one to another. Automator can record what you do and turn these actions into a workflow, or you can manually construct a workflow from predefined actions. Note that at no point do you need any programming ability—Automator workflows are built around intuitive building blocks, although you can add AppleScript if you want.

A predefined action can be used on its own, or, more commonly, the user can feed output from one action into another for further processing. For example, to create a workflow that grabbed a series of images from a web page, several actions would be needed. The first grabs the web page address, the second uses that data to work out the image links, the third uses the image link data to prepare for download, while the fourth actually grabs the image based on this data.

Recording a workflow is very different from manually creating a workflow from predefined actions and is akin to the macro-recording feature you might have used in applications like Microsoft Office. A workflow recorded in this way might consist of items such as "Click Safari in the Dock," followed by "Click the File Menu," "Save Image As," and "Click the Save Button."

Crucially, Automator workflows can be saved as applications that run when double-clicked or when a file is dropped onto their icon just like other apps. You can also save workflows as services and as folder actions.

You'll find Automator in the Applications list within Finder.

Tip 332

Use Option or Command for Shortcuts

If you're choosing from options in a drop-down list to change a keyboard shortcut in System Preferences, pressing `Shift`, `Control`, `Option`, or `Command` while the drop-down list is open will show additional keyboard combinations involving those keys.

For example, let's say you want Mission Control to activate when you hit `Command`+F9 rather than when you simply hit F9. Open System Preferences (Apple menu→System Preferences), and click the Mission Control pane. Click the drop-down list next to Mission Control to redefine its keyboard shortcut. While the list is open, try pressing `Shift`, `Control`, `Option`, or `Command`—you'll see that the shortcut changes accordingly. Selecting an entry in the list with one of the modifier keys pressed will switch it to that combination.

You can combine keys as well—you can make Mission Control appear when `Shift`+`Command`+F9 is pressed, for example; just activate the drop-down list, and press `Shift`+`Command` at the same time.

Tip 333

Use a Gesture to See App Windows

Swipe down with three or four fingers, and you'll activate the Application Windows mode of Mission Control for the app you're working in. In other words, you'll see previews of all currently open program windows and can click to bring any to the foreground.

What you might not know is that this trick can be extended to view application windows or other apps that aren't currently active. Just position the mouse cursor over any app's icon in the Dock, and swipe down with three or four fingers. Doing so will activate Application Windows mode for that particular app. Swipe back up to return to the desktop.

Tip 334

Change Alias Destinations

Most Mac users know an alias can be created for any file, folder, or application by clicking and dragging it to the new location and holding `Option`+`Command` before the mouse button is released. Aliases are akin to shortcuts under Windows.

Few people know that you can edit an alias to make it point to a different file. To do so, select the alias, hit `Command`+`I`, and in the info window that appears, click the Select New Original button. Note that the name of the alias won't change to match the new file, but its icon preview will change if the alias now points to a different kind of file.

Tip 335

Re-create the Dock from Scratch

The following has never happened to me, but some people report it as a frequent annoyance: when dragging several files to a Dock stack, accidentally missing the target will result in all the files being added to the Dock. Because the Dock scales with size, this can make it unusable.

If deleting all the new icons seems like a little too much work, you can reset your Dock's icons to the default state (that is, as if you've just booted your Mac from new) by deleting its configuration file. Open Finder, hit `Shift`+`Command`+`G`, and type ~/Library/Preferences. Then move the com.apple.dock.plist file to the trash. Immediately log out and back in again.

Tip 336

Reorder the "Menulets"

The small icons next to the time display in the top right of the desktop are known as *menulets*. They're usually arranged in the order in which they start.

To reorder them at any time, just hold down `Command` and click and drag them. Ensure the other menulets slide out of the way to make space before releasing the mouse button, and be careful not to drag the icon off the menu bar before releasing the mouse button because that will remove the menulet. Note that it's impossible to move the Spotlight and Notification Center icons, which always remain in the top-right corner of the screen, and several icons that belong to third-party apps might also be immutable.

You should be able to restore any missing icon by opening Finder, hitting `Shift`+`Command`+`G`, typing /System/Library/CoreServices/Menu Extras, and then double-clicking the .menu file corresponding to the missing menulet.

Tip 337

Wake Troublesome Macs

If you open the lid of your Mac and find that it's having trouble waking up—perhaps it refuses to let you type your password or perhaps the screen backlighting illuminates but the screen itself remains black—then simply close the lid for a minute or so and reopen it. Often things will work properly the second time around.

If after this the computer still refuses to wake, you'll need to forcibly reboot your computer, which you can do by holding down the power button for five seconds. Once the computer has powered down, press the button again normally to boot.

If the wake-from-sleep problems continue, try resetting the PRAM—see Tip 184, *Reset Hardware Settings*, on page 209.

Tip 338

View the True Size of an Image

You can change a setting within Preview that, when you opt to view a photograph at its actual size (View→Actual Size), what you see will mirror the physical dimensions of the image when printed at native resolution. Putting that in simpler terms, if you held the printed page up next to a picture viewed at its actual size once the setting has been activated, the two will be identical.

You might wonder why such a setting is necessary, but on-screen images usually appear smaller than they look when printed, even when viewed at the 100 percent zoom setting.

To make the change, start Preview (it's in the Applications list of Finder), and click the application menu and then Preferences. Then click the Images tab and click the radio button next to Size on Screen Equals Size on Printout.

Tip 339

Convert Audio and Video Files

OS X makes it easy to switch audio or video files to different formats within Finder.

Transcoding Audio

If you have an AIFF or WAV audio file that you'd like to convert to iTunes' native MP4 audio format, which usually has the .m4a file extension, just right-click it and select Encode Selected Audio Files (you might have to click Services →Encode Selected Audio files). Then select the format you'd like from the Encoder drop-down list. Arguably, the High-Quality option in the list is fine for most needs—this will match the quality of the majority of MP3 files currently available, although if you hover the mouse over each option in the list, you'll see a tooltip explaining what the technical settings are. Once you're done, click the Continue button to start the encoding. The new file will be outputted alongside the old one.

Downsampling Video

Want to shrink a 1080p or 720p movie to a smaller frame size? Right-click it, and select Encode Selected Video files (you might have to click Services→ Encode Selected Video Files). Then choose the settings you want from the dialog box that appears and click the Continue button to convert the file. Note that it's not possible to upsample a file; that is, you can't convert a 480p movie to 720p, for example. You can only downsample movies—converting a 1080p movie to 480p, for example.

Tip 340

Extend Quick Look's File Knowledge

http://qlplugins.com has a range of plug-ins that allow Quick Look—the window that appears when you select a file and hit `Space` to preview it—to view all kinds of additional files not typically understood by Macs. Other plug-ins available at this site replace existing Mac plug-ins, such as one that allows you to view pictures alongside all the technical information about them (known as EXIF data). Some plug-ins are free of charge, while others must be paid for.

Most of the plug-ins come with installers, but some you'll need to place in the /Library/QuickLook folder manually (hit `Shift`+`Command`+`G` in a Finder window and type the previous path to browse straight to the folder). The plug-in should work instantly, but if not, you can always force the system to update by opening a Terminal window (open Finder, select the Applications list, and then in the list of applications double-click Terminal within the Utilities folder) and typing qlmanage -r.

To remove the plug-in later, simply visit the /Library/QuickLook folder and delete it.

Tip 341

Use a Hidden Stacks Animation

This is a subtle tip but worth a try for those who truly like to personalize their Mac experience!

When a stack is set to Grid view, the folders appear to pop out with a particular animated effect. You can change this to an alternative that is arguably smoother and prettier.

First ensure you know what the existing effect looks like by right-clicking one of your Dock stacks and selecting Grid from the menu under the heading View Content As. Expand and contract the stack a few times by clicking the stack icon.

Then open a Terminal window (open Finder, select the Applications list, and then in the list of applications double-click Terminal within the Utilities folder), and type the following:

```
defaults write com.apple.dock use-old-grid-animation -bool TRUE;killall Dock
```

The changes take effect immediately, so try clicking the stack again to see the change. You should find that the pop-out window pops up into view more elegantly and doesn't fade into view, as it did previously.

If you decide to revert to the previous pop-out effect, open a Terminal window, and type the following:

```
defaults delete com.apple.dock use-old-grid-animation;killall Dock
```

Tip 342

Google Highlighted Text

Highlight some text in (almost) any application, and tap Shift+Command+L; Safari will automatically Google the text for you—even if it's not already open! This should work in any app that hasn't defined the Shift+Command+L keyboard shortcut for another function.

Tip 343

Use a Secret Gesture to Switch Spaces

There's a secret gesture you can use with Mac multitouch trackpads that lets you double-tap with four fingers to switch back to the most recently used desktop space (tap, not click!). For example, should you switch to the Dashboard space from the main desktop, double-tapping in this way will switch back to the desktop. Note that this gesture involves merely tapping the trackpad and not clicking. This remains true even if you have Tap to Click turned off in System Preferences.

To activate the gesture, you'll need to use a hidden setting. Open a Terminal window (open Finder, select the Applications list, and then in the list of

Repairing Disk Permissions

To repair disk permissions, start Disk Utility, which can be found in the Utilities folder within the Applications list of Finder. In the Disk Utility program window, select the partition on which OS X is installed—usually it's the indented second entry in the list of disks at the top left of the Disk Utility window. Then make sure the First Aid tab is selected. Now click the Repair Disk Permissions button. The process usually takes about five to ten minutes to complete. See Figure 51, *Repairing permissions for a smooth-running computer* for an example.

Figure 51—Repairing permissions for a smooth-running computer

Repairing the Disk

Although you might see the Repair Disk button in the same program window, don't click it. In fact, it's impossible to repair the disk while OS X is up and running. Instead, you must boot to the recovery system—reboot the computer, and then press and hold Command+R just before the boot-time Apple logo appears. Release it when the recovery screen appears, and select the Disk Utility option. As for repairing the disk, select the OS X partition and click the First Aid tab, but this time click the Repair Disk button. Again, the repair will take a few minutes to complete. Once done, click the Restart option from the main menu.

Tip 349

Tear Off Tabs

Some OS X apps, such as Safari and Terminal, make use of tabs. The standard keyboard shortcut in such apps to create a tab is `Command+T`. In most cases, the tabs can be "torn off" to create a new program window containing just that tab—just click and hold the tab, drag down, and then position the new window where you want before releasing the mouse button.

Tip 350

Move Time Machine to a Larger Disk

If you use Time Machine, you might find the backup disk beginning to get full. You'll know this because OS X will start to warn you that it's deleting old backups to make space. The solution is to buy a bigger disk. Migrating your Time Machine backups to the new disk is easy. Here's how. (These tips assume the disk is new and blank.)

1. Attach the new backup disk directly to your computer's port, rather than via a hub, to make the whole process of swapping backup disks much faster. Try to have a free USB/FireWire port on your computer ready for attaching to the old backup disk (although you shouldn't do so at this stage).

2. You'll need to partition and format the new disk in a Mac-compatible way. Many commercial hard disks are preformatted for Windows, which your Mac can work with in normal circumstances, but Windows formatting isn't compatible with Time Machine. Start Disk Utility. This can be found in the Utilities folder of the Applications list in Finder.

3. In the Disk Utility window, select the new disk on the left side of the window (select the main entry for the disk and not the indented entry beneath that shows the partition). Ensure you select the new disk and not the old one, or you could accidentally wipe your old Time Machine data!

4. Click the Partition tab within Disk Utility. Then, in the drop-down list beneath Partition Layout, select 1 Partition.

5. Give the disk a name in the relevant field (something like New Time Machine would be great), and then make sure the Format drop-down reads Mac OS Extended (Journaled).

6. Click the Options button. In the dialog box that appears, click the GUID Partition Table entry, and click OK. Finally, click the Apply button to partition the disk ready for use. This process might take a minute or two—watch the progress display at the bottom of the Disk Utility window.

7. Once it's finished, close Disk Utility and open Finder. Locate the new disk in the list in the side pane. Select it and hit Command+I.

8. In the dialog box that appears, look at the very bottom. Expand Shared & Permissions, and ensure there's not a check next to Ignore Ownerships on This Volume. If the box is checked, click the padlock icon to unlock the dialog, enter your password when prompted, and then click to remove the check. Close the info window when you're done.

9. Attach the old Time Machine disk, ideally in its own USB/FireWire port on your computer, rather than via a USB/FireWire hub. This will make the cloning process much faster. Then open System Preferences (Apple menu→System Preferences), and click the Time Machine entry. Temporarily turn off Time Machine by clicking the switch.

10. Open a Finder window and locate your old Time Machine disk under the Devices heading in the side pane. Browse the contents of the disk, and click and drag the Backups.backupd folder to the new Time Machine disk. This will copy across the backup files and will probably take some time to complete. Remember that while this is happening you aren't protected by Time Machine backups, so it might be wise to avoid working on the computer for this period.

11. Once the copy has finished, eject and remove the old Time Machine disk. Again, activate System Preferences, and click the Time Machine icon.

Click the Select Disk button, and then select your new Time Machine disk. Then click the Use Disk button.

12. Reactivate Time Machine by clicking the slider control.

This is all that's required. Check that your new Time Machine disk works by entering Time Machine in the usual way and browsing back through your file history. Once you're 100 percent sure everything is OK, it's a wise idea to blank the old backup disk by repartitioning and reformatting it as described in the previous steps. If you don't, each time you attach it to your computer OS X will attempt to make a backup to it, which could prove confusing.

If you find there's an issue with the new Time Machine disk, simply turn off Time Machine, eject the new disk, and reattach the old disk before repeating all the previous steps to format the old disk for use with Time Machine.

Tip 351

Let Spotlight Search More Files

Put simply, Spotlight will index only the content of files it understands, with a bias toward everyday files such as office documents. If you regularly use a different kind of file created by a specialist application, then you might find Spotlight won't index it.

The solution is to find a Spotlight plug-in that does so. You'll find many online or at some download sites,[24] but you might also simply Google for the name of the program that generates the file, adding the text *spotlight plugin* to the search query.

Installing Plug-Ins

In most cases, installation of the plug-in should be just like any other program, so you'll need to run an installer. In some cases, however, you might simply download a file with an .mdimporter file extension, in which case the file will need to be manually copied to the ~/Library/Spotlight directory (open a Finder window, hit Shift+Command+G, and then type in the directory to visit the folder). If the Spotlight folder doesn't already exist, you'll have to create it.

24. For example, http://mac.softpedia.com/get/Spotlight-Plugins---Utilities/

Then open a Terminal window (open Finder, select the Applications list, and then in the list of applications double-click Terminal within the Utilities folder), and type mdimport -r, followed by the full path and location of the new plug-in. This will install it. For example, I downloaded a Spotlight plug-in called Tarimporter,[25] which lets Spotlight index the contents of .tar archives. Tar archives are the default archive type under Unix. After creating a Spotlight folder in my Library folder—because it didn't already exist—and then copying the plug-in there, I typed the following to install it:

```
mdimport -r ~/Library/Spotlight/tarimporter.mdimporter/
```

Note the trailing slash; because .mdimporter files are actually package bundles, they appear at the command prompt in their true form as folders.

Uninstalling Plug-Ins

To uninstall a Spotlight plug-in, simply delete it from the ~/Library/Spotlight directory and then log out and back in again, or see the plug-in's home page for instructions on how to uninstall it.

Tip 352

Supertip: Optimize Screen Sharing

OS X includes a tool whereby you can use one Mac to remotely view the desktop of another Mac across a network or Internet connection. This can be useful if you want to do something on an iMac in your home office while using your MacBook in a downtown cafe, for example.

Getting a working Screen Sharing setup can involve modifying arcane network settings in order to make the remote Mac accessible from the Internet. However, with Back To My Mac offered as part of iCloud, Apple has created an idiot-proof setup, as follows:

1. While sitting in front of it, enable Screen Sharing on the Mac you want to access while out and about—its checkbox is within the Sharing pane of System Preferences, which you'll find on the Apple menu.

2. Ensure you're signed into iCloud on both computers using the same Apple ID, and then enable Back To My Mac on both computers—the remote Mac

---

25. http://www.macupdate.com/app/mac/21178/tarimporter

and the one you intend to use to access it remotely. This can be done within the iCloud pane of System Preferences. Back To My Mac invisibly creates a secure network connection between computers across the Internet, with no need to alter firewall settings or configure Internet routers.

You can then connect to the remote Mac while out and about by finding the remote Mac's entry under the Shared heading within Finder and clicking the Share Screen button at the top right of the Finder window.

If you decide not to use Back To My Mac, the remote Mac will need to be Internet accessible. This can be done several different ways, such as configuring the demilitarized zone (DMZ) of the remote Mac's Internet router to pass incoming Screen Sharing (also known as VNC) requests to the Mac. Alternatively, a popular choice is to use a third-party Dynamic DNS service like DNS2GO,[26] if the Internet router is compatible with it.

Note that the remote Mac's firewall is automatically configured when you activate Screen Sharing to allow incoming connections. No modification or setup is necessary on the computer you want to use to connect to the remote Mac.

Once setup has been completed, here are some tips to make using Screen Sharing more productive.

No Need to Log In

There's no need to leave the remote Mac logged into your desktop. In fact, although it needs to be left switched on, you can simply leave the remote Mac at the login screen. You'll still be able to connect to the screen of the remote Mac, as described earlier. When you do, you'll see the login screen of the remote Mac, where you'll be prompted as usual to select a user account and then log in with the password. However, remember that—once you're logged in—anybody able to view the remote Mac's screen will see everything you're doing.

Log In as a Different User

Let's say the iMac in an office has two user accounts: one for Jane and one for Gary. Jane is using the iMac to do some word processing. Meanwhile, Gary is in a cafe on the other side of the city, with his MacBook Air in front

---

26. http://www.dns2go.com

of him, and would like to connect to his account on the iMac via Screen Sharing to check some files.

Even though Jane is using the iMac, there's nothing stopping Gary from remotely logging into his desktop via Screen Sharing. If Gary specifies his *own* username and password, he'll be asked if he wants to get permission to access Jane's desktop or log into his own account and see his own desktop. If he selects the former, Jane will see a dialog box asking her to give him permission. If he clicks the latter, Gary will be shown the iMac's login screen, where he can log in to his own desktop as if he's sitting in front of it. Jane won't be aware of any of this and can continue working (the desktop Gary sees is described as being *virtual* and only he can see it). In other words, Jane and Gary will be able to access their desktops on the iMac, simultaneously.

There are a few things to note, however. First, this won't work if Back To My Mac is used when setting up Screen Sharing. It will work only if—as mentioned during the setup instructions earlier—the Internet router the iMac is connected to has been configured to allow incoming Screen Sharing connections. Gary will also need to connect to the iMac manually via the Screen Saver app—see the instructions in "Manually Connect to Screen-Sharing Computers."

Second, this assumes that Gary has an administrator user account on the iMac. This is the default type of account, so he probably does. However, if he's merely a standard user, on the iMac it's necessary during screen-sharing setup to open System Preferences, click the Sharing icon, select Screen Sharing in the list on the left, and click the radio button alongside Allow Access for All Users.

Avoid Sharing Your Clipboard When Screen Sharing

One caveat when using OS X's Screen Sharing tool is that any items copied or cut to the clipboard on either computer are automatically transferred to the clipboard on the other computer. This includes not only text but also files, images, and so on.

This can be annoying, but turning it off is simple: when the Screen Sharing app is running and you're connected to the remote computer, simply click Edit→Disable Shared Clipboard.

This will affect only the current screen-sharing session. To make the change permanent, click Screen Sharing→Preferences, and remove the check from Use Shared Clipboard.

Note that you'll still be able to share clipboard contents after this if you need to—just click Edit→Get Clipboard to get the clipboard contents of the remote computer, or click Edit→Send Clipboard to pass your Mac's clipboard contents to the remote computer. You can also click the buttons on the toolbar.

Drag and Drop Files While Screen Sharing

You can drag and drop files and folders onto the window showing the remote Mac in order to instantly transfer them to that computer. This works the other way too—you can drag files and folders out of the window to transfer them to the Mac at which you're working.

Adjusting Image Quality

By default OS X will attempt to get the best image quality it can bearing in mind the speed of the Internet or network connection you're using. It's pretty good at this, and generally the image quality is excellent, but you can force Screen Sharing to always show you the best-quality image, often at the expense of making the connection jerky, by clicking View→Full Quality. To switch back to OS X managing the image quality, select View→Adaptive Quality.

Note too the Screen Sharing window can be resized in the usual way by clicking and dragging its edges, which will shrink the image. This can make it easier to access a remote Mac on a laptop, for example, although it can make text on the remote Mac a little more difficult to read.

You can switch the remote Mac's image within Screen Sharing to grayscale using a secret command. I find this makes it easier for me to identify the remote Mac's desktop and not confuse, say, a Finder window on the remote Mac with one on the Mac I'm using!

To switch to grayscale images, close Screen Sharing if it's open, open a Terminal window (open Finder, select the Applications list, and then in the list of applications double-click Terminal within the Utilities folder), and type the following:

```
defaults write com.apple.ScreenSharing controlObserveQuality 2
```

To reactivate full-color connections later, quit Screen Sharing if it's open, and then type the following into a Terminal window:

```
defaults delete com.apple.ScreenSharing controlObserveQuality
```

Create Font Families

Although most of us don't get beyond bold and italics, many of OS X's fonts include other style variations, such as Light or Condensed.

The OS X font manager app, Font Book, lets you create font *collections* in which you can place such fonts to organize them for ease of access. Collections are like folders that hold files within Finder, although fonts aren't actually copied or moved into collections. They're merely a way of categorizing them, and one font could be in several different collections.

Crucially, however, font collections are displayed in the Fonts palette that appears whenever you hit Command+T in apps like TextEdit of Pages. Microsoft Word offers a Font Collections submenu at the top of its font listing too, where you can select to use collections.

Creating a New Smart Collection

You can easily create a new collection in Font Book by starting the app (it's in the Applications list of Finder) and then clicking the plus icon at the bottom left of the window. Then drag and drop fonts into it. However, you can also create *smart collections*, which are collections automatically sorted according to certain criteria. You could have a smart collection of only Condensed fonts, for example, or a collection of Light fonts.

To create a smart collection, select the entry on Font Book's File menu. In the dialog box that appears, give the collection a name (i.e., Light Fonts), and then select Design Style in the left drop-down list on the bottom left of the dialog box. In the drop-down list alongside, select whatever style of font you'd like to include in the smart collection, such as Condensed or Bold. If the option you want isn't there, instead select Style Name from the bottom-left drop-down, and then type the font style into the field alongside. If you wanted to create a collection of Light font styles, for example, then you would type Light. Once done, click OK.

Your new smart collection will appear on the left side of the Font Book window.

Removing a Collection

To delete a font collection (whether created manually or a smart collection), just right-click it and select the Delete option from the menu that appears.

Tip 355

Speed Up Making SSH/SFTP/FTP Connections

If you regularly create command-line connections to remote computers, you can speed up the process by creating bookmarks for the computers within Terminal.

Creating Bookmarks

This requires Terminal be added to the Dock, so do so by clicking and dragging it there from the Utilities folder within the Applications view of Finder. Start Terminal, right-click its icon, and select New Remote Connection in the menu that appears.

In the window that appears, select the type of connection you'd like to create (that is, SSH, SFTP, FTP, or Telnet), click the plus button under the Server list, and type the fully qualified domain name (FQDN) or IP address of the remote computer in the dialog box that appears. Then click OK to save the new bookmark. Then to test it, select it from under the Server heading, and click Connect to open a new Terminal window that, when it's connected, will prompt you for your username and password in the usual way (you can speed up the procedure a little by typing your username into the User field of the aforementioned dialog box).

Making Connections

The bookmark is now stored. To make the connection in the future, start Terminal if it's not already running, and then right-click it and again select New Remote Connection. Then in the window that appears, select the bookmark you created, and click the Connect button.

Many different server bookmarks can be defined in this way.

Connecting via Back to My Mac

If you have the Back to My Mac feature activated on the remote Mac (see *Exploring OS X: iCloud*, on page 211), there should be no need to create a shortcut, assuming the following:

- Both the remote and local computer are logged in with the same iCloud ID.

- The remote computer has Remote Access enabled.

If this is the case, you could find that the remote computer is automatically listed when you select the Secure Shell (SSH) option within the New Remote Connection dialog box, as mentioned earlier. All you need to do is select it, type your username in the field, click the Connect button, and then type your password when prompted in the new Terminal window that appears.

Tip 356

Add Your Signature to Docs

Preview is OS X's general-purpose image and PDF viewer, but recent versions have brought substantial PDF annotating capacities similar to Adobe Acrobat (open a PDF file, and click Tools→Annotate). OS X includes the ability to add your written signature to PDF files, provided your computer has an iSight/FaceTime HD camera or an attached webcam.

Putting a Signature on File

Here are the steps required to add your signature to Preview:

1. Start by grabbing a white piece of paper and signing your name with a black pen, ideally one with a thicker rather than a thinner nib. Don't use lined paper or paper with a margin—it must be entirely white. If possible, don't underline your signature or add any other kind of flourish, which can confuse the scanner tool.

2. Start Preview (it's in the Applications list in Finder), and click the application menu and then Preferences (or hit `Command+,`).

3. In the dialog box that appears, click the Signatures icon. Then click the Create Signature button.

4. You'll see a preview of what the camera sees (see Figure 53, *Adding a written signature to a PDF file*). Hold the written signature you created so that it rests on the blue line in the middle of the preview and fills the interior lightened square within the preview window. After a few seconds, you'll see snapshots of the signature start to appear on the right of the window. When you see one you're happy with, click the Accept button. Then close the Preferences dialog box.

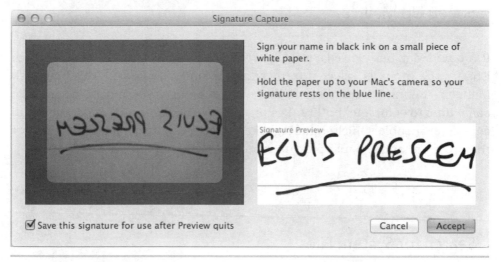

Figure 53—Adding a written signature to a PDF file

Inserting the Signature

Once the signature is stored on file, inserting it each time you need to is easy.

1. Make sure the PDF into which you want to insert the signature is open. Click Tools→Annotate→Signature. Then click the signature button on the annotations toolbar that appears—it's ninth from the left and looks like an S placed on a line.

2. The cursor will change to a crosshair; click anywhere to insert your signature. Click and drag the handles at the corners to resize it if necessary.

You can add several signatures in the way described earlier—just click the plus button at the bottom left of the Preferences dialog box after selecting the Signatures tab.

Clicking the application menu and then Preferences, and then the Signatures icon will let you delete stored signatures—select it in the list and click the minus icon at the bottom left.

Tip 357

Speed Up Mail

If you find Mail has slowed a little, try rebuilding its message index databases. Ensure the Inbox is selected (rather than a single mailbox), and then click Mailbox→Rebuild. Depending on how many messages you have, it might take some time to complete, but it takes place in the background, and Mail is still completely usable while rebuilding takes place. You can even quit and restart the program, and it'll just pick up rebuilding where it left off.

Tip 358

Search for System Files

OS X works hard to keep users separate from system files, and this can make tracking down files outside of your Users folder tricky. However, here are two ways to do so.

Using Spotlight

In terms of files, Spotlight searches only those in your personal User folder. This is very limiting, especially if you're used to the more wide-ranging search tools of other operating systems that can be used to track down system files too.

There's no way to make the main Spotlight tool search for system files, but you can use Finder's Spotlight search tool to uncover them. Here's how.

1. Hit Option + Command + Space to reveal the Finder Spotlight window, no matter which app you're currently using (if that key combination doesn't work, try Control + Option + Space).

2. Click the plus button next to the Save button. This will add a new filter for the search. Click the Kind drop-down list, and select Other.

3. In the list that appears, put a check next to System Files, and click the OK button. Back in the Finder window, change the drop-down list next to System Files Are Included.

4. Finally, type your search query into the Spotlight field at the top right of the Finder window, and ensure This Mac is selected alongside the Search heading. After a few seconds, you should start seeing the results, which will include system files.

5. If you click the Save button, located just beneath the search field, you can add the system file search to the sidebar of Finder, to be used again (just select it each time and type the search query as described earlier). Otherwise, you'll have to repeat these steps each time you want to search for a system file.

Using the locate Command

As a version of Unix, OS X comes complete with the locate command, which can be used at the command line to track down any kind of file—a system file or a user data file. locate relies on a database of file locations and names that are periodically and automatically updated (as such, unlike Spotlight, locate knows only the names of files and doesn't index their contents).

However, locate isn't activated by default. You can do so by opening a Terminal window (open Finder, select the Applications list, and then in the list of applications double-click Terminal within the Utilities folder) and typing the following, entering your login password when prompted:

```
sudo launchctl load -w /System/Library/LaunchDaemons/com.apple.locate.plist
```

This needs to be done only once.

To use locate in the future, just specify the search query after typing locate -i. For example, to search for the location of the hosts file, you could type the following:

```
locate -i hosts
```

The -i flag tells locate to ignore case sensitivity. Note that it will take some time for the initial locate database to be created, in which case you'll see error messages when you try to use the locate command.

To deactivate locate, type the following, which will deactivate the periodic updating of the locate database:

```
sudo launchctl unload -w /System/Library/LaunchDaemons/com.apple.locate.plist
```

Tip 359

Set the Default Operating System

If you have Microsoft Windows installed on your Mac alongside OS X, you might always want to boot to it rather than to OS X. Holding down `Option` when booting will offer a choice of operating systems, but to make Windows the default boot-time choice on your computer, open System Preferences (Apple menu→System Preferences), click the Startup Disk icon, and select the Windows option in the listing. Then hit Restart to restart your computer and make the change permanent.

To revert to OS X being the default boot-time choice, boot to your Mac installation and repeat the previous steps, this time selecting the Mac hard disk in the list before clicking the Restart button.

Tip 360

Dump a Snapshot of Your Mac

There might be certain situations where you need a snapshot of your computer. For example, if you spot a bug in a program, the developer might need to know what your computer is doing when the bug occurs.

Taking a Snapshot of Everything Happening Right Now

The sysdiagnose command will dump all technical information about your computer's state and configuration into a series of files. You can use sysdiagnose one of two ways: at the command line by simply typing it or by holding down `Shift`+`Control`+`Option`+`Command`+`.` (period). If you choose to use the key combination, sysdiagnose will take about a minute to complete, although there will be no sign of its progress. Eventually a Finder window will open that shows the data that's been gathered. This is stored in /private/var/tmp.

Be aware that some personal data is included in the dump, including the serial number of your computer, the computer name, and your username. Don't hand over the sysdiagnose data to somebody you don't trust.

Creating a Hardware and Software Snapshot

If you just want to dump all the hardware capabilities of your Mac into a file, along with what software you have installed—perhaps for sending to somebody else via email—you can open a Terminal window and type the following:

```
system_profiler -xml -detailLevel full > ~/Documents/systemprofile.spx
```

This will generate a systemprofile.spx file in your Documents folder that, when double-clicked, will open in the System Profiler app for easy reading. Thus, this is the best format for sending to another Mac user. If you want a plain-text version for viewing on just about any computer, the following command will output a simple systemprofile.txt file in your Documents folder containing the same extensive information:

```
system_profiler -detailLevel full > ~/Documents/systemprofile.txt
```

Once again, be aware that personal information is included in the dump, such as your username and Mac's hardware serial number.

Tip 361

Search for Carriage Returns and Tabs

Holding Option while hitting Tab or Return within a Find or Find and Replace dialog box in most OS X apps will insert an "invisible" tab or carriage return character, allowing you to search for tabs and carriage returns within the document. Such invisibles can be combined with any other search term.

Tip 362

Work Better in Sunlight

If you have a portable Mac, you might know how difficult it can be to see the screen in very bright and sunny conditions, even with the screen illumination turned up full. One solution is to invert the screen colors so that any text becomes white against a black background. To do this, hit Option+Command+F5 so the Accessibility palette opens, and then check Invert Display Colors under the Display heading. Repeat later to restore screen colors to normal.

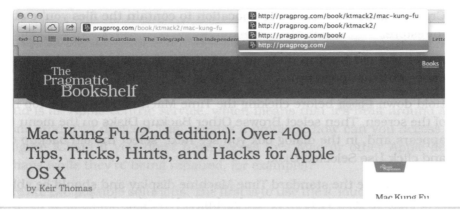

Figure 54—Quickly navigating to a site's home page in Safari

Tip 369

Reorder Finder Sidebar Headings

You can click and drag any of the sidebar headings (Favorites, Shared, Devices, and so on) to reorder the list. Want the Devices listing at the top of the Finder sidebar? Just click and drag the Devices heading up there! Whatever heading is already there will move out of the way to make space for it.

Tip 370

Switch Tabs Quickly

In an app that uses tabs, like Safari, you can switch between tabs by holding Control and tapping Tab. Add Shift also to move left in the tab selection. Note that this won't work in Terminal, because the Control key is used at the command line for other functions.

Tip 371

Quickly Adjust Preferences for Any App

Hitting Command+, (that's the comma key) will open the Preferences dialog box for the app you're currently using.

Tip 372

Grab Files from Your Mac While Miles Away

There are a variety of ways of accessing files on your Mac's hard disk while you're away from it. Of course, for these tips to work, your Mac will need to be left turned on when you're not sitting in front of it, and you'll have to ensure it isn't set to go into sleep mode after a period of inactivity (look at the Energy Saver settings within System Preferences).

Using the Back To My Mac Service

The easiest and most fuss-free way of accessing files is to use the Back To My Mac service, which is offered as part of iCloud (see *Exploring OS X: iCloud*, on page 211). However, this can be accessed only via another Mac.

Back To My Mac makes it seem like the home Mac and remote Mac are on the same local area network—as if they're in the same home or office. It does this via a secure tunnel across the Internet.

Back To My Mac requires both the home Mac and the Mac you're using to access the files to be signed in with the same iCloud ID.

Some setup is necessary, as follows:

1. On the home Mac, open System Preferences (Apple menu→System Preferences), and then click the iCloud icon. Then check the Back To My Mac box. Note that you might see a warning about enabling Universal Plug 'n' Play or NAT Port Mapping on your Internet router, and if so, you should consult the router's documentation. Back To My Mac will work without this enabled but will be slower than it could be.

2. Click the Show All button in System Preferences, and then click the Sharing tab. Check File Sharing.

3. There's no need to select a folder to share because, by default, those logging in with the username and password of an account get access to that user's home directory automatically.

4. When done, close System Preferences.

5. On the remote Mac, you'll need to repeat step 1 to enable Back To My Mac, but there's no need to repeat steps 2 and 3 to enable File Sharing.

Once you've enabled Back To My Mac on the remote Mac, the home Mac will appear in the Finder sidebar under the Shared heading, where you can click it to automatically log in and access its files. Remember that in all likelihood file transfer will be pretty slow!

When you've finished transferring files, click the Eject button alongside the computer's entry.

Sharing Files Using SSH

OS X features SSH, software that allows command-line logins from remote computers across a network or the Internet. A component of this software is SFTP, which is essentially a secure version of File Transfer Protocol (FTP), which you might have encountered if you've ever created a website. SFTP lets you retrieve and transfer files from a computer without the risk of snoops (although on your Mac it is supported only at the command line and not via Finder).

SSH can be enabled by starting System Preferences (Apple menu→System Preferences) and then opening the Sharing pane. Check the Remote Login box in the list on the left. On the right you can allow either all of the users on the system to log in remotely or just some (although this is moot if you're the only user of your system).

You can use SFTP from the command line of another computer if it has the correct software, but most graphical FTP clients include SFTP support.

Remember that you'll also need to ensure your Internet router hardware allows SFTP connections. This can be done within its configuration panels. There is no need to deactivate or alter any setting of the OS X firewall—it is automatically opened to allow incoming SSH/SFTP connections.

Configuring FTP

For what it's worth, OS X includes a standard FTP server that you can enable by typing the following:

```
sudo -s launchctl load -w /System/Library/LaunchDaemons/ftp.plist
```

This will run in the background as a service, and there will be no sign it's running. It will persist across reboots. To permanently deactivate FTP, type the following:

```
sudo -s launchctl unload -w /System/Library/LaunchDaemons/ftp.plist
```

However, bear in mind that every security expert agrees that FTP is too unsecure to use, especially when SFTP is available, which in terms of features is virtually indistinguishable yet is encrypted throughout.

Tip 373

Move Back and Forward in Apps

Apps like Finder, System Preferences, and App Store have back/forward buttons so you can easily move back and forward in your browsing history. However, they don't obey the usual back/forward trackpad gesture of swiping two fingers left/right. However, OS X offers two other ways to move back and forward in your history:

- Hold down Command, and then hit [or] to move backward and forward, respectively.

- If your Mac has a multitouch trackpad, you can hold down Option and swipe three or four fingers left or right on the trackpad.

Tip 374

Play Games

Are you flying across the country, intending to work for the journey but found your mind just isn't cooperating? In addition to the venerable Chess app within the Applications view of Finder, some very simple games are included in OS X as part of the Emacs command-line text editor. To play Tetris, open a Terminal window (open Finder, select the Applications list, and then in the list of applications double-click Terminal within the Utilities folder), and type emacs; then hold down `Esc`, and hit `X`. Then type tetris. Use the Left/Right cursor keys to move the blocks and the Up cursor key to rotate them. Hit `Q` to quit the game and then `Control`+`X` followed by `Control`+`C` to quit Emacs.

Other games to try—specify them instead of tetris, as described earlier—include pong, solitaire, snake, gomoku, and dunnet (a text adventure game). To see the full game list at the command prompt, type ls /usr/share/emacs/22.1/lisp/play—the name to type in Emacs is the filename for each game but without the file extensions.

Tip 375

Run X11 (XQuartz) Apps Full-Screen

If you regularly use any apps that require X11 (now known within OS X as XQuartz),[32] such as the Inkscape vector graphics editor,[33] then you might be used to the confusion of each XQuartz app utilizing its own menu bar. A way to make XQuartz apps easier to work with is to integrate XQuartz with Mission Control's spaces and to run XQuartz full-screen. Here are the steps:

1. Create a space specially for XQuartz. This can be done by starting Mission Control using either the keyboard hotkey or `Control`+Up and then holding `Option` and pressing the plus button in the top-right corner of the screen.

2. Switch to the new space, and start XQuartz by hitting `Command`+`Space` and typing XQuartz. Hit `Return` to start the program.

3. Right-click the XQuartz icon in the Dock, and click Options→This Desktop.

4. Click XQuartz's application menu, and then select Preferences. Select the Output tab in the dialog box that appears, and check the boxes Full-Screen Mode and Allow Menu Bar Access in Full-Screen Mode.

5. Close the Preferences dialog, and then quit XQuartz (right-click its Dock icon and select Quit).

---

32. X11 is not part of the default Mountain Lion (and newer) installations of OS X; it is now known as XQuartz and can be downloaded from http://xquartz.macosforge.org.

33. http://inkscape.org

From now on, any apps you start that require X11/XQuartz will automatically switch to the new space to run, and they will start in full-screen mode without the Dock or OS X menu bar present. However, by nudging the mouse cursor at the top edge of the screen, you can make the main OS X window appear. Here you'll be able to quit X11 once you've quit the app running within it.

X11 takes over the keyboard so all keyboard shortcuts and hotkeys that allow you to switch spaces or activate Mission Control no longer work. However, a curious trick (or possibly a bug!) will let you get around this—nudge the cursor at the top of the screen so that the OS X menu bar appears, and then click the Help menu. Full-screen XQuartz will disappear, revealing the desktop. You can now switch spaces in the usual way or use Mission Control. To return to full-screen XQuartz, just click the XQuartz icon on the Dock, click Window, and select the app from the list beneath. This will also switch you back to the XQuartz desktop space.

Tip 376

Get Cool Wallpapers from Screensaver Packages

The images included within screensavers on OS X can be explored, and the high-quality images they use can be extracted and used as desktop wallpapers.

There are two stashes of screensaver files. The first contains old screensavers with lower-resolution images, and the second contains new screensavers with very high-resolution images. You can extract images from both as follows:

1. Start by creating a folder within your Documents folder where you can store the wallpaper files you're going to extract. It doesn't matter what you call this.

2. We'll start with the folder containing the old screensavers. Open a Finder window, hit Shift+Command+G, and type /System/Library/Screen Savers. You should see screensavers listed by name. We'll start by extracting the images from the Beach screensaver, although the technique is the same for all the files in the folder with a .slideSaver file extension, such as Cosmos.slideSaver. Right-click Beach.slideSaver and, in the menu that appears, click Show Package Contents.

3. Use Finder to navigate to the Resources folder. Here you'll find the images listed, usually in sequence and usually in the JPEG format. In the Beach

screensaver, for example, they're named Beach01.jpg, Beach02.jpg, and so on. Click and drag them all to the new folder you created earlier.

4. Repeat the steps for any other screensavers you'd like to take images from, such as Cosmos.slideSaver or Forest.slideSaver. Only .slideSaver files contain images—ignore the other screensaver files.

5. Once you've finished, you can move onto the second stash of new high-resolution screensaver images. In a Finder window, again hit Shift + Command + G, and this time type /System/Library/Frameworks/ScreenSaver.Framework/Versions/A/Resources/Default Collections/, before hitting the Go button.

6. You'll see four folders numbered 1 to 4, each also describing their contents (for example, 1-National Geographic). Dip into each folder, and drag and drop the images into the folder you created earlier.

7. Open System Preferences (Apple menu→System Preferences), click the Desktop & Screen Saver icon, and then click the Desktop tab. Open Finder, locate the folder containing your new wallpaper images, and click and drag it to the left of the System Preferences window under the Folders heading. The folder will be added, but note that it's only a link to the folder you created—if you delete the original folder, the images will disappear from the list.

Tip 377

See What Disk Space Is Taken Up by Media

OS X's About This Mac application can show in a crude way how much of your hard disk is taken up by music, movies, photos, apps, and backups (that is, Time Machine snapshots—see Tip 160, *Back Up Without a Time Machine Disk*, on page 185). Additionally, if there are any external storage devices attached, you'll see the same information for those.

To access the application, click the Apple menu, and select About This Mac. Then in the window that appears, click More Info. In the new program window, click the Storage menu button. For an example, see Figure 55, *Seeing at a glance what kind of files fill your hard disk*, on page 387.

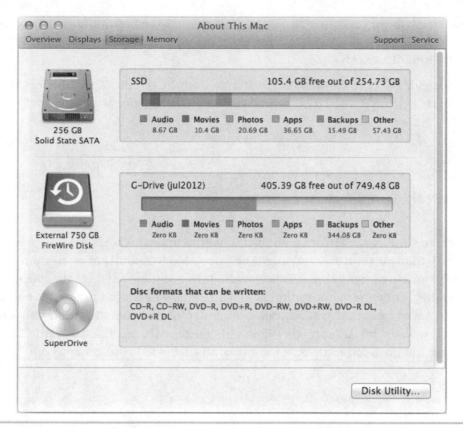

Figure 55—Seeing at a glance what kind of files fill your hard disk

Tip 378

Switch Dashboard Back to Overlay Mode

Up until OS X Lion, the Dashboard magically overlaid the main desktop when it was activated. In recent releases of OS X, however, it's been converted into a desktop space.

If you prefer the old way of working, open System Preferences (Apple menu→ System Preferences), select the Mission Control icon, and remove the check next to Show Dashboard as a Space. This change will take effect immediately.

You'll now have to switch to Dashboard either by using its hotkey, if your Mac's keyboard has one, or by hitting F12 (Fn+F12 on portable Macs and Macs with aluminum keyboards).

A nice side effect of making this switch is that the "ripple" special effect that formerly appeared when a new widget added to the Dashboard is also restored.

Tip 379

Tweak iTunes Visualizations

If you're a fan of the iTunes visualizations that appear when music is playing (View→Show Visualizer), you might be interested to know that often there are configuration options that can be tweaked. To see them, just hit the question mark key while the visualization is playing. This will show a menu indicating other keystrokes that will change the nature of the animations. If you use the classic visualization mode (View→Visualizer→iTunes Classic Visualizer), hitting the question mark key for a second time will bring up a second help menu.

Tip 380

Add Finder to Launchpad

If you're a fan of Launchpad, you might notice a strange omission—you can't open a Finder window from within Launchpad. There's no Finder icon.

The solution is simple. Open a Finder window using the Dock icon, hit Shift+Command+G, and type /System/Library/CoreServices. Then look for a file called Finder (it'll have the same icon as the Dock's Finder icon), and drag and drop it on top of the Launchpad icon in the Dock.

Activate Launchpad, and, hey, presto—you now have a Finder icon! It will probably be at the bottom of the first page of app listings or perhaps on the last page of the Launchpad app listing. You can move it to the first page by clicking and dragging it to the left edge of the screen.

Tip 381

Create an Instant Wired Network Between Macs

To create an instant network between two Macs, just connect them via a standard network cable. Your Mac will take care of the rest. Then enable file sharing on one or either Macs—open System Preferences (Apple menu→System Preferences), and click the Sharing icon. Then check File Sharing. The other Mac should now appear in Finder under the Shared heading. You'll need to log into the other Mac using the account you have on that computer.

Tip 382

Use Full-Color Emoticons

Emoji are similar to emoticons you might already use: things like :-) for a smiley face, for example. The difference is that they're full-color high-quality images, and they're usually distributed as a special font. They're popular in Japan and are rapidly spreading to the West.

OS X includes default support for Emoji, as does iOS, the operating system that runs the iPad, iPhone, and iPod touch. Therefore, you can add them to email messages, for example, and text documents created with apps like TextEdit, although apps such as Microsoft Word don't currently support Emoji.

Setting Up Emoji Access

Emoji can be inserted using the Special Characters palette, which you can activate in most apps by clicking Edit→Special Characters (or by hitting Option + Command + T).

If that option isn't visible, you can add the Special Characters app to the Dock, where you can click to activate it in all apps. To do so, open a Finder window, and hit Shift + Command + G. In the dialog box that appears, type /System/Library/Input Methods. Then look for the file called CharacterPalette. Click and drag it to the Dock to create a shortcut for future use. Alternatively, you can drag it to the desktop, but before releasing the mouse button, hold Option + Command to create an alias.

Inserting Emoji

Start the Special Characters app in either way described earlier, and in the left of the program window select Emoji. Then select a category of Emoji icon from the column next to this—People, Nature, Objects, Places, or Symbols. Finally, select the icon you want from the list of icons, and then click and drag it to where you want to insert it into your email, document, and so forth. See Figure 56, *Accessing Emoji characters*. Alternatively, if you activated the Special Characters palette via the Edit menu or keyboard shortcut, you can position the text cursor where you want the Emoji to appear and then double-click the Emoji in the Special Characters window.

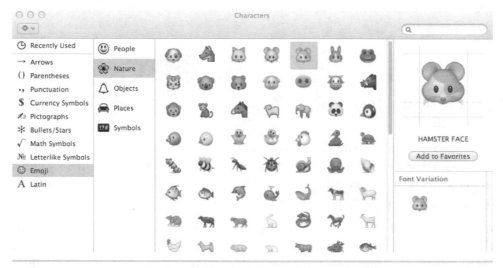

Figure 56—Accessing Emoji characters

Click the cog icon at the top left of the Special Characters window to alter the size of the icon display—selecting Large will show more detail, but be aware this will also affect an icon's size when inserted into documents. To alter the size of an Emoji once it's been inserted into a document, select it and use the standard font point size adjustment tool, usually available on the formatting toolbar.

Remember that any Emoji you insert into emails and documents will appear when opened by other OS X computers (running Lion or Mountain Lion) and on iPads and iPhones, but they won't appear on Windows or Linux systems or on Macs running pre-Lion releases of OS X. Instead, users will see a missing character symbol instead (usually a question mark symbol within a box).

Using Emoji for File and Folder Names

Emoji can also be used in file and folder names. The best technique for inserting them is to open a TextEdit document, insert the Emoji you'd like to use (as described previously), and then copy and paste this when you come to save a file or when you rename a file.

However, although OS X seems happy to allow Emoji to be used in file and folder names, I suspect this might cause future problems. Should you share a file with a Windows or Linux computer, for example, the filename will appear to be corrupted, although in my brief testing the files still seemed to open correctly.

Tip 383

Supertip: Be a TextEdit Power User

As its name suggests, TextEdit started life as a simple text-editing application. However, it has grown into a fully fledged word processor to the extent where it's good enough for light to moderate use. It can be found within the Applications list of Finder, and here are a few tips to help you get the very best out of it.

Type and Spell-Check Foreign Languages

This is less of a tip and more of an observation, although it's worth knowing. If you start typing in a non-English language, TextEdit will automatically switch its spell-check dictionary to that language. Start typing in German, for example, and it will spot any errors in the German words you type. Right-clicking a misspelled word underlined in red will bring up a list of suggested German-language corrections.

Start typing in English, however, and TextEdit will again realize and switch the dictionary for that particular part of the document to English.

Go to a Particular Line

There's a hidden keyboard shortcut within TextEdit that lets you jump straight to a particular line number. This can be useful for programmers, even though there is no option within TextEdit to actually display line numbers! To jump to a particular line, just hit Command+L, and then type the number in question.

Copy the Font Style of Some Text

Let's say you're working on a complicated document in TextEdit and want to add a paragraph. However, you also want to copy the same font and style as a paragraph earlier in the document. Simply place your cursor within the older paragraph, and hit `Option`+`Command`+`C`. Then place the cursor where you'd like to type, and hit `Option`+`Command`+`V`. If you start typing, you should find it matches the font and style.

Search Better

If you search for a word or phrase in TextEdit, you'll see that the document view is dimmed, and any instances of the search term are picked out in stark white. Additionally, you can click the left and right arrow buttons in the Find toolbar to move a yellow "blob" highlight through the document that shows instances of the search term.

The problem is that the yellow "blob" expands beyond the boundaries of the word or phrase and covers letters to the left and right, which can make it difficult to see whether this particular instance of the found search term is the one you're looking for.

The solution is to click anywhere within the document. This will deactivate the screen dimming. The search toolbar won't disappear, and if you keep using the left and right arrows to find the search term, the yellow blob will contract to a simple highlight of the word or phrase, within a second or two of finding it. It's a subtle but useful difference.

Replace Text Within a Selection

At first glance, TextEdit doesn't seem to offer any way of replacing text within a selection you've made in a document. However, if you hold the All button on the Find/Replace toolbar, a pop-out menu will offer the option. See Figure 57, *Replacing text within a selection in TextEdit*, on page 393 for an example.

Add Word Counting

TextEdit lacks one key feature that students and professional writers might miss: word count.

This feature can be added using a little AppleScript, as follows (with many thanks to tip creator Mike Riley, author of fellow Pragmatic Bookshelf title *Programming Your Home*):

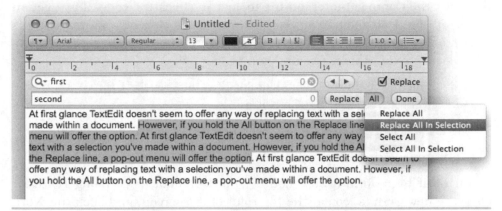

Figure 57—Replacing text within a selection in TextEdit

1. Open a Terminal window (open Finder, select the Applications list, and then in the list of applications double-click Terminal within the Utilities folder), and then type the following:

```
mkdir ~/Library/Scripts/
```

Close the Terminal window.

2. Start AppleScript Editor, which you'll find in the Utilities folder within the Applications view of Finder.

3. Click the program's menu, and then select the Preferences entry. In the dialog box that appears, ensure the General tab is selected, and check the Show Script Menu in Menu Bar heading. This will add a new icon to the top right of the screen, which you can ignore for the moment. Close the Preferences dialog box.

4. Back in the main AppleScript Editor window, type the following code:

```
tell application "TextEdit"
set wc to count words of document 1
if wc is equal to 1 then
set txt to " word."
else
set txt to " words."
end if
set result to (wc as string) & txt
display dialog result with title "Word Count" buttons {"OK"} default
        button "OK"
end tell
```

5. Click the Compile button on the toolbar to check the code. If you get an error, check to ensure you've typed everything correctly. If everything is fine, you should see that AppleScript reformats the code slightly so it's easier to read—this is fine and can be ignored.

6. Click File→Save. In the Save As dialog box, hit Shift+Command+G; then type ~/Library/Scripts/, and hit the Go button.

7. Give the script the filename Word Count, and then click the Save button.

8. Quit AppleScript Editor.

If you want to perform a word count on a document when using TextEdit, click the new Scripts icon at the top right of the screen, and click the Word Count entry, which will probably be at the bottom of the list.

To remove the word count feature, open a Finder window, hit Shift+Command+G, and then enter ~/Library/Scripts/, before hitting the Go button. Then delete the Word Count file. Open AppleScript Editor once again, open its Preferences dialog box, and remove the check next to Show Script Menu in Menu Bar.

Copy a Ruler from One Doc to Another

Did you know that you can copy a ruler within TextEdit, complete with a set of tabs you might have created, from one document to another? Or from one place in a document to a later or earlier position? Just hit Control+Command+C to copy the ruler; then, after positioning the cursor where you want to apply the rule, hit Control+Command+V. Alternatively, you can click the options on the Format→Font menu.

Create a New Document from a Text Selection

Ever wanted to instantly create a new document within TextEdit from text you've selected? For example, if you're writing a letter and want to create a nearly identical duplicate, you could highlight the text you want to be in the duplicate and then hit a keyboard shortcut to instantly create a new document containing it.

OS X makes it easy to set up a new keyboard shortcut and menu option to allow just this, as follows:

1. Open System Preferences (Apple menu→System Preferences), and click the Keyboard icon. Then select the Keyboard Shortcuts tab.

2. Select the Services heading in the list on the left.

3. Scroll down the list on the right to the Text heading. Underneath this, several entries down in the list, will be New TextEdit Window Containing Selection (although it might appear truncated as "New TextEdt Window Contai..."). Check it. This will add it to the menu that appears when you right-click text in TextEdit.

4. If you'd also like to assign a keyboard shortcut, click the small, almost invisible, word *none* at the right of the line within the list. Then click the Add Shortcut button that appears. Adding shortcuts can be tricky because you mustn't use a shortcut already in use.[34] In this case, I find that Control + Option + Command + N works well.

5. Restart TextEdit for the changes to take effect.

You can now right-click selected text and select New TextEdit Window Containing Selection from the menu that appears, or you can select text and hit Control + Option + Command + N.

To deactivate the function later, repeat the previous steps, but simply remove the check alongside the TextEdit Window Containing Selection entry in the list within System Preferences. You'll have to restart TextEdit for the changes to take effect.

Instantly Zoom In or Out

If you have a trackpad, you can zoom in or out in TextEdit using the pinch-to-expand gesture (that is, placing your finger and thumb together on the trackpad and moving them apart; contracting them again will zoom out).

Change Page Color

You can switch the page color in TextEdit by opening the Text palette (Command + T) and then clicking the fourth icon from the left on the palette—the one that looks not unsurprisingly like a page icon! Then just select a color from the pinwheel that appears. It will be applied instantly.

Note that the page color is merely for your viewing ease and pleasure. Although the color choice will be saved with the document and will reappear when you open the document in the future, the background color won't appear when the document is printed. Nor will it appear if the document is opened in any

---

34. A reasonably comprehensive list of keyboard shortcuts used in OS X can be found on Apple's support pages: http://support.apple.com/kb/HT1343.

other word processor apart from TextEdit. Currently there's no way to implement background colors within TextEdit.

Note that this same trick works when writing an email, although you must first click within the body of the email before bringing up the Color palette. Unlike with TextEdit, the background color will appear in mails sent to other Macs (and if the mail is viewed by http://icloud.com), but in my tests it didn't appear if the email was viewed using Microsoft Windows email clients. Therefore, you should be careful if you select to use white text against a dark background color—for any recipients of your email using Windows, the mail will appear to be white text against a white background and therefore be unreadable!

Tip 384

Migrate from Windows to Mac Without Losing Data

If you're setting up a Mac for somebody who's switching from a Windows computer, head over to http://support.apple.com/kb/DL1415 to download the Windows Migration Assistant. This runs on Windows and exports to the new Mac email from Outlook, Outlook Express, Windows Mail, and Windows Live, alongside contacts, calendars, the iTunes library, personal files within the home directory, browser bookmarks, and localization settings. It transfers this data to a computer running OS X via its network connection (either Wi-Fi or Ethernet), so both computers will need to be online and part of the same network.

Once the Windows app has been started, it will search the network for a Mac computer ready to accept the data. If the Mac has already been set up, start the Migration Assistant app within the Utilities folder of the Applications list within Finder. If the Mac has not yet been set up (that is, it's new and hasn't even been booted for the first time), switch it on and follow the OS X setup steps until you reach the Transfer Information to This Mac stage. Then, from the list of possible sources, select From a Windows PC.

Whichever route you take, you'll be prompted to confirm the computer you want to import from, and a short numeric passcode will be shown on the screen of both computers so you can confirm it is the correct computer.

Following this, on the Mac you'll be prompted to select the kind of information you want to transfer. Clicking the Continue button should start the import process.

Be careful not to wipe the Windows computer too quickly after the process has finished. Check to make sure all your files have been transferred across first.

Tip 385

Shrink and Expand Fonts in Docs and Emails

If you use the Text palette to set fonts and font sizes (hit `Command`+`T` when editing a document or email), you can set font sizes by specifying multiples of existing sizes, rather than specifying exact point sizes.

To do so, highlight some text, click in the Size text field, and, rather than typing a point size, type an asterisk followed by a decimal multiple. For example, to increase the text size by 1.5x, you would type *1.5. To double the font size (2x), you would type *2. You can specify a number less than 1 to reduce the text size: *0.7 will reduce the font size to 70 percent of what it was (10-point text will be reduced to 7 point, for example).

This tip comes into its own when globally modifying all fonts within a document. For example, if you've written a letter and want it to fill a page, you can highlight everything (hit `Command`+`A`) and then type *1.1 to grow all the fonts in the document by 10 percent. Or if text overflows onto the next page by two lines and you want to make the letter fit a single page, you could reduce all the fonts to 90 percent of their original sizes by typing *0.9.

Tip 386

Use Safari While Booted to the Recovery System

Hold down `Command`+`R` before the Apple logo appears during booting, and you'll boot to the recovery system. Here you can perform disk checks, restore the system via Time Machine, and even reinstall OS X. See Tip 322, *Make Use of Boot-Time Options*, on page 335.

You can also unofficially launch apps that are installed within the main OS X installation. It isn't intuitive to do so, but you might want to launch Safari to be able to research a problem you're having.

While booted to the recovery system, click Utilities→Terminal, and then type the following:

```
/Applications/Safari.app/Contents/MacOS/Safari
```

Once you've finished, hit Command+Q twice to quit Safari as well as the Terminal window that launched it. This will return you to the main recovery options dialog box. To restart the computer, click the Apple menu, and then select the Restart option.

Tip 387

Expand QuickTime Player's Knowledge of File Types

This book has largely avoided recommending third-party tools you can download, but there are two exceptions: Windows Media Components for QuickTime and Perian.[35] These are system add-ons that allow your computer to play practically all movie and audio file formats. This is needed because OS X's support for movie files doesn't go much beyond its own QuickTime formats and DVD movie discs.

Once installed, Perian will add an entry within System Preferences (Apple menu→System Preferences) by which you can configure some of the options for audio output and so on (although there's usually no need to do so). Windows Media Components for QuickTime includes a special player application, accessible within the Applications view of Finder, but you can ignore this because, as the name implies, after installation you'll find that QuickTime Player is compatible with Windows Media files.

To play all types of media files, many people ignore QuickTime Player completely and use the third-party app VLC instead. Visit http://www.videolan.org/vlc/download-macosx.html for more information.

---

35. http://windows.microsoft.com/en-US/windows/products/windows-media-player/wmcomponents and http://perian.org/, respectively

Tip 388

Read Apple Manuals for Your Products

It's often claimed that, beyond a few pamphlets, Apple doesn't produce manuals for its products. The truth is that the company does in fact create all kinds of documentation, including manuals. Apple just doesn't include them in the box with the product.

Head over to http://support.apple.com/manuals, where you'll find various types of documentation for Apple software and hardware products, including OS X.

Alternatively, if you just want to read the manual for your Mac hardware, click the Apple menu and then About This Mac. Click the More Info button in the dialog that appears, and in the new program window click the Support menu button at the right. Then click the User Manual link.

Tip 389

Use a Non-Apple Keyboard with Your Mac

It's possible to use a standard PC keyboard with your Mac. However, in my experience the modifier keys sometimes get mixed up.

Ideally, the "Windows key" (that is, the key with the Windows logo) should operate as the Command key, usually identified on genuine Mac keyboards with a ⌘ symbol, while Option and Control should work as marked on the keys. However, for some reason, Option and Command sometimes get swapped.

Yes, it's very confusing. But here's how to fix it:

1. Open System Preferences (Apple menu→System Preferences), and click the Keyboard icon. Make sure the Keyboard tab is selected.

2. Click the Modifier Keys button. At the top of the dialog box that appears, select Unknown External Keyboard in the drop-down list next to the Select Keyboard heading.

3. Using the drop-down list next to the Option ⌥ Key heading, select ⌘ Command.

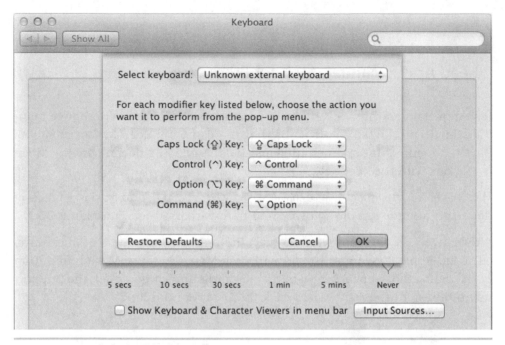

Figure 58—Changing modifier key designations for a PC keyboard

In the drop-down list next to the Command ⌘ Key heading, select ⌥ Option. Everything should look like Figure 58, *Changing modifier key designations for a PC keyboard*. Click OK, and close System Preferences.

The changes will take effect immediately.

Tip 390

Connect to Network Shares at Login

If you work in an office or have more than one computer in your home, you might be used to connecting to shared folders across the network. However, you'll also know that your Mac expects you to create a new connection every time the computer boots. This can be annoying.

It's possible to automatically connect to shared folders upon login, as follows:

1. You'll first need to make connected servers appear as icons on the desktop. To do so, first open Finder, and click the application menu and then

Preferences. Make sure the General tab is selected, and check Connected Servers, under the Show These Items on the Desktop heading.

2. Connect to the shared folder if you're not already connected (usually you can do this by clicking the shared computer's icon in the side pane of the Finder window, under the Shared heading, but see Tip 309, *Connect to Stubborn Shared Folders or Servers*, on page 324 if you can't). In the login dialog box, be sure to put a check next to the option for remembering the password in the keychain.

3. Open System Preferences (Apple menu→System Preferences), and select the Users & Groups icon. Unlock System Preferences if necessary by clicking the padlock icon; then make sure your account is selected on the left of the screen. Click the Login Items tab on the right.

4. Then simply click and drag the desktop icon for the server to the list of login items. Note that there's no need to put a check next to the new entry in the list—that's used to force login items to start minimized and isn't relevant here.

And that's it! If you want to hide desktop icons showing network connections, you can repeat the previous step that activated the display of server icons on the desktop, but this time remove the check next to Connected Servers.

Note that it might take a few seconds after the desktop appears when you boot before the Finder window pops up showing the shared computer.

If in the future you want to stop connecting to the server at start-up, just repeat the steps and remove the server entry from the list of login items for your user account by selecting it and clicking the minus button to the bottom left of the list.

Tip 391

Invert a Selection of Files

Let's say you've just downloaded 100 images from your digital camera. You want to copy all but three of them to another folder. How would you select just the 97 you want to copy?

Finder features a neat little trick to let you do just that quickly and easily. However, it works best on the desktop or in Icon view within Finder.

Start by selecting the files you *don't* want to include in your selection. In my previous example, that would be the three files that we don't want to copy. This can be done by holding down `Command` and selecting them.

Then press and hold the `Command` key and use the mouse to rubber-band select *all* the files—including the three you've already selected. You should find magic happens—the selection inverts so that files that weren't selected now are and those that were are automatically unselected. In my example, 97 files would now be selected.

This technique works in Finder's List and Column views too but is difficult to pull off correctly: you must start the elastic-band selection within the listing of files and not outside the boundaries of the list, or you'll cancel the original selections.

Tip 392

Open Duplicates of Dashboard Widgets

Here's a tip that might be obvious to some but mind-blowing to others.

You aren't limited to just one representation of any Dashboard widget. In other words, you could have as many clocks as you want on the Dashboard, each showing the time in a different time zone—just repeatedly add new clock widgets from the Manage Widgets selection at the bottom of the screen.

You could also have several versions of the weather widget showing conditions at different locations or several versions of the Stickies widget with different colored notes.

Tip 393

Cue Second-by-Second in Movies

You might already know that if you click the blob within the timeline on the QuickTime Player controller bar, you can cue back and forth in the movie you're watching, something known as *scrubbing*. However, if you click and hold the blob without moving it, you'll see white bars appear in the timeline.

Each of these indicates one second, and the entire timeline will be changed to represent ten seconds. Dragging the blob will now allow precise movement through the movie. Releasing the mouse button will return the timeline to normal.

Additionally, when the movie is paused, tapping the Left/Right cursor keys will advance the motion frame by frame. Pressing and holding either key will play the movie in slow motion.

Tip 394

Turn a Website into an App

If you want to simply double-click an app icon to open a website on your desktop, avoiding a full-blown browser, this tip is for you. Here are the steps to turn a website into an app:

1. Start the Automator app. It's located in the Applications list in Finder.

2. In the document chooser that appears when Automator starts, double-click the Application icon—its icon is a robot. If this doesn't appear, click File→New.

3. In the list of actions beneath the Name search field, scroll down until you find the Get Specified URLs entry. Double-click it to open it on the right side of the window.

4. Under the new Get Specified URLs heading, double-click the Apple website address and replace it with that of the site you want your new app to visit, including the http:// component. Hint: If you want to specify one of Google's web apps, you might have to append /?browserok=true to the end of the URL. In other words, something like http://docs.google.com will need to read http://docs.google.com/?browserok=true. Appending the URL causes Google to stop checking to ensure the browser is compatible, which can cause problems.

5. Back in the list of actions under the Name search field, locate the Website Popup entry. It'll probably be at the bottom of the list. Again, double-click to add it to the right of the window.

6. Under the new Website Popup heading, you can leave most entries as they are. However, in the Site Size and User Agent drop-down lists you

can select either iPad or iPhone, which will not only shrink the app window to the size of an iPad or iPhone but also access the iPad or iPhone versions of a site. These are often optimized for small screen sizes, which makes them ideal for our new app.

7. Once you're done, click File→Save, give your new app a name, and then click the Save button. Once that's done, you can close Automator. The app is ready to use, so double-click it to try it.

The new app window has Cancel and OK buttons at the bottom right, and both quit the app. You can also quit the app by clicking the cog icon at the top right of the screen and clicking the close button alongside the entry for your website app.

You can edit the app at any time by starting Automator again and opening it using the File menu.

You can change the icon for your new app to something more identifiable with the site by following Tip 116, *Personalize Every Icon*, on page 127.

Another way to get websites on your desktop within discrete program windows is to create a Dashboard web clip of the site and then follow Tip 117, *Bring Widgets to the Desktop*, on page 128.

Tip 395

Use Quick Look to Skim Sites

Here's an interesting way of viewing web pages that might be useful for those who are frequently in a hurry and just want to skim the front pages of sites without first loading Safari.

Some setup is required, as follows. Create a new folder, and then use Safari to visit the first of the websites you want to regularly skim. Click and drag the small icon just before the web address to the new folder. This will create a .weblo file—a web location file that's nothing more than a file-based bookmark for a site. Repeat with the other websites you want to regularly skim. You might choose to rename the web location files to make them easier to identify at a glance. This won't affect which website they point to.

Setup is now complete. In the future, all you need to do to skim the sites is select the first web location file in the list and then hit Space to view the site using Quick Look. The Quick Look window will load the site, looking like a stripped-down version of Safari. Once you've finished reading, click the next web location file (or use the Left/Right cursor keys to move between the web location files). This will then open in the Quick Look window. Keep going until you've finished, and then hit `Space` to close the Quick Look window.

Tip 396

Create a New Folder Anywhere

Want to create a new folder? Just hit `Shift+Command+N`. This will work on the desktop, in a Finder window, in a Save As dialog box, and even within a File Open dialog box. In short, practically anywhere you come into contact with files, it should work, with the exception of File Open/Save dialog boxes showing iCloud files—see Tip 13, *Create iCloud Folders*, on page 25.

Tip 397

Grab Files from FTP Servers Using Finder

Finder includes basic FTP accessing functionality. You can browse files and folders on an FTP server and download them, but you can't upload files. For that you'll need to use a third-party FTP client. SFTP isn't supported either.

To connect to an FTP server, open a Finder window, and click Go→Connect to Server. In the dialog box that appears, type ftp:// followed by the address into the Server Address field. For example, to connect to the server at ftp.example.com, I would type the following:

```
ftp://ftp.example.com
```

Then click the Connect button. You'll be prompted for your username and password once you've connected. The protocol to log into public FTP servers is usually to specify anonymous as the username and then provide your email address as the password.

To disconnect from the server, click the eject icon alongside the FTP server's entry under the Shared heading in Finder's sidebar.

Tip 398

Turn Off the Caps Lock Key

Some people find they accidentally hit the Caps Lock key while typing. Under OS X you can turn it off so that pressing the key does nothing—you won't even light up the key's indicator light. To do so, open System Preferences (Apple menu→System Preferences), and click the Keyboard icon. Then make sure the Keyboard tab is selected, and click the Modifier Keys button. In the drop-down list next to Caps Lock Key, select No Action. The change will take effect immediately.

To reactivate Caps Lock later, repeat the steps to access the modifier keys dialog box, and select Caps Lock from the Caps Lock Key drop-down list.

Tip 399

Make Keyboard Lighting Work

If your Mac's keyboard has backlighting, you can adjust it using the keyboard hotkeys (usually on the F5 and F6 keys, above the 5 and 6 keys on the keyboard). However, sometimes the lighting might refuse to activate—you'll see a "no entry" sign when you tap the hotkeys no matter how many times you press them.

Don't worry—nothing is broken. It's simply that your Mac has detected that the ambient light in the room is bright enough to illuminate your keyboard naturally and so backlighting isn't needed. Place your finger over the iSight/FaceTime HD camera above the screen; this should fool your Mac into thinking it's dark and should restore your ability to adjust the keyboard backlighting.

If you want to avoid this confusion in the future, open System Preferences (Apple menu→System Preferences), and click the Keyboard icon. Make sure the Keyboard tab is selected, and then remove the check next to Adjust Keyboard Brightness in Low Light. You should now find yourself able to adjust the keyboard backlighting no matter what the ambient conditions are, although beware that using the backlighting drains battery life more rapidly.

Tip 400

See the Condition of Your Battery at a Glance

This is a tip for anybody with one of the MacBook series of computers.

If you hold down `Option` and click the battery life display at the top right of the screen, you'll be told the condition of your battery. On most Macs this reads Normal, which means the battery is in good condition. If instead you see Replace Soon, Replace Now, or Service Battery, there's likely a fault with the battery, and you should take your computer for repair as soon as possible. However, before you do that, consider resetting the System Management Controller, as described in Tip 184, *Reset Hardware Settings*, on page 209. This will remove the possibility of the status being incorrectly reported by corrupted system settings.

To see many more details about the battery, click the Apple menu, hold down `Option`, and click the System Information entry on the menu. In the window that appears, click Power in the list on the left side, and then look at the details under the Battery Information heading on the right side.

Tip 401

Magnify Sections of Photos or PDFs Easily

When viewing photos or PDFs in Preview, you might use the magnify buttons on the toolbar to get a better view of details. But try this instead: hit the backtick key (left of the top number row on most keyboards, but sometimes left of the `Z` key), and a magnifying glass will appear. If you have a multitouch trackpad, you can use the pinch-and-expand gesture to make the glass zoom in and out. Everybody else can tap the plus and minus keys (hold `Command` at the same time to also zoom the image/document). To get rid of the glass, just hit the backtick key again or hit `Esc`.

Tip 402

Tell Your Mac to Do Things

We can file this tip under "innovative features introduced some time ago."

Your Mac has powerful speech recognition software, which you might already know about. What you might not know about is a different kind of speech recognition on offer that lets you issue commands to your Mac to do things like start apps or select options within dialog boxes. For this to work, you'll need a Mac with a built-in microphone, although all modern portable Macs and iMacs have this.

Activating Spoken Commands

To activate spoken commands, open System Preferences (Apple menu→System Preferences), and click the Accessibility icon. Then click the Speakable Items icon in the list on the left, ensure the Settings tab is selected, and click the On radio button next to the Speakable Items heading.

A new circular floating window will appear at the top right of the desktop, which lets you know that your Mac is waiting for voice input. All you need to do is hold down Esc and speak a command, releasing Esc when you've finished.

To learn what commands you can speak, hold down Esc and say "Open speech commands window." This should then show a pop-up window displaying all the commands recognized by default. You can also use Finder to browse to ~/Library/Speech/Speakable Items (open Finder, hit Shift+Command+G, and type the path into the dialog box before clicking Go). Any files you see there relate to commands you can issue—a file called Quit this application means that you can issue that command.

Calibrating the Microphone

It's very likely you'll need to calibrate the microphone to get the best results. To do this, click the Calibrate button in the Speakable Items pane within System Preferences; in the window that appears, drag the slider beneath the audio meter to around 25 percent. Then try speaking some of the test phrases listed on the left of the window. They'll flash if they've been recognized, and you'll hear a "squip" sound. If none seems to work or the results are spotty, try dragging the slider to the left or to the right. Note that on the MacBook Pro I used for testing, I had to drag the slider to the very first bar near the Low heading to get consistently accurate speech recognition, despite the audio meter display appearing to show a perfectly acceptable input at higher settings. See Figure 59, *Calibrating speech recognition*.

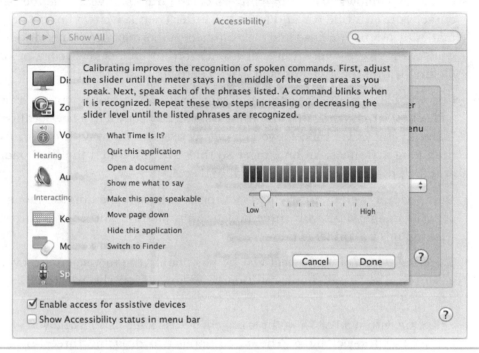

Figure 59—Calibrating speech recognition

Having Fun

Try saying, "Tell me a joke." OS X knows quite a few jokes, so try it several times.

Tip 403

Use Three Fingers and Revolutionize Your Mac Use

If your Mac has a multitouch trackpad, open System Preferences (Apple menu →System Preferences), click the Trackpad icon, make sure the Point & Click tab is selected, and check Three Finger Drag.

This will activate several useful features, as follows:

- Moving windows: You can move windows by positioning the mouse cursor over the title bar and dragging three fingers on the trackpad.

- Coasting windows: Place three fingers on the trackpad when the mouse cursor is over a title bar and move it a little. Then leave two fingers permanently on the trackpad and flick with a neighboring finger—the window will "coast" for a while (think of a puck on an air-hockey board or of flicking within a list on an iPhone/iPad screen).

- Copying files: In Finder windows, if you position the mouse cursor over a file or folder and drag with three fingers, you can copy it to a new location instantly (hit `Esc` to cancel if you change your mind midway through). To drag long distances, lift one finger so that two still touch the trackpad, and flick that finger to "coast" (try it and see).

- Downloading web images: When viewing web pages, position the mouse over an image, drag with three fingers on a picture, and copy it to the desktop or to a Finder window.

- Selecting text: You can select text by positioning the mouse cursor over a sentence in a paragraph, putting three fingers on the trackpad and dragging.

- Selecting within a list: Drag three fingers across a file listing, and you can rubber-band select them. The same applies to dragging three fingers within any other list within OS X, such as the Inbox in Mail.

Note that when the three-finger drag is activated, the three-finger gesture is switched to four fingers—swiping four fingers left or right will switch spaces, and swiping four fingers up will activate Mission Control.

Tip 404

Use AirDrop Even on Incompatible Macs

AirDrop allows you to share files between compatible Macs (see *Exploring OS X: AirDrop*, on page 161), but by altering a hidden setting, some computers that Apple states are incompatible can also join the AirDrop network (although all the computers must be running OS X Lion or Mountain Lion).

However, unlike regular AirDrop networking—which lets users share files even if they're connected to different Wi-Fi networks—AirDrop enabled this way works only if the Macs to which you want to send or receive files are part of the same network. However, unlike with regular AirDrop, this network can be either wired (Ethernet) or Wi-Fi.

It's important to note that this is strictly an unofficial tweak—you might find it works perfectly, or it might not work at all. Just give it a try! If it doesn't work, simply disable the tweak as described at the end of this tip.

Enabling AirDrop on Incompatible Macs

Open a Terminal window (open Finder, select the Applications list, and then in the list of applications double-click Terminal within the Utilities folder), and on the Mac not supported by AirDrop, type the following:

```
defaults write com.apple.NetworkBrowser BrowseAllInterfaces -bool TRUE
```

Then restart the computer. Repeat this tweak on every other Mac to which you want to transfer files via AirDrop, *even if they are already compatible with AirDrop.* Reboot each after making the tweak.

Using AirDrop on Incompatible Macs

Once enabled on all the computers concerned, you should find AirDrop works exactly as described in *Exploring OS X: AirDrop*, on page 161—just drag and drop files on the icons of other Macs that appear within the radar view that appears when AirDrop is selected in Finder. Their users can drag and drop files on your icon to transfer files to you, too.

You might find that some Macs don't appear on your AirDrop radar, even though you appear on theirs. Once someone has transferred a file to you, however, you should find that that Mac becomes visible.

Bear in mind that the standard AirDrop service is intentionally limited by distance because it's intended for sharing files with those physically nearby. Enabling this tweak will open up AirDrop to each Mac in the network, which, in an office environment, could cover an entire building—or more.

Disabling the AirDrop Setting

To disable this tweak, open a Terminal window, and type the following, again rebooting your computer afterward:

```
defaults delete com.apple.NetworkBrowser BrowseAllInterfaces
```

Don't forget to do so on all the computers on which you made the tweak.

Tip 405

Supertip: Get Some Must-Have Mac Apps

In this book I've deliberately avoided recommending third-party apps. There are a handful of exceptions where apps are needed to make up for rare deficiencies in OS X's functionality—for example, Tip 387, *Expand QuickTime Player's Knowledge of File Types*, on page 398—but throughout the book a DIY approach and faith in OS X's extensive built-in toolkit are encouraged.

That said, there are some add-in apps that are part of a standard Mac setup for many users. I've listed a handful here. Unless otherwise marked, the apps are free of charge and can be downloaded from the websites mentioned.

- ClamXav (http://www.clamxav.com): Adds on-demand virus scanning to OS X. Unlike other antivirus programs,[36] ClamXav doesn't remain present in memory. You can run it to scan any files that look suspicious, such as those you've downloaded from a less reputable website. This is available via the App Store.

- Xcode (http://developer.apple.com/technologies/tools/): Apple's own programming toolkit and integrated development environment is free of charge via the App Store for anybody who purchased OS X. It allows you to create apps for OS X and iOS and also create Dashboard widgets.

- The Unarchiver (http://wakaba.c3.cx/s/apps/unarchiver.html): This significantly expands OS X's knowledge of compressed file formats, specifically adding in the ability to expand RAR, 7-zip, LhA, and StuffIt formats (the official app by the creators of the StuffIt format, StuffIt Expander, which is a free download from the App Store). This is available via the App Store.

- Transmission (http://www.transmissionbt.com): There are a variety of BitTorrent clients for OS X, but this is perhaps the most fully featured and is frequently updated with new features.

- Cyberduck (http://cyberduck.ch): This is a file transfer program that works with FTP, SFTP, WebDav, Amazon S3, Google Storage (including Google Docs), Microsoft Azure, and Rackspace Cloud Files. This can be purchased via the App Store, but a free-to-try older "donationware" version is available

---

36. For example, Sophos Anti-Virus for Mac Home Edition: http://www.sophos.com/en-us/products/ free-tools/sophos-antivirus-for-mac-home-edition.aspx

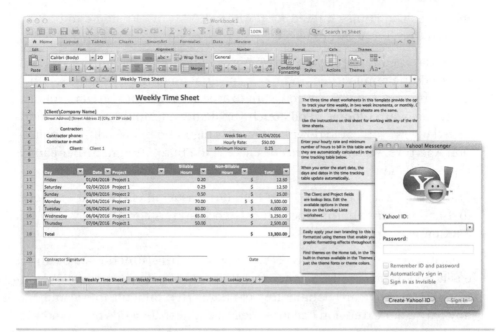

Figure 60—Continuing the Mac adventure with third-party apps

from the website. Also worth mentioning as an FTP/SFTP client is FileZilla,[37] which is available free of charge but lacks the polished finesse expected of Mac apps.

- iWork (http://www.apple.com/iwork/): This is Apple's own office suite, consisting of Pages (word processor), Numbers (spreadsheet), and Keynote (presentations). All are packed with features plus the ease of use and excellent design expected of Apple products, but, perhaps crucially, the apps also integrate 100 percent with OS X's features, such as Versions and iCloud, and there are versions available for the iPhone/iPad too. Each component of iWork for OS X is purchased individually from the App Store.

- VMware Fusion (http://www.vmware.com/products/fusion/overview.html): This creates virtual computers within software that let you run Microsoft Windows, Linux, or even additional installations of OS X. Fusion is useful if you need to run some Windows software or games but not enough to warrant a full Bootcamp installation of Windows, and you can also access prebuilt

---

37. http://filezilla-project.org

machines sometimes offered for download. VMware Fusion can be purchased from the VMware website.

- iPhoto (http://www.apple.com/ilife/iphoto/): Apple's photo cataloging, sharing, and basic editing app is loved and hated in equal amounts by Mac users but is a requirement on OS X if you want to access your Photo Stream—photos taken on your iPhone, iPod touch, or iPad and stored within iCloud. Alternatively, you could download Apple's high-end photo-editing application Aperture, which also provides access to Photo Stream. Either can be purchased via the Mac App Store.

- Adium (http://adium.im/): This is an instant messaging client that supports just about every chat protocol in existence and integrates fully with OS X's Contacts app.

- Safari extensions (https://extensions.apple.com): Safari's functionality can be easily and dramatically expanded with the aid of *extensions*—small plug-in programs that are usually free of charge. It's difficult to recommend any particular extension because their usefulness depends on an individual's browsing habits, but the Top 10 list is a good place to start and can be seen by clicking the link given. To browse for new extensions, you can also click the application menu and then Extensions, and you can remove or adjust extensions by opening Safari's Preferences dialog box and then clicking the Extensions tab.

Additionally, it should be noted that the makers of most major Windows software usually produce an OS X version too. There's a Mac version of Microsoft Office,[38] for example, and Mac versions of Skype and Yahoo Messenger (see Figure 60, *Continuing the Mac adventure with third-party apps*, on page 413).[39] Additionally, you'll usually find Mac versions of major open source projects such as LibreOffice and Gimp.[40] Note that some open source software uses X11, which is installed upon demand on OS X Mountain Lion, although can be manually downloaded if needed from http://xquartz.macosforge.org (you should download and install the latest XQuartz package).

Adobe Flash Player isn't a default installation on new Macs, so it must be installed manually.[41] This is for a reason: Apple claims the Flash plug-in

---

38. http://www.microsoft.com/mac/
39. http://www.skype.com/intl/en-us/get-skype/on-your-computer/macosx/ and http://messenger.yahoo.com/mac/, respectively
40. http://www.libreoffice.org and http://www.gimp.org/macintosh, respectively
41. http://get.adobe.com/flashplayer/

reduces battery life on MacBooks. However, Flash is still ubiquitous on websites, and its absence can lead to a substandard browsing experience. An effective solution is to install the Flash plug-in and also the free ClickToFlash Safari extension (click Safari's application menu, and then select Safari Extensions and search for *ClickToFlash*). This blocks Safari in all web pages unless you explicitly select to run it.

Index

Learn iOS Programming

Ready to learn how to program on iOS? We've got you covered.

Welcome to the new state of the art development for iOS, with the radically overhauled Xcode 4 toolchain and iOS 5 SDK. With this book you'll accelerate your development for iPhone, iPad and iPod Touch. You will learn the new tools like Storyboards, practice on new APIs like the Twitter framework and use the latest features of the Objective-C 2.0 programming language.

Chris Adamson and Bill Dudney
(300 pages) ISBN: 9781934356944. $35
http://pragprog.com/titles/adios

Core Data is Apple's recommended way to persist data: it's easy to use, built-in, and integrated with iCloud. It's intricate, powerful, and necessary—and this book is your guide to harnessing its power.

Learn fundamental Core Data principles such as thread and memory management, discover how to use Core Data in your iPhone, iPad, and OS X projects by using NSPredicate to filter data, and see how to add iCloud to your applications.

Marcus S. Zarra
(250 pages) ISBN: 9781937785086. $33
http://pragprog.com/titles/mzcd2

Welcome to the New Web

You need a better JavaScript and better recipes that professional web developers use every day. Start here.

CoffeeScript is JavaScript done right. It provides all of JavaScript's functionality wrapped in a cleaner, more succinct syntax. In the first book on this exciting new language, CoffeeScript guru Trevor Burnham shows you how to hold onto all the power and flexibility of JavaScript while writing clearer, cleaner, and safer code.

Trevor Burnham
(160 pages) ISBN: 9781934356784. $29
http://pragprog.com/titles/tbcoffee

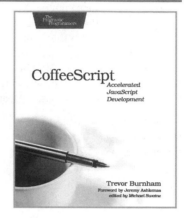

Modern web development takes more than just HTML and CSS with a little JavaScript mixed in. Clients want more responsive sites with faster interfaces that work on multiple devices, and you need the latest tools and techniques to make that happen. This book gives you more than 40 concise, tried-and-true solutions to today's web development problems, and introduces new workflows that will expand your skillset.

Brian P. Hogan, Chris Warren, Mike Weber, Chris Johnson, Aaron Godin
(344 pages) ISBN: 9781934356838. $35
http://pragprog.com/titles/wbdev